RETIRE
&
THRIVE

RETIRE
&
THRIVE

REMARKABLE PEOPLE SHARE THEIR

CREATIVE, PRODUCTIVE & PROFITABLE

RETIREMENT STRATEGIES

BY ROBERT K. OTTERBOURG

KIPLINGER BOOKS, Washington, D.C.

Published by
The Kiplinger Washington Editors, Inc.
1729 H Street, N.W.
Washington, D.C. 20006

Library of Congress Cataloging-in-Publication Data

Otterbourg, Robert K.
    Retire & Thrive: remarkable people share their creative,
productive and profitable retirement strategies / by Robert K.
Otterbourg. — 2nd ed.
        p.   cm.
    Includes bibliographical references and index.
    ISBN 0-938721-64-X (cloth)
        1. Retirement—United States—Planning.   2. Retirement—United
States—Case studies.   3. Retirees—United States—Attitudes—Case
Studies.   I. Title.   II. Title: Retire and thrive.
HQ1063.2.U6077   1999
306.3'8—dc21   99-10133
                                                                    CIP

This publication is intended to provide guidance in regard to the subject matter
covered. It is sold with the understanding that the author and publisher are not herein
engaged in rendering legal, accounting, tax or other professional services. If such services
are required, professional assistance should be sought.

Second Edition. Printed in the United States of America.

98765432

Dedication

TO SUSAN: We started this journey together as comparative youngsters and now we find ourselves as full-fledged members of the 50-plus set.

TO LAURA, KATHERINE, KENNETH AND SAM: One day you, too, will face the challenges presented in this book.

AND IN MEMORY OF ARTHUR WEISSMAN, my son-in-law, an energetic and persevering newspaper reporter, and a good guy who tragically will never have a chance to retire and thrive.

Acknowledgements

Writing an acknowledgement for a book seems akin to preparing an acceptance speech to deliver at an Academy Awards ceremony. You want to thank everyone starting with your first grade teacher.

After nearly 18 years of running my own public relations firm, I decided in the late 1980s to change careers or, better yet, return to writing, my initial occupational port of entry. *Retire & Thrive* represents my second and hopefully not my last published book. But even more importantly, researching and writing this book has proven to be an absolute joy, both for having the chance to get to know my sources and their stories, and to reactivate sometimes long-dormant skills.

And now I would like to thank just a few people who were my invaluable partners. Patricia Burton read the initial manuscript. Her pithy and oftentimes humorous comments forced me to focus on the real issues. My literary agent, Edward Knappman, of New England Publishing Associates, provided thoughtful insight and perspective into the publishing world.

I'm grateful to the following people who pointed me toward some of the problems and challenges facing downsized managers and early retirees: Sara Craven, director of the Duke Institute for Learning in Retirement; Anita Lands, an outplacement consultant and instructor with New York University's School of Continuing Education; William Stanley, also an outplacement consultant; and Sterling Dimmitt, a senior vice president of Lee Hecht Harrison. A special thanks to Tom Otwell of the American Association of Retired Persons' staff for cheerfully fielding my many questions.

I am especially grateful to the reference librarians at Durham County Public Library, who, on numerous occasions, showed me ways to reduce what might have been hours of endless research. At times, I find that researching the old-fashioned way is a pleasant break from the computer screen.

My special thanks once again go to David Harrison, director of Kiplinger Books and Tapes, and Jennifer Robinson, managing editor, for making the second edition of this book possible. I especially appreciate their keen analysis and commentary and their upbeat attitude throughout the editorial process. Thanks, too, to Cynthia Currie, and Heather Waugh, members of Kiplinger's design department who refreshed the book with a new clean look, and to Allison Leopold for her careful copy editing.

My wife Susan receives double recognition, first in the dedication and here again. As usual, she was an invaluable and much-needed sounding board.

ROBERT K. OTTERBOURG
Durham, North Carolina

Table of Contents

"Work Is Still My Only Hobby"
The Making of a Community Activist
Computers, an Ally in Real Estate Sales
Just Got Bored in Retirement
Out of the Frying Pan and Into the Fire

Introduction

RETIREMENT, LIKE THE OL' GRAY MARE IN THE FOLK song, "ain't what it used to be." As a matter of fact, retirement today bears so little resemblance to its old self that we should probably retire the word "retire." Years ago, retirement was short and not-so-sweet. The typical retiree lived about a decade in modest circumstances, sedentary activities and declining health. Private and public pensions were not so generous, if one had them at all. Old age correlated inevitably with frailty and ill health, which is blessedly not the case today.

We're living today in an era of the 20-year retirement. What we call retirement is actually one-quarter of our lives, maybe more—and it is far from sedentary. Financial planning and improving health have made possible a full, satisfying and highly active two decades of retirement.

Recently, these trends have intersected with dramatic changes in the American workplace...downsizing of large corporations, more-frequent changing of jobs and whole careers, and a surge in entrepreneurship among people of all ages.

What this means is that more and more men and women in their fifties and early sixties are giving a lot of thought to their futures:

- They are retiring from one career only to launch a new one.
- They are starting businesses of their own.
- They are going back to college to learn new skills, either for fun or profit.
- They are becoming paid consultants or volunteer advisers.
- They are lending their knowledge to small businesses and nonprofits.
- They are turning hobbies into businesses.
- They are turning their businesses over to the younger generation, while staying involved via mentor or emeritus roles.

Whether officially "working" or "retired," they are leading full, satisfying lives.

In this wonderful book by Bob Otterbourg—himself a dynamic retiree—you'll meet dozens of creative, highly energetic men and women who caught their second wind. They retired and thrived, and their stories will show you how you can do it, too. Full of practical lessons you can apply to your own experience, *Retire & Thrive* provides countless ideas to make your retirement decades of living every bit as exciting as the middle years.

On behalf of all of us at the Kiplinger organization, my best wishes to you, as you begin the next stage of an exciting journey.

Knight Kiplinger

Knight A. Kiplinger
Editor, *The Kiplinger Letters*
Editor in Chief, *Kiplinger's Personal Finance Magazine*
Washington, D.C.

What's Next?

WHEN I RECEIVE *THE SCENE*, COLGATE UNIVERSITY'S alumni newspaper, I first turn to the class note section. I've always enjoyed reading about the professional and personal achievements of classmates. That's how it went for nearly 35 years.

Then something happened. These same dynamic classmates switched the tone of their correspondence—from career to retirement. One sold his business, packed up and moved to Florida. Another opted for early retirement and reported that he was golfing every day. Still others chatted about activities I couldn't imagine being part of my lifestyle. What they were doing seemed to me to be about as enjoyable as a month of Sundays.

How, I wondered, do they fill the 2,000 to 2,500 hours or more a year that they once devoted to their careers? Why would anyone even want to retire? Retirement was something that I had never considered, not even when I exited the public relations field to become a writer.

With those musings, the die was cast. The result is *Retire & Thrive*, a source of ideas, reassurance and inspiration for those who want to catch a second wind in "retirement," however and whenever it comes.

Early, Late or Never

The first edition of this book was published in 1995. The initial intention was to focus on people 55 to 65 years old, including those who became victims of corporate downsizing and its close kin, early retirement, as well as those who elected to work indefinitely and not retire.

I soon found that I was limiting my editorial horizons by excluding those ages 50 to 54, many of whom were losing their jobs or prematurely retiring. As a result, I packaged everyone from ages 50 to 65 into what I called the 50-plus set. By using age 50 as the starting point, I deliberately set a trap for the older members of the baby-boomer generation, who would begin to turn 50 in 1996. They, too, should be asking, "What's next?"

A generation ago, an out-of-work 52-year-old executive would most likely have found an equivalent or even better new job. Early retirement in the face of lay-offs and downsizing were not common occurrences. The message is now loud and clear for those severed from the workplace: To survive, they need to adopt different career and lifestyle objectives. In looking for another job, chances are they will not be able to duplicate the one they just lost. Furthermore, within the employment marketplace there is little discernible difference between a 52-year-old and a person ten years older. For those who are resourceful, inventive and willing to do things differently, the future is bright. The others have less reason to be cheery.

NEED A BETTER CRYSTAL BALL. This second edition reflects the mood of the late 1990s. I'm amazed how fast the world has moved in the past few years. I should have used a better brand of tea leaves to help me forecast many of the trends noted in the first edition. As such, this edition recognizes both the ongoing events and the trends that presently or will soon affect the 50-plus set:

As a starter, computers and data communications have really come of age. In the mid 1990s, the PC was hardly in its infancy. Even so, other than business users, comparatively few consumers of all ages were routinely corresponding by e-mail or browsing the Web in search of information. Nowadays, electronic transmission has become nearly ritualistic. One exchanges e-mail addresses with friends and business associates as readily as a telephone or fax number.

The statistics tell the story. In 1995, says Forrester Research, 22 million consumers used e-mail, each sending an estimated 2.4 messages a day. Three years later, 75 million users transmitted and average of three messages a day. By 2005, e-mail participation is projected to skyrocket to 170 million users who will average 29.4 daily messages. In recognition of this change, Web site addresses have been included in this edition.

BABY BOOMERS GROW GRAY WHISKERS. Now that baby boomers, once cute little kids in diapers and later young adults who vowed never to "trust anyone over 30," have begun to turn 50, men and women in this "never-going-to-get-old" age group are actively considering future workplace and lifestyle alternatives. AARP's *Modern Maturity* magazine noted this trend by creating two demographic editions—one directed toward those age 50 to 65, and the other to its older readers. More than a ploy to attract advertisers, it shows that the retirement years affect a broad spectrum of ages—and interests.

Along with the graying of the baby boomers is a parallel phenomenon, aptly called the Sandwich Generation. As Americans live longer, the 50-year-old as well as the 65-year-old are helpmates to one or both living parents. In addition to paying college tuition and wedding expenses for their children, a typical 50-year-old might be attending to an 80-year-old mother or father—or both parents.

What Lies Ahead

The first chapter sets the stage by exploring attitudes about retirement and describing a number of 50-plus-set trends. Chapter 2 discusses how to plan for these life events. The next three chapters concentrate on what I find are the three most vibrant non-work activities: becoming a student, working as a volunteer and pursuing a hobby. The concluding chapters focus on the dynamics in the workplace: staying on, though very likely with a change of pace or focus; changing careers or becoming self-employed; or escaping from retirement and returning to the workplace.

The editorial guideline for *Retire & Thrive* is clear-cut. The introductory part of each chapter highlights societal and demographic information, and relevant how-to information; the balance of the chapter is given to human-interest profiles. It is not the intention of this book to be encyclopedic. Rather, the groups and activities cited were selected because they would have particular appeal to a diverse 50-plus-set audience. Simply put, *Retire & Thrive* is intended for anyone age 50 to 65, in or out of the workplace.

The anecdotal profiles support the theme of each chapter. They are organized so you learn what 50-plus set people are presently doing and, just as important, the different routes they took to reach their present lifestyle. A number of the men and women portrayed are in their late sixties and seventies, but in nearly every instance they adopted their present lifestyle formula before they were 65.

Do not for a moment think that this book profiles only the affluent. Several are wealthy. But nearly all the others, even those with secure pensions and sound investments, are living on smaller incomes than when they were in the workforce. While financial issues are right up there in your mind as retirement looms, dealing with them is not the primary thrust of this book. Finding ways to make the most of your time and energy is the goal.

I had initially hoped to profile an equal number of men and women. Unfortunately, the potential pool of women executives and professionals in the 50-plus set is still comparatively small. There is an explanation for this disparity: In the years when today's mature women would have been students, most professional schools accepted few if any female students. In addition to this imbalance, the rungs in the corporate ladder rarely reached to the top for those women who made it into corporate America.

Few newsmakers are profiled. Why interview the rich and famous when we can profile people just like you who have produced real-life solutions in their 50-plus set years whether through a hobby, volunteerism, part-time work, attending school, starting a new business or career, continuing with their lifetime work or even returning to the workplace after trying retirement?

A few of the people I interviewed agreed to share their stories, but asked that I preserve their privacy by giving them pseudo-nyms or using an abbreviated form of their names. I honored their requests.

No Formulas

The editorial placement of many of the profiles provided a particular challenge. Those profiled could have easily been featured in several different chapters since their range of interests typifies the diversity that underscores the 50-plus set.

It would be much simpler if we could fit everyone in the 50-plus set into neat little boxes, but real people defy that type of classification. Rather they are discovering and implementing different lifestyle plans. Some of the solutions might lead you to think that 50-plus-set members are dabblers. Hardly the case. A retiree might work as a part-time professional three days a week, serve as a volunteer two mornings and then spend an equal amount of time with a hobby. More often than not, the people profiled selected a lifestyle that includes a combination of interests described so wonderfully by futurist Charles Handy (profiled on page 41) in *The Age of Unreason* as "portfolio careers."

Though they would deride such a description, the people in *Retire & Thrive* are, in a special sense, adventurers. They have created a 50-plus lifestyle uniquely their own whether as volunteers, managers turned consultants, or the owners of small businesses with no intention to retire but the flexibility to see themselves in a new role. By doing so, they reinvented themselves. Some developed new skills, but most took existing talents and reshaped them to meet new objectives.

The people you are about to meet, regardless of their interests, are all active and energetic. None are "couch potatoes." I've included seven new profiles in this edition. Six of them use computers, four rather avidly. Only one of the newcomers lives in the typewriter age. They, as everyone else in this book, thrive on variables in an environment where it is no longer business as usual. If nothing more, the 50-plus set adheres to the sentiments that Frank Sinatra lyrically depicted in "My Way": "And more, much more than this, I did it my way."

What's All the Fuss About Retirement?

IF YOU'VE BEEN COASTING ALONG CONTENTEDLY toward midlife, the American Association of Retired Persons knows how to elevate your blood pressure: A membership invitation arrives on your 50th birthday. So much for immortality. For an $8 membership fee, you're entered into AARP's expanding database of 33 million members, and you have taken the first step as a participant in the great retirement game.

When we become 50 we are understandably ambivalent, if not indifferent, about retirement. Youth, we rightfully maintain, is still on our side. Retirement seems like an event in the distant future. But sooner than we anticipated, retirement is on our doorstep. It may even be accelerated by the twin effects of downsizing and early-retirement buyout plans. Retirement-related questions begin to surface, and at best, we have entered into uncharted waters.

As the many profiles in this book will make clear, it's difficult to define "retirement." We've euphemistically called retirement the "golden age" and the "leisure years." The French call it "The Third Age" or the age of living (which follows the ages of learning and working), possibly the most accurate of these descriptions. Contrary to the dictionary definition, retirement need not be a "withdrawal from one's position or occupation, or from active working life."

In fact, looking at the current environment of corporate restructuring and those affected by it, the AARP found that "those nearing retirement no longer seek it as a sharp break with the past." Rather, today's "preretired" seek continuity. Many anticipate "retiring" from their lifelong career only to continue working, either in a new job in the field they've been in or in an unrelated area.

Much depends on how you feel about your career. As much as some people enjoy their work, they might be emotionally burned out and physically exhausted after 30 to 40 years; they're ready to take a break or do something different. Countering those emotions may be a feeling of guilt, especially among "Depression-age babies" who were born in the late 1920s and 1930s. They were inoculated with a self-perpetuating work ethic that makes it difficult to accept retirement of any sort.

When counseling retirees, Boston gerontologist and sociology professor David Karp finds that "some feel that there are important things left unfinished in their work lives. As would be expected, people with unfinished agendas were relatively more engaged in work and least likely to look on retirement favorably."

William Stanley's job provides an ideal perch for observing the corporate retirement process. Bill spent 30 years as a human-resources manager with Fortune 500 and smaller companies before he became an outplacement consultant, specializing in representing workers over 50. Several years ago Bill surveyed the Yale class of 1946 and his own Princeton class of 1956 on their attitudes toward retirement. Compared with the Yale alumni, who had already retired and seemed content, many of Bill's classmates were still working, yet were very anxious about the future. Typical of their comments about the prospect of retirement:

- Why retire when there's so much left to do?
- There's no structure in retirement.
- I must learn a new routine.
- I want to be busy but not stressed or rushed.

Where's the Equal Opportunity?

Of course, feelings and decisions about retirement may be complicated by a husband or wife's attitude toward it. Alas for many of the husbands who are ready to leave corporate America and perhaps enjoy some leisure time with their wives, their partners have more recently joined it. Many women now in their fifties and sixties are far from ready to retire, having only entered the workplace in their early to mid forties once their children were in high school or college. "They are too busy making a mark," says gerontologist David Karp. "In their fifties, many men feel an urgency to do things that their occupational lives had made difficult, whereas many women feel an urgency to do occupational things their family lives have made difficult." He notes, not surprisingly, that men and women of the same chronological age often talk very differently about their work. "Many women are 'turning on' at the same age that their male counterparts are 'turning off.'" The good news for many male retirees, whatever their reason for retiring, is that their wives are providing a financial safety net. As many of the profiles in this book show, a wife's income and benefits package give her spouse flexibility in decision making that he might not otherwise have.

A working wife also gives her retired mate a breather in making the transition from the workplace to a new lifestyle. She avoids the homebound wife's cliché, "I married you for better or worse but not for lunch." In this changeover period, perhaps it is best that each spouse has some space.

> ## POINTS TO REMEMBER
>
> - So-called retirement age comes faster than anyone thinks it will—and faster yet for those who are ousted by downsizing or offered early retirement.
> - There's no one definition of retirement. How you view it is strictly a personal thing.
> - Longer life expectancy means more years to spend in retirement.
> - Your role models may not provide much help in preparing for it.
> - It's becoming increasingly difficult though not impossible for 50-plus-set managers to find another good job.
> - Women view retirement differently than men.
> - The age of retirement differs among professions and vocations.
> - Believe it or not, CEOs have retirement problems much like your own.

The Generation Gap

Our closest role models may not be much help in thinking about retirement. Growing up, I knew very few people who had retired. My parents and their friends were self-employed professionals or owners of small businesses who worked, as was the custom a generation ago, until they died or were physically unable to work. Since my father had virtually no retirement savings or benefits, retirement was not a part of the household vocabulary.

The formula was rather simplistic for our parents' generation. People worked longer and died earlier. In 1900, people who survived to age 65 could expect to live another 12 years, and 80% of men 65 or older were still working. Compare that with more recent figures. In 1995, men and women who made it to age 65 could expect to live another 17.4 years, with women outliving men by 3.3 years. Interestingly, only 3.7 million, or about 12%, of the men and women age 65-plus remain in the workforce. So we're living longer and leaving the workforce sooner. Simple arithmetic proves that most retirees need to find ways to redirect the 2,000 to 2,500 hours or more a year that were once spent at work.

A FINANCIAL CHANGE OF FORTUNE. A generation or two ago, a retirement package, if one existed, consisted of a testimonial gift together with a relatively small pension and equally small social security benefits. A pension was not always an inherent right. Less than 60 years ago, the average American worker, unless handicapped or ill, never considered retirement—or could afford to. The Social Security Act was passed in 1935 in response to the financial hardships caused by the Great Depression and to provide workers with the type of social benefits many Europeans had been enjoying for 50 years before.

For most Americans in the mid 1930s, retirement with an assured pension was limited to the wealthy and to a few long-term corporate and government employees. In an era when life expectancy was around 63 years, Congress set 65 as the age of eligibility to collect $30 a month in benefits.

Over the next 55 years, social security coverage was broadened to include nearly all wage earners. New features were

HOW DO YOU FEEL ABOUT RETIREMENT?

Many of the questions raised in "Gearing Up for Retirement," a workshop co-sponsored by the American Medical Association (see page 33), apply to anyone, not just medical practitioners. Use them to check your pulse about retirement.

- Do you see retirement as a reward for a lifetime of hard work or as a punishment for growing old?
- Is it an opportunity to learn and do things you've always longed to pursue?
- Is retirement like a banishment from a way of life that you've cultivated over the years?
- Is retirement something you've determined never to do, based on someone else's experience?
- Are you looking forward to it, planning and dreaming over it?

added in stages—in 1965, medicare insurance coverage and in 1974, the pegging of retirement benefits to the consumer price index. Even with these enhancements to the social security system, the average retiree in 1973 received a $166 monthly check, compared with approximately $780 in 1998.

Not only have government-mandated benefits improved, but so has discretionary income. Marketers have discovered that the golden years for Americans between 55 and 64 are indeed bright in terms of discretionary income. While their incomes on average are slightly lower than the older baby boomers, these folks over 55 often have a financial advantage since their children have completed college and are self-supporting.

How High Is Up?

How much money do I need to retire and live comfortably? That's the question that clouds much thinking about the otherwise fulfilling possibilities of retirement. While hardly of retirement age, Sherman McCoy in *The Bonfire of the Vanities* pointed out that he was "going broke on a million dollars a year." Paul Terhorst, a renegade from corporate accounting, advises readers in *Cashing In on the American Dream—How to Retire at 35* on a variety of ways to

A TAKE ON RETIREMENT

"Retirement is a bad word in this society, particularly, as it turns out, for those who have not yet retired. There is no doubt that it represents a major turning point in life. It is also a major opportunity. Common belief is that those who retire either shrivel up on park benches or fritter away the rest of their lives playing bingo and shuffleboard in senior-citizen centers."   From *Growing Old,*
by Christopher Hallowell

live comfortably on $50 a day. You'll probably want to be nestled somewhere between these two extremes.

But it is critical that you develop some form of game plan, one tailored by you to meet your specific needs and interests. You should be comfortable with this plan. Above all, remember you're a newcomer to retirement and you don't know how you might feel about it in six months' time. It makes little sense to write any game plan in indelible ink. Chapter 2 gives you an opportunity to realistically assess your financial needs and resources for retirement. But in the meantime, as you're adjusting your attitude toward retirement, keep these key points in mind:

LEARN HOW TO LIVE ON A NEW BUDGET. You'll discover a different pattern of expenses—a shift in wardrobe from suits to less costly casual sports clothes, less expensive midday lunches and the elimination of commuting costs, to name a few. These new guidelines may remain constant even if you return to the workplace or become a consultant depending on the new work environment you choose.

KEEP DEBT LOW. Until you know your expenses, it makes little sense to pick up additional financial burdens, such as a boat or second home.

DON'T USE MONEY AS YOUR SOLE EXCUSE FOR NOT DOING SOMETHING. Instead, be creative. If you want to go on a two-week trip to Greece, you can spend $12,000 a person on a luxury tour or less than $4,500 through Elderhostel (see page 63). Being creative means looking for alternatives that complement your pocketbook.

ABOVE ALL, BE KIND TO YOURSELF. Before you decide on a more permanent course of action, don't feel guilty if you linger over a second cup of morning coffee and the crossword puzzle. Chances are you're not down to your last dollar, so when something nice happens to you, celebrate appropriately. It's okay to be conservative, but there's no need to start squealing when you spend.

My Own Story

Unlike my father and his peers, I've already come to grips with certain aspects of retirement. Without labeling it as such, I innocently took my first step in the late 1980s in executing my version of retirement. Nearly 20 years of running my own public relations firm was enough. After a number of excellent years, I lost several accounts. Such setbacks in the past were usually only temporary. I would recharge my batteries and replace the lost business. But at 58, I was no longer as resilient or as patient. "If this is a problem at this age, what will happen when I am 65?" I asked. Up to then, I had never considered retraining for another career or retiring.

The first step was to phase out of public relations. I discharged my secretary and embarked on a new career as a freelance writer. Two years later, my office lease ended, and I moved a truncated business into a spare room at home. Without much fanfare, I had created a new business lifestyle, bordering on semi-retirement.

> ## A TAKE ON RETIREMENT
>
> "Some men can retire with dignity and security as early as 50, others as late as 70. Within this range, the age at which a man retires from formal employment, and especially from a position of direct authority over others, should reflect his own needs, capabilities and life circumstances."
>
> From *The Seasons of a Man's Life*,
> by Daniel Levinson

The transition was easier than I anticipated. A few factors were in my favor: I knew what it was like to be self-employed, and I enjoyed being a writer. I was also a hobbyist as well as an officer and trustee of several not-for-profit groups. My daytime calendar was usually full. I anticipated few problems in my career and lifestyle switch.

As part of my changeover, I gave myself a 60th birthday present which I renewed five years later: I set a goal to work as a full-time writer for the duration. In looking back over the past ten years and, more importantly, looking ahead, I'm pleased with my decision. I've blended writing, hobbies, volunteerism and family life into a rewarding lifestyle. Fortunately, my wife and I share similar lifestyle goals and views toward retirement.

Baby Boomers Come of Age

The demographers are having a field day interpreting what's going to happen to the baby-boomer generation. Some boomers are already in their early fifties, and retirement may be just around the corner if they intend to retire early. For other boomers, retirement means only shifting gears, an opportunity to change careers or start a business.

Still other boomers have had retirement forced upon them. As downsizing victims, many have found it difficult to get another job that matches the one they lost. Some—especially those who walked away with generous severance packages—don't care. They want to work only part-time or find a less pressured job.

Boomers can also read the longevity charts. They know that they represent 45% of the workforce and they're the biggest consumer-spending age group. Unlike their parents and their older siblings, they don't intend to cease being consumers once they retire. At age 52, they expect to live another 30 or more years.

Even for many who have plenty of money in their retirement nest egg, work is an important part in their retirement planning. Boomers, says a recent AARP report, are not about to become an idle generation. Here's how boomers react to workplace and retirement issues: 80% expect to work at least part-time during their retirement; only 16% have no interest in any type of job. Of those interested in staying in the workforce, nearly one-third plan to work part-time primarily for the interest and enjoyment it brings, compared with 23% who would like to work part-time for the money. Slightly less than 20% are considering buying their own business.

Why are boomers so job oriented? The AARP says their generation needs more money than their parents' generation to live comfortably and they are more self-indulgent. It adds up to this: A retirement income based on pension, social security and personal investments will not pay the bills for consumer-oriented boomers.

Workplace Realities

Not everyone gets to pick the date when they'll retire, as Robert McCord discovered. He'll never forget the day the *Arkansas Gazette,* the oldest daily newspaper west of the Mississippi, was sold to the *Democrat,* its Little Rock rival. With its sale, Bob lost his job and could have ended his journalism career. Since the mid-1950s, Bob had held nearly every editorial position on the *Gazette* and *Democrat.* When Gannett, the *Gazette*'s owner, sold the paper, Bob's career nearly ended at age 62.

Many of the other older *Gazette* reporters and editors retired before the sale because the *Democrat* was not interested in hiring the *Gazette*'s senior and better-paid staff members. Bob was fortunate. His financial stresses were few. His expenses were fixed. The mortgage was paid, and the three McCord children were self-supporting. His wife, Muriel, did not work. What Bob really needed was a professional challenge.

Among the local media, Bob was well known and regarded, so it was not surprising when he got a call from one of the local

A TAKE ON RETIREMENT

"I've seen a lot of old bulls retire, and I've watched what happens to them after they get out of harness," says Ivar Thorsen [a ranking New York City police officer, to Edward Delaney, a retired policeman]. "A few of them can handle it but not many.... You'd be surprised how many drop dead a year or two after putting in their papers. Heart attack or stroke, cancer or bleeding ulcers. I don't know the medical or psychological reasons for it, but studies show it's a phenomenon that exists. When the pressure is suddenly removed, and stress vanishes, and there are no problems to solve, and drive and ambition disappear, the body just collapses.... Or other things happen. They can't handle the freedom. No office to go to. No beat to pound. No shop talk. Their lives revolved around the Department and now suddenly they're out. It's like they were excommunicated."

From *The Third Deadly Sin,*
by Lawrence Sanders

television stations asking him to write and broadcast three editorials a week. Next, the *Arkansas Times* asked him to write a weekly political column. "I don't go downtown to work anymore," says Bob, "but I'm better off than a lot of other guys who lost their jobs and careers when the *Gazette* folded."

The result of the continuing round of corporate purges is a labor force of more than 20 million Americans between ages 50 and 65 who face the distinct possibility of working fewer hours, being laid off or pushed into some form of early retirement, and most likely never finding as good a job as the one they just lost.

In 1998, the American Management Association (AMA) released a survey on corporate downsizing that reported that 60% of the surveyed companies had undergone at least one round of job cuts in the 1990s, and 23% had cut jobs in three or more calendar years since 1990. Some of the factors contributing to job elimination included organizational restructuring, re-engineering of business processes, business downturn, outsourcing and merger and acquisition. Middle managers continue to be a favorite target for cuts. While comprising from 5% to 8% of the total corporate workforce, they accounted for nearly 27% of those downsized in 1998.

Downsizing victims can no longer expect to receive extensive outplacement services as an automatic corporate right, says Eric Greenberg, AMA's director of management studies. He reports that 64% of the surveyed companies provided some form of outplacement services in 1997, compared with an 84% rate five years earlier, The AMA cautions that actual assistance ranges from full services by a professional outplacement firm to photocopied handouts featuring simple how-to tips on writing résumés.

Early-retirement buyout packages are proving to be more

MEDIAN RETIREMENT AGE

Years Including	Men	Women
1950-55	66.9	67.7
1955-60	65.8	66.2
1960-65	65.2	64.6
1965-70	64.2	64.2
1970-75	63.4	63.0
1975-80	63.0	63.2
1980-85	62.8	62.7
1985-90	62.6	62.8
1990-95[1]	62.7	62.6
1995-2000[2]	62.3	62.0
2000-2005[2]	61.7	61.2

[1]Based on 1990 actual and 1995 projected data.
[2]Based on projected data.
Source: *Monthly Labor Review*, U.S. Department of Labor

popular than their corporate designers imagined, often stripping a company of too many high achievers. That's why corporate leaders such as DaimlerChrysler, Eastman Kodak and Pacific Gas & Electric have scaled down their early-retirement packages. There is a sound reason why buyout packages are often oversubscribed: Managers anticipate what will happen to those who remain with the company and choose to escape the corporate fallout of downsizing. Those who remain with the company gamble on doing equally well on a subsequent round of buyouts. Too often, they discover their strategy does not pay off.

After You're Out

The employment picture for the 50-plus set used to be a bleak one. Most unemployed workers over age 50 in nearly all job categories could not expect to find a new job commensurate with their abilities. And the older the workers got, the gloomier the employment opportunities became. When they did find work, chances were they'd be working for less money than in their previous job.

Companies driven by the need to cut costs tended to exhibit a negative attitude toward older workers, and large companies—those with 1,000 or more employees—were often the most negative. This strategy might have made corporate sense, but it threatened workers, particularly those with a desire to work again.

How times have changed. As America ages, businesses are discovering they will continue to need older workers. Writing in the Conference Board's *Across the Board* magazine, Harvard psychologist Douglas Powell reported that companies will find fewer managers and professionals in the 24-to-44 age group to replace retiring workers. The alternative is to encourage the 50-plus set to defer retirement. Powell suggests that companies conduct career-strategy workshops for employees, starting in their early fifties, to help them decide if they want to stay on full-time, continue working an alternative schedule or retire. In short, he says companies need to retain a portion of the aging boomers in the organization.

In tracking workplace trends, the Conference Board also notes that while companies may need and want the services of

experienced workers, "many employers still appear more interested in getting people of retirement age off their books and
rehiring them as contingent workers." Even at the managerial
and professional level, the trend is to shift the workload to independent consultants or temporaries because different work rules
apply and management no longer has to offer health care, retirement and other benefit programs.

Setting the Work Rules

If you survive cutbacks and ignore the inducements of early-
retirement payouts, you can, in theory, work indefinitely. The
Federal Age Discrimination in Employment Act of 1967 made it
illegal to discharge or fail to promote a worker between ages 40
and 65 due to age. Ten years later, the age was raised to 70, and
in 1987 the age ceiling was eliminated.

Although corporate officers and partners in professional service firms usually sign employment contracts that specify their
date of retirement, even here there are some admonitions.
Federal regulations stipulate that employment may be terminated at age 65 only if the executive has been in a high policy-mak-
ing position considered critical to the mission of the organization for the past two years and has earned a pension that will
pay at least $44,000 a year. The act also addresses the issue of
age discrimination as it relates to benefits: If it's more expensive
for an employer to provide benefits for older employees, it may
reduce the level of benefits, but it can't charge older employees
more for them.

Some workers in hazardous jobs are governed by mandatory
retirement. The Federal Aviation Administration requires that
pilots on the larger regional and all national airlines retire at age
60. The Age Discrimination Employment Act permits cities to
retire police and firefighters at age 55. But even when retirement
was voluntary, most police and firefighters retired in their fifties
after 20 to 30 years of service, frequently due to job burnout or
work-related health problems.

The Equal Employment Opportunity Commission monitors
workplace conditions, including those that pressure employees

ARE YOU A PAMPERED CORPORATE BABY?

In the '90s, it's dangerous to assume that you can retire according to your own schedule. Your employer may have other ideas. Here are some warning signs that you've become a pampered corporate chicken, one who may suffer the ax without a clue.

- I'm 55 and expect to retire from my job at age 65.
- We've never downsized before, or we've already had staff reductions. Why do I need an updated résumé?
- They wouldn't touch me after being here 30 years.
- I always do well in my annual job review.

WAYS TO AVOID BECOMING ONE

- I play "what if" games.
- I have a game plan tucked away in my drawer just in case.
- I'm going to school at night to upgrade my skills.
- I'm continually updating my computer skills and résumé.
- Job fairs and business shows keep me alert to new trends.
- I have a special emergency fund to cover a job loss.

to accept retirement as a way to reduce the workforce. In 1995 the EEOC received nearly 88,000 new charges of discrimination, a 40% increase over charges received in 1990. The EEOC also had a backlog of 100,000 cases, double the 1990 rate.

The steep climb was accelerated by factors such as changes in federal law that have virtually eliminated mandatory retirement in the workplace and class-action suits brought by workers after downsizing. In screening complaints, the EEOC is on the lookout for companies that ax employees rather than retrain them or that reassign them to jobs hardly commensurate with their ability. Conversely, the EEOC will dismiss the action if the employee turned down the chance to learn a new skill.

THE SOCIAL SECURITY PENALTY. Employees ages 62 to 70 who elect to work indefinitely yet want to receive social security benefits need to be aware of the penalties on excess work-related income. Between ages 62 and 65, the government deducts $1 of benefits for each $2 received in salary or commissions exceeding $9,600 in 1999 (that threshold rises slightly each year). The ratio becomes more favorable for the pensioner between age 65 and 70, when the penalty is reduced to $1 for each $3 earned over $15,500 in 1999. And starting at age 70, the ceiling on job-related income is removed for social security recipients—you can earn any amount of money without sacrificing benefits.

Collecting social security while continuing to work is still an issue that fuels passions, particularly when you're a double and in some instances a triple dipper who collects salary, pension and social security. The purists argue that if you work you should not collect social security. But multiple pensioners have their supporters. "I paid into the system all these years so why not collect?" is a typical response, from retired blue-collar workers as well as corporate executives. Groups such as the AARP and the National Committee to Preserve Social Security and Medicare have successfully lobbied to raise the earned-income barriers for older workers to $30,000 by 2002.

All this said, however, the penalty on earned income isn't as onerous as most people think. See the discussion beginning on page 272, which examines this issue in more detail.

What's Happening in the Professions?

Even here, the term "retirement" is difficult to define, and in some cases, expectations are changing. In accounting, architecture, law and medicine, for example, the practitioner who satisfies state licensing requirements and meets other professional obligations, such as continuing education, is still considered a member of the profession regardless of age and hours spent in active practice. However, there are practical limits:

When I had an annual medical examination a while back, I asked my doctor what retirement rules applied to physicians. "None whatsoever," said Dr. Bruce Tapper. Normally the type of medical specialty dictates to some extent when a physician retires, as do the amount and nature of physical activity required. As Bruce asked, "Would you use a 74-year-old doctor for complex surgery?"

The median retirement age for all but a few medical specialists is 65. Emergency-room doctors retire from that demanding environment somewhat earlier, while psychiatrists work, on average, to age 70. Psychiatrists might even enjoy age as a possible ally. Somewhat like older judges, artists and musicians, their wisdom seems to grow with age in the public's eye, often allowing them to take on the persona of sage.

From a practical standpoint, partnership agreements often help winnow out older partners. Less productive partners are forced to leave firms whose partners are required to work a specific number of hours a year or bring in a sufficient volume of new business consistent with the terms of their partnership agreements. The paternalistic, "clubby" relationships, once the hallmark of many midsize to large partnerships, have nearly vanished, along with laissez-faire arrangements that once permitted older partners to work indefinitely, often on a reduced basis. Smaller firms have fewer rules and, of course, solo practitioners can operate indefinitely.

Thomas Evans, formerly of counsel to the law firm of Andrews and Kurth, notes that a lawyer's professional career life cycle has changed at most firms. "Until recently, the law-firm associate was young, underpaid and overworked. It was a form of apprenticeship. The next step was promotion to a junior partner. The pay was better, yet the partner was still required to work long hours. Eventually a lawyer age 50-plus moved to senior partner status. Lifestyle changed once again. The older lawyer worked fewer hours but was very well paid. It was a rite of passage to pay one's dues for 20 to 25 years and then reap the rewards in later

---

WHICH ONE ARE YOU?

Lydia Brönte, in her book, *The Longevity Factor,* describes retirees as follows:

- **Homesteaders,** who stay in the same field all their lives and remain endlessly fascinated by the work they chose;
- **Transformers,** who find their dream job only after a major career shift;
- **Explorers,** who, in the pursuit of opportunity and growth, make periodic career changes throughout their lives;
- **Long Growth Curver and Late Bloomers,** who reach the highest peak later in life;
- **Retirees and Returnees,** who thought they were leaving work permanently but returned to work having missed the activity and challenges.

life." But the partner's life tenure in all but a few midsize to large firms has virtually disappeared, and bloodletting has become more widespread. At one of Chicago's larger law firms, 20 of its 180 partners were dismissed on the same day, a situation that was explained to the *Wall Street Journal* this way by the head partner: "In today's economy, everybody has to pull his or her own weight. Everybody has to make a sustained contribution."

The news is better for about 500,000 tenured college and university professors.

As of January 1, 1994, the federal government eliminated the mandatory retirement age of 70 for college faculty members. More professors are delaying their retirement, reports the Teachers Insurance and Annuity Association/College Retirement Equities Fund, the nation's largest provider of pensions to educators. In 1997, 84% of TIAA-CREF participants receiving annuity income that year were under age 70 and 16% were age 70 or older. Ten years earlier, in 1987, the proportion under age 70 was 89%, and the proportion age 70 or older was 11%.

SUGGESTED READING

- Brönte, Lydia, *The Longevity Factor* (HarperCollins, 1993). How some well-known Americans view retirement.
- Dychtwald, Ken, *Age Wave* (Bantam Books, 1990). A gold mine of demographic information.
- Friedan, Betty, *The Fountain of Age* (Simon & Schuster, 1993). Lively reading about retirees.
- Glassner, Barry, *Career Crash: The End of America's Love Affair With Work* (Simon & Schuster, 1994). Written primarily for the baby boomers, but parts apply to the 50-plus set.

- Saltzman, Amy, *Downshifting* (HarperCollins, 1992). What it is like to downshift your career into a slower gear.
- Sonnenfeld, Jeffrey, *The Hero's Farewell* (Oxford University Press, 1991). An insightful look at retirement trends among CEOs.
- Handy, Charles, *The Age of Unreason* (Harvard University Press, 1993). A futurist speaks his mind on how we'll be working in the future.
- Manheimer, Ronald, *The Second Middle Age* (Visible Ink Press, 1995). This book traces important trends affecting retirees.

In North Carolina, a study of employment records at the state's three largest universities—Duke, University of North Carolina and North Carolina State University—shows that the tenured faculty is delaying its retirement. The proportion of working faculty members over age 65 increased to 6.3% in 1998 from 3.6% in 1988.

Colleges are fighting back. They're trying various incentives to encourage older faculty to retire, according to the *Chronicle of Higher Education.* They offer a financial bonus or permit them to shift to part-time teaching.

> ### A TAKE ON RETIREMENT
>
> "The self-employed live longer than those who work for others, and the reason most often given is that they are free to plan their own work. This independence seems to be the reason that farmers live almost as long as professional men in spite of the physical hazards of farming....The power to determine the course of one's career affects longevity more than the actual job description." From *The Good Years,* by Caroline Bird

The Corporate Lions

The attitudes of senior corporate executives toward retirement have attracted a number of observers, including author Jeffrey Sonnenfeld, who was smitten with the topic when he was teaching at the Harvard Business School in the 1980s. He tracked how 50 CEOs, all running billion-dollar companies, were able to handle the transfer of power and their departure from active corporate life.

In his book, *The Hero's Farewell,* Sonnenfeld categorizes how CEOs retire—if at all. He divides executives and their attitudes toward retirement into four groups:

- **The Monarchs** leave involuntarily or die, in the best tradition of a Hollywood saga, with their boots on.
- **The Generals** also leave involuntarily, but during their retirement years they plot a return. The General enjoys playing the role of the returning savior, and hopes to remain around long enough to take the firm and himself toward even greater glory.
- **The Ambassadors,** by contrast, quit gracefully and frequently serve as post-retirement mentors. They often remain on the

company's board of directors, do not try to sabotage their successor, and provide continuity and counsel.

- **The Governors,** who serve a limited term, depart for other interests and maintain very little ongoing ties with their company once they leave.

"When the time comes to step aside for newer and almost always younger leaders, many high corporate officers are beset with fears....Leaving office means a loss of heroic stature, a plunge into the abyss of insignificance, a kind of mortality," says Sonnenfeld.

Senior executives innately resist stepping down. "Violinists in retirement," says Sonnenfeld, "can still offer solo performances or play with small ensembles. A conductor, however, needs the full orchestra to be employed, and thus a conductor's skills are not usually portable in retirement. The lack of portability of their skills makes retirement threatening to chief executives....the transition for leaders means finding new, involving and challenging tasks."

Don't dismiss the problems facing CEOs as totally different from your own. While on the surface they may appear dissimilar, most 50-plus managers and professionals view stepping down much the same way as Sonnenfeld's monarchs, generals, ambassadors and governors.

ONE OF THE LIONS

Al Kronick

DEPARTMENT STORE CEO TURNED CONSULTANT

As spectacular as the corporate career of Albert Kronick had been, the announcement of his retirement was totally unexpected. Al retired voluntarily in the early 1970s when he turned 50. He was chairman and CEO of Abraham & Straus, then the leading retail group within the Federated Department Store chain. Other than the several years that he spent as president of another Federated store in Dallas, Al's entire career since graduating from Harvard Business School had been spent at A&S. The Lazarus family, which then controlled Federated, was known for its strong leadership, and Al was one of its highest achievers. Al left at an age when most executives are just hitting full stride.

> **The secret of Al's success? Learn when it's over, and don't look back and second-guess.**

"When I resigned from A&S, people wondered whether I was crazy or was actually fired. Considering these questions, I let them believe in the latter. They could not understand how I could step down at the height of my career while I was in excellent health and had a bright future."

"I had no plans to retire but I decided I would like to leave A&S on my terms while I was still a top performer. I liked my work and I enjoyed running one of the New York's largest stores." There were other factors in his favor. He had saved enough money over the years, his two children were completing college and he had an excellent financial package, including stock in Federated and a vested pension plan. "I also felt that if I earned only another $30,000 a year, Joan (my wife) and I could live very well."

"I was also fortunate in other ways. As CEOs go, my ego was rather small. I had spent 25 years in retailing, but my life was never tied to the job. Friends were in other business fields or were professionals."

Though he had discussed his plans with Joan, Al had not developed a detailed, step-by-step plan for his retirement. "At first I thought I'd like to use my business skills in the nonprofit world, perhaps as a provost of a university. When I looked into these opportunities, I found that the lifestyle was actually very much like the business world that I had just left."

Throughout his career, Al had a reputation as a highly effective corporate manager working in a high-pressure field for a demanding employer. That combination attracted interest from a number of prospective employers. "I was offered other retail jobs but turned them down. The opportunity to continue working came when several companies asked me to be a paid consultant."

Now more than two decades later, Al has reduced the pace of his consulting assignments and concentrates his duties as a director of three companies and as the volunteer treasurer of the Brooklyn Botanic Gardens.

As we've seen throughout the chapter, circumstances have changed since Al Kronick left Federated and chose consulting as his retirement-career alternative. But one thing has remained constant, for Al and for anyone considering retirement: "The secret of Al's success," Joan says, "is to learn when it's over, and not look back and start to second-guess."

Planning for Retirement

MANY OF US SPEND MORE TIME PLANNING OUR next vacation than we do formulating a retirement strategy. That's no great surprise. You've been busy living your life. Who has the time to schedule every nuance of life far into the future? Then one day you get the wake-up call, maybe an early-retirement buyout offer or an invitation to attend a retirement planning session. You're confronted with retirement head-on, especially the questions: What will I do next? How can I afford to do it?

It is never too early to start retirement planning, one reason that companies like Adolph Coors and Polaroid have opened their preretirement workshops to all employees, regardless of age. Nearly two-thirds of preretirees, according to a Merrill Lynch survey, feel that they, rather than their employers or the government, have the prime responsibility for producing their retirement income.

Still, other than emphasizing the need for a sound level of savings, some career counselors warn about the potential for retirement-planning overkill. "Unless the person has retired or is on the verge of doing so," notes Chicago-based outplacement consultants Challenger, Gray & Christmas, "retirement-oriented considerations will necessarily prove theoretical. It takes an extremely well-organized person to really plan a retirement that is still in the future."

Don't take it for granted that your employer will provide retirement planning. Only a handful of larger companies offer a comprehensive retirement-planning program, and then only to their high-echelon employees. What seems like disinterest in corporate-sponsored retirement planning parallels the other trends.

- **Companies are now providing fewer support services to their terminating employees,** according to a 1997 survey of corporate severance practices by Coopers & Lybrand. These services, says the auditing firm, are being axed as companies look for ways to cut the costs of decreasing their workforce. When offered, outplacement services are more often provided to executives than non-executives.
- **Some companies are purposely limiting the scope of their financial planning workshops,** to some extent out of fear of liability from employees if investment advice turns sour.
- **The Conference Board noted a decline in corporate paternalism,** including a shift toward making employees more responsible for financial self-management.

Almost everyone has been feeling the effects of these corporate cutbacks. For example, until a few years ago, IBM offered a retirement education assistance program to all of its employees. This popular benefit program reimbursed employees up to $2,500 for course work they took in nearly any subject, ranging from computer training to golf lessons. IBM eliminated the program and now offers retraining to employees only as part of its special downsizing packages.

Simply put, you need to explore all avenues for retirement planning that are available through your employer, recognizing that as corporate cutbacks continue, these benefits will likely be reduced in many companies. That means you will have to depend on yourself to solve the twin dilemmas—or opportunities—of managing time and your money in retirement.

This chapter will help you change mental gears and show how to take charge of your upcoming retirement life.

Getting Ready to Go
Going Plural: A Model for Your Future?

Call it what you may, many in the 50-plus set believe that a portfolio, or patchwork, work-and-lifestyle formula represents smorgasbord living at its best. British consultant and author Charles Handy champions this cause in his book, *The Age of Unreason,* by showing how to combine various work and non-work interests into "portfolio" careers. (See the profile on page 41 for more on Charles Handy.)

It is only natural that professionals and the self-employed put into play all types of flexible work and lifestyle game plans in preparation for living in retirement. They have the option to reduce their work schedule yet stay put in the workplace. Corporate managers, by contrast, are guided by more rigid employment practices in the workplace. But once they leave their jobs they are free to create new lifestyles and structure different career patterns.

In the United Kingdom, KPMG Career Consultancy Services, part of the worldwide KPMG Peat Marwick accounting and consulting empire, promotes the idea of a balanced lifestyle for some clients. KPMG partner Roger Shipton tells of one 50-year-old client who lost his job. Instead of returning to a traditional 9-to-5 job, he has "gone plural," with three separate yet concurrent paid positions: board chairman of a company in the industry in which he worked, British sales representative for a Far Eastern manufacturing firm, and franchisee in the ice business.

Going plural also describes the lifestyle approach taken by

> ### POINTS TO REMEMBER
>
> - Retirement planning is an individual responsibility.
> - Corporate paternalism is diminishing, and few employers offer help in retirement planning.
> - Retirement provides the chance to juggle many interests—work and play—at once.
> - You can find plenty of opportunities for ideas and support before and after retirement.
> - More than ever, this is the time to think flexibly and creatively.
> - It's also time to become computer literate.
> - It's never too soon to take stock of your financial needs and resources in retirement.

New York City's ex-mayor Edward Koch. "I never thought I would have a third career. To be honest, I never counted on a second, but there it was," he wrote in *Citizen Koch*. "And now, here I am, nearly three years into my new life as an attorney, radio talk-show host, newspaper columnist, television news commentator, syndicated movie reviewer, public speaker, university lecturer, commercial spokesperson and author (of mystery books). That's nine jobs by my count, which suits an old workaholic like me just fine." Though he did not reveal his income, he said it surpassed his former pay as mayor and member of Congress—and that didn't include what he makes now that he is a television judge on "The People's Court."

Ron Rich launched his version of a patchwork career when he lost his job as an elementary school teacher and principal. Ron decided to pursue a career in children's literature by starting a newsletter for librarians, teachers and parents. For the second leg in his program, he created "Let's Read a Book," in which he visits elementary schools and acts out his favorite books for children. He was then hired as a salesperson at a local bookstore. After six months, Ron was promoted to children's book specialist. Though not by choice, Ron traded in his old career for a work portfolio with three paid assignments.

Whatever route you take to get there, you can be sure that your new lifestyle will resemble the oft-used pie chart. How you apportion the different pieces of the pie is your choice.

Time to Say Goodbye to Computer Illiteracy

"Not one of us has a PC in our home or in our office," said J. Richard Munro, the former co-chairman of Time Warner Inc., describing himself and his fellow directors when he resigned from IBM's 18-member board of directors in 1993. Munro's revelation of computer illiteracy is embarrassing enough considering IBM's product line, but unfortunately his personal plight applies to many other 50-plus executives who might very well need computer skills to survive in their post-retirement lifestyle. Put Dick's situation aside because he has the resources to obtain administrative help, but what about you? Knowing how to operate a desktop computer is no longer an optional skill.

Take Tom R., a soon-to-be retired corporate executive who plans to become a self-employed financial consultant. Despite his financial expertise, Tom is handicapped because he is computer illiterate. But Tom appears unconcerned. His homemade solution is to have a former secretary, also retired, process his handwritten notes into reports and letters. With this alternative, he sees no reason to learn how to operate a computer. In principle, that may be true. But practically speaking, he'll have less flexibility in how he gets his work done, and his approach will increase his lag time in responding to clients' requests for reports and impair his ability to handle assignments. He'll miss out on software tools that would permit him to work more efficiently and to better serve his clients. Simply put, the computer-illiterate manager stands little chance of getting a new full- or part-time job. Bottom line, Tom runs the risk of looking like a dinosaur.

Be smart, and avoid following in Tom's footsteps. Like it or not, chances are you'll be required to be proficient in basic computer skills in most postretirement careers. Computer know-how is the "open sesame" to reentering the job market, starting a business, changing careers or becoming a consultant.

Instead, take a lesson from former President George Bush, who while in the White House learned to use a computer to write memos and personal correspondence. As a starter, at least learn the fundamentals of word processing. It's best to start your lessons before leaving the active workplace, where you can more easily learn programs within the context of your daily work and call on those in the know to help out in a pinch. You might even ask a co-worker or one of your company's programmers or systems managers to teach you the ABCs. As a last resort, chances are one of your children—nowadays even a seven-year-old grandchild—can teach the fundamentals. As with any new skill, becoming proficient takes practice. After taking a few lessons, just turn on the computer and go for it.

If you can't get help within your company or from your own family members, there are nearly unlimited opportunities available within your community. Start the search at your local community college, where you will find low-cost courses in word processing, spreadsheet analysis and database management. If you feel uncomfortable in a group setting, don't give up. Ask for a referral to someone who can work with you one-to-one. Three to four lessons should have you on your way.

THE SENIORNET CONNECTION. Also see whether SeniorNet operates within your community. It could be the perfect place to learn computing. SeniorNet was founded in 1986 by Dr. Mary Furlong. Like other adult education programs, SeniorNet caters to retirees who want to learn in a classroom with their peers. Its forte is teaching computer skills exclusively to older adults who have never used a computer and feel uncomfortable at a keyboard—and who would feel even more uncomfortable learning how to use a computer in a classroom filled with younger students.

SeniorNet has grown to include 140 centers in 35 states, the District of Columbia and New Zealand, with a membership exceeding 30,000 retirees. Since its founding, SeniorNet has trained over 100,000 retirees. Cost varies slightly by location; the center serving Raleigh, N.C., for example, charges $60 ($25 for the Raleigh Center and the balance for one-year SeniorNet membership) for six or seven two-hour sessions. By the time you're finished with the introductory course, you'll know the basics: how to boot-up a computer, do basic word processing, use e-mail and access Web sites.

SeniorNet sponsors online discussion groups in 345 different areas, ranging from cooking and recipes, gardening, home and auto repair to current events. The centers also provide follow-up courses in database management and genealogy. To learn if there is a center in your area, contact SeniorNet at 121 Second St., San Francisco, CA 94105 (415-495-4990; www.seniornet.org).

MORE ON COMPUTERS. "Never before in our history has a medium so sharply divided the population along generational lines," says Cheryl Russell, executive editor of *The Boomer Report*. She notes that only 5% of people age 55-plus have been online during the past 30 days.

"In the long run, the technological divide will shrink as

boomers replace older generations in the 50-plus group." The "want-nots," as Russell describes them, "have a distinct demographic profile. Rather than being the poorest and most marginal among us, they are, on the whole, comfortably well-off. Most want-nots are older Americans."

SeniorNet, however, developed other information that indicates much higher computer usage among users over 50. In 1998, about 40% of people age 55 to 74 owned a personal computer, nearly double the number who had them in their homes just four years earlier. As computer prices continue to decline and more retirees get "hooked" by e-mail and the Web, computer usage should climb even higher among the senior set.

Move or Stay Put?

When it comes to retirement migration, your guess is as good as mine on the number of people age 60-plus who retire and relocate. Sociologist Charles Longino of Wake Forest University finds that approximately 4.5% of the retirement-age population relocates out-of-state each year and about the same number move within their home state.

But there's more to relocation than statistical analysis. Even though most retirees might never buy a retirement home, chances are they'll shop the marketplace for a city or town that complements the lifestyle they seek.

Starting at age 50 and continuing for the next ten to 15 years, hordes of curious Americans are on the road searching for potential places to move. They tour the Sun Belt states, look at communities and homes, examine the lifestyle, and return home. Some buy and others decide to stay put.

Why Move?

Family, friends and nostalgic haunts glue them to home base. Yet home base need not be a four-bedroom home on a one-acre lot. The alternatives are plentiful. Some stay put in the same home town but buy or rent a smaller home or apartment. Others hedge their bets by remodeling an existing home. And there are those folks who maintain both a winter and a summer home, ranging from a plush apartment on New York's Park Avenue and a home in Nantucket to retirees with a modest home and a recreational vehicle or a small condo in Florida.

The change in the tax law is a boon for retirees who want to buy a home more suitable to retirement, and at the same time augment their nest egg and their monthly cash flow. Gone is the one-time $125,000 capital-gains exclusion on the sale of a home. The 1997 Taxpayer Relief Act increased the ante for homesellers to $250,000 for a single taxpayer, and $500,000 for a couple filing jointly. The new rules represent a form of financial downsizing that makes sense to the 50-plus set. What better incentive than to sell a home, replace it with a less expensive apartment or home, and pocket the balance.

Tom Sawyer, Iris-Rose Ruffing, Art Lebo, Armando (Mickey) Henriquez and Herbert Halbrecht, all profiled in this book, moved to North Carolina for different reasons. Too young to retire at age 58, Tom, an ophthalmologist, came from Milwaukee to join a Pinehurst-based practice. Iris-Rose retired as a Girl Scout director in Chicago. A native of North Carolina, she was returning home. Art was in search of an area that offered good sports, educational and lifestyle features.

Tom, Iris-Rose and Art live in Fearrington Village, an upscale retirement community near Chapel Hill. Mickey took a different route. Mickey's son was on the Duke University faculty when he relocated from the metropolitan New York area to Durham. Mickey wanted no part of a retirement community. Instead, he built a house in Durham surrounded by neighbors of all ages.

Herb Halbrecht also moved from suburban New York to Durham. To gain the full flavor on his relocation, see what Herb has to say about his priorities. "We wanted to live on or adjacent to a golf course. Gayla [his wife] is obsessive about golf and after 30-years-plus of being married to me, it was payback time. I wanted to be close to a major university to provide access to an intellectual ferment. And, as one reaches retirement age, close proximity to world-class medical facilities becomes increasingly relevant. I also wanted to be near inner-city schools so I could volunteer as a tutor." And finally, like other retirees who move south, Herb poses this question: "Who needs ice storms and blizzards? Then again, who needs the summer humidity? But these are bearable and avoidable. The airport is convenient and so are highways to cooler summer weather in the north."

What About a Retirement Community?

Retirees face a dilemma when they ponder whether to move or stay put. If they do decide to relocate, what type of community will they select after they have lived in the same home for 30 or more years? Do they favor a balanced urban or suburban residential area with neighbors of all ages, or would they prefer to move to Sun City, Arizona, by far the nation's largest retirement community with its 46,000 older residents?

Del Webb, which has developed a number of large-scale retirement communities, surveyed baby boomers who were about to turn 50. Approximately 50% said that they planned to move to another state when they retired. Another 21% said they intended to move to another city in the same state, 18% expected to relocate in the same community where they'd been living, and the remaining 10% were undecided on where they'd live.

Given this variety of preferences, Del Webb, which already has built eight Sun Belt communities with about 100,000 residents, is hedging its bets. It built a retirement community 20 miles northeast of Sacramento for the 55-plus set who prefer northern California to the Sun Belt. The average home there costs about $210,000. About 70% of the homeowners previously lived in the San Francisco Bay area, and somewhere between 30% to 40% of the residents work full- or part-time. The same rationale prompted Del Webb to break ground for a community of nearly 5,000 homes a mere 45 miles from downtown Chicago.

Factors to Consider

Before looking at home sites, it's best to do your homework. Start off by knowing the difference between retirement communities. A leisure-oriented retirement community such as Sun City or Leisure World appeals to retirees who relocate when they first retire, in their mid fifties and sixties. A country-club lifestyle is the theme. As retirees age, many move again to a managed-care facility. Here they live independently, yet take their meals in a central dining room. The facility also provides amenities such as shuttle bus service to shopping malls and evening concerts, and on-site health care professionals.

If you're considering a move, the site selection possibilities should include:

- **A large city.** Surprisingly, a number of suburbanites relocate to the city to be nearer the array of activities that a large city has to offer.

- **A college community.** There's lots to do in terms of sports, adult education and cultural activities. It's even better when you're an alumnus.

- **A summer community.** Retirees are taking summer cottages and remodeling them for year-round rather than seasonal usage. That might sound like a great idea but it's best to visit these towns in the off season. The weather could be dismal and the community desolate. In short, it might be a wonderful summer lifestyle but an impractical one for 12 months.

- **Returning home.** When both husband and wife are from the same area, returning home is often rewarding even if the couple hasn't lived there for many years. This is particularly delightful when there are fond memories of hometown USA.

- **Moving outside the U.S.** Mexico and Costa Rica appeal to some retirees. Guadalajara, Mexico, is home to 30,000 Americans and Canadians. The living is definitely cheaper but be aware that medicare does not apply cross the border.

- **Take to the road in a recreational vehicle.** According to a University of Michigan study, nearly one-half of the RVs on the road are owned by people over 55. The question is, do you want to live in an RV year-round or use it on a seasonal basis? Many RV folks are snowbirds. They live in the north from April to October. Come fall, they hop into their RV and travel south.

- **Rural America.** Lots of Americans are trying to escape from congested metro centers for the quieter, and usually less expensive, lifestyle of a smaller community. Be cautious about this type of move unless you know and understand how life in a small town works. Be prepared to find that there may be few, if any, coffee bars, ethnic restaurants or other amenities associated with suburbia and large cities.

Now it's time to examine the merchandise. Take these factors into consideration as you consider possible places to relocate to:

- **Health care services.** What about the local hospital and the medical community in general? This should be a prime consideration for anyone over age 60. Rural America might be scenic, but traveling 150 miles once a week to see a medical specialist makes little sense—and could be dangerous. So think ahead.
- **The job market.** Retirees often want to work part- or full-time. Even if you think you might not want to work after you settle down, investigate whether there's a demand for your skills.
- **Taxes.** Check the state and the city income, property and nuisance taxes. Otherwise, you might be in for a shock when you prepare your first tax return after you've moved.
- **Weather.** Sections of the Sun Belt might be a great place in January, but what about the hot and humid summer days?
- **Sports.** Like to play tennis, golf, fish and take walks? Is there a good golf course nearby? If it is a private club, is it affordable?
- **Religion.** Are there churches or synagogues in the community you're considering? Would you feel comfortable there?
- **Transportation.** How many miles is it to the airport? This is an important feature for retirees who want to visit children or take frequent vacations.
- **General amenities.** Good restaurants, retail stores, libraries and other activities are often taken for granted back home. Check to see if the area you're considering has enough of a variety for your needs.
- **Security.** Crime exists in the smallest hamlets. It's not just exclusive to metro centers. If you're particularly concerned, move to a gated community.
- **The politics.** Don't go where the prevailing political sentiment goes strongly against your grain.
- **Adult education.** Is there a community or four-year college in easy reach?
- **The emotional factor.** You probably don't want to think about it, but is this the place where you'd like to live the rest of your life?

Sources of Ideas & Support

The resources below range from the structured program offered by the American Medical Association to a do-it-yourself group organized by retired New York City teachers. There's nothing proprietary in the way these or other groups have approached retirement planning. What applies to physicians could be duplicated by other professionals. And literally anybody can start a self-help group. One thing remains constant: You need to take the initiative and personally put the ball into play.

A Little Life Planning

If your employer doesn't offer a retirement-planning program, you might be able to find one locally that's similar to Duke University's "What Are You Going to Do With the Rest of Your Life?" or New York University's "Over 50? What's Next?" The NYU seminar, conducted by its Center for Career & Life Planning, "used to be called 'Over 55, What's Next?' but we lowered the age to attract more early retirees and those whose companies downsized," says Anita Lands, seminar leader and an independent, late-career and retirement planner who does consulting. It takes Anita four sessions, two hours each, at a cost of about $100 per participant to cover the basics in retirement planning. The seminar focuses on ways to clarify goals, manage change and develop a personal plan based on self-assessment and exploration of realistic alternatives in both work and leisure areas. Information and inspiration similar to what Anita offers in her course is available through many other college-sponsored programs, independent counseling and self-help groups.

Anita's preamble at the first session sets the tone for the seminar and is a realistic primer for most soon-to-be retirees. "Whether you're thinking about changing jobs, working part-time, retiring or simply remaining productive, you can make a better decision when you see where the road is heading. Ongoing life and career planning is a must if you want to create and sustain a desirable level of satisfaction from your job and life."

The participants at one workshop series included nine women

and four men, all 50-plus, who had either recently retired or were considering it. Their objectives differed: to change jobs or careers, reenter the job market, return to school or start their own businesses. David, a building supply company's chief financial officer, said he felt "stuck in the mud trying to figure it out. I'd go into my own business, but I'm not sure I want to take the risk." Then there was Maureen, a just-retired bank officer, who said, "I'm bored out of my mind. What's the next step? Will I be 'bad' if I don't go back to work immediately?"

DON'T RETIRE. INSTEAD, RETREAD. In guiding the class, Anita employs many of the tools that she uses with her corporate outplacement clients. She encourages students to think creatively, to consider different career or retirement options, and above all to take a fresh look at themselves, evaluate their work and leisure skills, set goals and implement an action plan.

Potential couch potatoes squirm as Anita talks:

"We have to learn how to transfer skills and develop new ones. We get locked into old skills, things that we do too easily.

"Remember, the way expenses are increasing, we are all under some pressure to earn extra money. One secret is to take an avocation and perhaps turn it into a vocation.

"Please rid your vocabulary of such baggage as 'should have,' 'would have' and 'could have.' Why turn 84 and still have the attitude of I 'should have' done something else after I retired?

"Avoid being referred to as a former VP. You need a new identity and it only comes by acquiring new skills, activities, and life values.

"Whether you work part- or full-time, you're still part of the work force. It is time to plan your life on your terms. Up till now there have been scripts for school, work and family. The old scripts no longer apply. It's up to you to write a new one.

"Above all, don't retire—rather, retread."

Physicians Look Ahead

In a conference room in the St. Moritz Hotel in New York City, 20 physicians in their mid fifties to mid sixties and their spouses attended "Gearing Up for Retirement," a workshop co-sponsored by the American Medical Association. The workshop is designed for physicians who expect to retire within the next five years, are considering a second career and want to understand their post-practice options. Its objective is to help physicians consider all facets of retirement, from new lifestyle to investment and portfolio management, retirement income and estate planning.

The attendees wondered how they would deal with possible boredom after an exciting and useful professional life. Would they be able to find an equivalent new lifestyle? What about a loss of self-esteem when they are no longer actively practicing medicine? "Are you prepared to face possible boredom when you no longer work 70-hour weeks?" asked Patty Dunkel, the workshop's former moderator. "How will you replace the professional relationship with patients and colleagues, and the loss of self-esteem?"

No quick cure-alls are prescribed. The suggested antidote is for the attendees to plan and develop practical new strategies that deal with the day when they will no longer be part of the workforce. Attendees are encouraged to prepare a checklist of what they plan to do and how they'll do it. For example, do they plan to leave medicine totally or would they like to continue to work in the health care field, perhaps on a pro bono basis or as a part-time worker? What about developing hobbies, making travel a part of their lives, or perhaps relocating to another part of the country?

Though the workshop is directed at physicians, 50-plus-set professionals and managers in other fields can benefit from its message: You can enjoy a satisfying, active new career without a full-time practice, using your skills—or developing new ones— as a consultant, volunteer, speaker or hobbyist.

FOR MORE INFORMATION. Members of professional and business societies in other fields should consult their organizations to see if they conduct retirement planning sessions. Physicians should contact AMA Solutions at 200 N. LaSalle St., Chicago, IL 60601 (800-366-6968; www.ama-assn.org).

Small-Company CEOs
Seek a New Paradigm

CEOs of small to midsize companies have a different set of options than their brethren from larger companies when planning their switch from business to a different lifestyle, and corporate-sponsored outplacement usually isn't one of them. One possible solution is to retain a specialist who is familiar with the problems facing owner-managers. Interestingly, what such specialists suggest applies to other managers and professionals.

Carl Samuel's gun is for hire. As founder in 1986 of Business Life Transition and a management consultant since 1972, Carl assists business owners in considering and adjusting to the possibilities of a life beyond winning in business, for the period of life he calls "the fourth quarter." "They have a need to find something to organize their life around. It's hardly an easy process for the president of a company, a guy who enjoys making decisions."

Carl tries to help clients take a fresh look at themselves. "The first half of their lives, they lived from the outside in, and now they must discover how to live from the inside out." He describes this as a critical step toward a successful fourth quarter. Once retired from the workforce, most former CEOs have lost their corporate clout. This is a particularly difficult challenge for a person who is an achiever, motivated by money, recognition, success, status and power. To get them to shift their perspective, Carl often combines individual coaching with workshops and peer-group meetings. "We bring six to ten executives together in all-day group sessions once a month for a year. They hear how people with similar backgrounds are trying to make the changeover. They might listen to me in one-on-one counseling sessions, but they really listen to and respect these guys."

THE BIG ISSUES FOR ANYONE. The transition into retirement is hardly an overnight process, often taking a few years to accomplish. It takes time to realize that "business as usual" is being replaced by another lifestyle. During this period, Carl finds that CEOs have five primary concerns on their minds:
- **Aging.** How much time do I have; how do I want to spend it?
- **Security.** How do I know that I have enough money to maintain

my standard of living?

- **Self-identity.** Who am I besides my business, and what will I do?
- **Dreams.** What will give me meaning, purpose, vitality and relevance in my life?
- **Relationships.** What do I want, and who do I want to be with? During the CEOs' transition into retirement, Samuel suggests that they find some things to do temporarily while they're looking for activities with more long-term value.

FOR MORE INFORMATION. Write to or call Carl Samuels, Business Life Transitions, 2792 Main Way, Los Alamitos, CA 90720 (562-598-8117).

Letting Go Isn't Easy

Dr. Joel Goldberg in New Jersey is another niche consultant who advises CEOs on retirement. As president of Career Consultants and a consultant for 25 years in the techniques of change man-

---

SUGGESTED READING

- *Retire Worry-Free* (Kiplinger Books, 1998). An easy-to-read primer, written by the staff of *Kiplinger's Personal Finance Magazine,* that will help you determine your retirement needs and resources.
- Miller, Theodore, *Invest Your Way to Wealth* (Kiplinger Books, 1998). A common-sense guide to investing that will help you grow your nest egg and make the most of what you have.
- Savageau, David, *Retirement Places Rated* (Macmillan, 1995). Helps retirees weigh alternatives.
- Longino, Charles, *Retirement Migration in America* (Vacation Publications,

1995). An academic expert explores relocation trends.
- Parrott, William and John L, *You Can Afford to Retire!* (Prentice Hall, 1993). Questions answered on taxes, inflation and investments.
- Solomon, Salend, Rahman, Liston and Reuben, *A Consumer's Guide to Aging* (Johns Hopkins University Press, 1992). A detailed reference book. Several of the authors are physicians.
- Terhorst, Paul, *Cashing in the American Dream...How to Retire at 35* (Bantam Books, 1988). Interesting reading for planners and dreamers.

---

agement and organization development, Joel advises clients who are typically in their mid fifties to mid sixties, and, more often than not, are the founders and presidents of companies with less than $100 million in sales. All of Joel's counseling is done one-to-one.

Joel has not reduced his counseling services to a short-term fix or an easy-to-use checklist. "It takes time and planning. There's a need to think the problem through, take a look at different options, and learn how to detach. Whatever the approach, the shock of retiring is enormous. Thus, sufficient advance planning is critical.

"In the first meeting," Joel notes, "I find many of them to be restless, bored and tired, but they would like to work forever. They must face a central issue in their lives—letting go."

Severing ties with one's business has an emotional impact that often affects family relationships. Some business owners divorce after 40 or more years of marriage. They discover differences of opinion brought about by the process of retiring that are irreconcilable.

Clients are naturally concerned with managerial succession. It is often the first time that they have openly discussed this problem with an outsider. The CEOs of closely held and family-owned businesses have strong emotional attachments after running the company for 30 or more years. They need to be presented with alternatives—selling the company or turning ownership over to a new generation of family or nonfamily managers.

"I show them how to invent a new scenario. Remember, these are high achievers. They have more than ample incomes, and they are emotionally tied to their business. Most are good in their corporate planning but have done little of it in their personal lives. I get them to start reflecting on their lives. What would they like to do if they could do it all over again? It's a process that takes several years; it's not something that can be done overnight. I personally abhor the idea of retirement. I get them to think of it as redirecting their experiences into other areas—whatever they find satisfying."

Some of Joel's clients are interested in becoming directors of other companies or nonprofit organizations. He helps them prepare a résumé for those purposes and introduces them to companies and organizations that might need their services.

Letting go does not always produce a Cinderella ending. Joel tells about one CEO who was training his son to be his successor. But the CEO had no way to fairly evaluate his son's business skills. "We suggested that he establish an independent board to conduct the evaluation. They found that the son did not have sufficient management skills to run the business. As a result, the company was sold." A transition in management within the family was scuttled.

Sometimes, after evaluating the alternatives, the CEO decides not to retire. "It's their business and they can do what they want."

FOR MORE INFORMATION. Write to or call Joel Goldberg, Career Consultants, 1767 Morris Ave., Union, NJ 07083 (908-687-7350).

Say Hello to "Our Group"

When "Our Group" has lunch in a midtown New York City restaurant, they look like any other luncheon meeting of six midlife business and professional women. Their conversation varies from work to lifestyle issues. But the group actually has a different purpose. These former New York City teachers and administrators meet monthly as a postretirement support group.

Little did Mary R. and her friends realize that they were pathfinders when they started what they refer to as "Our Group," an organization that has no charter, official status, officers or dues. Ever since their first meeting more than 30 months ago, they have provided each other with informal and ongoing support that goes well beyond the assistance offered by many structured organizations.

The first lunch meeting after their retirement set the tone for future meetings. Little time was spent reminiscing—or as Mary puts it, "we have better things to discuss." They typically talk about part-time work, using free time and adjusting to a less hectic lifestyle that includes the freedom to have a leisurely breakfast, read the newspaper and not leave for work at 7 A.M. At one lunch, they chatted about a newspaper article they had read on Charles Handy's concept of "portfolio careers" and how his concept applies to them.

Our Group has found that six members is a practical number to meet and talk over lunch or dinner in a restaurant, or to meet in someone's living room. They see no need to expand beyond their present number.

Our Group has created a basic formula that could easily serve as a template for many other retirees.

- **The group shares a strong common thread**—for example, the same employer or similar professional training or jobs.
- **Its members know and generally respect each other.**
- **The group is small;** the meetings are informal but directed.
- **It avoids letting one or two of the members dominate** the group or its agenda, or letting the group become a stage for "show-and-tell" instead of mutual support and discussion.
- **The meetings, while informal,** depend for their continuity on the professional tone of the participants.
- **Above all, gossip is downplayed** at every meeting.
- **While there are no officers** in this "birds of a feather" group, it needs one or two active members to handle a few administrative functions such as sending out meeting notices or setting an agenda, informal as it may be.

FILLING A GAP FOR ITS MEMBERS. Our Group started in mid 1991 when the New York City Board of Education, as part of its downsizing plan, sweetened its retirement package to encourage teachers and administrators to retire ahead of schedule.

One of Mary's friends came to her soon after the board made its offer. She was uncertain about accepting the early-retirement package and asked Mary for her advice. The teachers' union had provided printed handouts digesting the key issues but offered little practical counseling. The union, too, seemed uneducated on the pros and cons of an early buyout. The future members of Our Group looked for advice from their peers. "I decided to lend an ear," Mary noted. "The word spread, and a few of us decided to get together informally and discuss the retirement package. We were not totally sold on early retirement or the advantages of the board's package. What it would mean? What would we do when we were no longer working? We were not mentally ready to retire."

Even with their reservations, they all accepted the board's buyout plan. They were aware of current buyout trends in corporate America, and knew that, as in industry, the board's next buyout offer might not be as generous. Looking back, their decision was correct. Future buyouts were skimpier as the board of education attempted to control early-retirement costs.

"Since my retirement decision was made so hastily," Barbara, another group member, noted, "I needed the group as a support. Though we each have different family setups, the group has become a sort of extended family. As old friends, we're frank and honest with each other. That's what you need when you've just left a job after 25 years and you're looking for new things to do."

Several in Our Group have already returned to work as part-timers or substitute teachers. Judith substitutes several days a month, Arlene teaches history at a community college, Mary is studying for a doctorate, Charlotte helps her husband in his business, and Frances is an artist. And Barbara, who discovered in retirement that she needed the discipline of a job, now works three days a week as a guidance counselor at a private school.

Our Group is "a continuation of a fulfilling work experience," says Charlotte. "We shared so many things over the years as colleagues and friends over cups of coffee or lunch in the teachers' room. As retirees we continue to share our experiences."

How They Planned Their Retirement

There are two types of retirees. Some switch from the active workforce on their own terms, often meticulously planning each step in advance. The others have a more abrupt transition. They report to work on Friday to learn that their job has either been eliminated or they have been asked to take early retirement.

The long-term planners do not necessarily have the advantage. Often they need to conduct their retirement planning in secrecy because a premature announcement might offend employers, co-workers or partners and could even put their current job in jeopardy.

The diverse group you will meet on the following pages includes the CEO of a small public company, a partner in a large law firm, a computer programmer with a large company, and two former corporate managers who use computers extensively.

MEET CHARLES HANDY AND HIS "PORTFOLIO CAREER"

Charles Handy

PERSONNEL EXECUTIVE, ECONOMIST AND TEACHER TURNED PORTFOLIO CAREERIST

Charles Handy practices what he preaches in his book, *The Age of Unreason,* by living a portfolio career. His lifestyle has been one of discovering "how the different bits of work in our life fit together to form a balanced whole." Charles believes that more people of all ages, not just early retirees and the 50-plus set, will soon be living portfolio careers as a result of technological, societal and corporate organizational changes.

To define the portfolio career, Handy divides work into two groups: paid work, consisting of wage work and fee work; and free work, which includes home work (work around the house, including tending to children), gift work (volunteerism) and study work (learning a new language or training for a sport). He estimates that approximately half of people over age 55 are already pursuing portfolio careers even though they might not label them that way. Because this lifestyle can extend right into the period usually known as retirement, Handy contends that "retirement" is not an accurate term and will become obsolete.

Charles is a graduate of both Oriel College at Oxford and the Sloan School of Management at the Massachusetts Institute of Technology. Sandwiched between the years at Oxford and MIT was a decade that he spent as a personnel executive at Shell International and as an economist for the Anglo-American Corp. When he left MIT, he joined the London Business School, to start and direct the Sloan program in England and to teach courses in managerial psychology and development. In 1977, he served as warden of St. George's House in Windsor Castle, a private conference and study center concerned with ethics and values in society.

Charles, thinker and author, looks at the future of work and the obsolescence of retirement as we've known it. He puts his theories into practice.

"My teaching concentrated on the application of behavioral science to organizations of all types. In particular, I was dealing with the management of change, the cultures of organizations, and the theory and practice of individual and organizational development. My current thinking focuses on the future of work, and on the changes that demography and technology will bring to organizations and to all our lives."

Charles was ready to put his theories to the test. "I was writing how the world would be. I was 49. It was time I bloody made some personal changes, and quick."

To make things happen requires a plan. "It is important to allocate the number of days and hours to be devoted to different segments of a portfolio career. I had to find ways to make money. In my case writing books has helped to build a reputation but hasn't exactly made me a lot of money. What makes money for me is running seminars and teaching managers.

"Elizabeth [his wife] and I are somewhat conservative, so we doubled the amount of money we thought we needed to support our lifestyle. How many days of teaching and running seminars would we have to work? The goal was not to maximize our income but to make enough so we could live somewhat more comfortably.

"Fortunately, Elizabeth is my manager. If I answer the telephone, I tend to say 'yes' to everyone. She keeps track of my hours. Every Christmas we review the hours we spent on different projects throughout the year to help us understand and manage the portfolio. It is a very disciplined approach."

DIVIDING HIS TIME

Besides 150 days of fee work, Charles devotes 50 days to gift work—or as he calls it, "my causes," such as the Carnegie Inquiry in the Third Age. As the Carnegie Inquiry's non-paid consultant, he has persuaded a number of foundations to provide $2 million to fund a two-year inquiry into a study of the Third Age. (The Third Age comes from the French idea that life divides into three sequential parts—learning, working and living.) His gift work also includes some church-related activities.

"I'm very interested in religion. I make myself available at no fee to bishops to run seminars for the church."

He devotes another 75 days to reading and keeping current. This portion is expanding. "I'm now learning Italian because we own a house in Italy. Of all the things I do, learning Italian is by far the most difficult."

There's a lighter side in his portfolio— the 90 days devoted to home work and leisure. "We live part of the year in London, which is our public life; we also have a country place in Norfolk, where I do my writing. In Norfolk I'm housekeeper. Elizabeth and I reverse roles. I buy and cook the food, maintain the house and do everything. Elizabeth is free to devote her time to photography. This change is very good for me. It makes me aware of what it is like to go shopping every day. It keeps me as a human being and [saves me] from becoming arrogant.

"One can write great books, but the secret is learning to cook a tasty omelet. This is important. When friends come to stay with us in Norfolk, they're more impressed by my cooking than by my writings." As part of his portfolio lifestyle, Charles completed a one-week Cordon Bleu course in French regional cooking.

The portfolio career concept is starting to attract the children of the 50-plus set. The Handy children are no exception. Kate and Scott, who are in their mid twenties, heed to such a lifestyle. "It is silly to have a single job," says Kate. "One needs to have three or four different paying jobs because employment conditions are so poor."

COMBATING COMPUTER ILLITERACY

Louis Powell

PRODUCTION MANAGER TURNED COMPUTER EDUCATOR

Louis Powell's business card carries an unusual line: teaching computer skills to adults born before Pearl Harbor. Hardly a wise-guy comment. Louis supervises a computer boot camp for retirees.

A native of Minnesota and a University of Minnesota graduate, Louis, 66, worked for IBM for 34 years. When he retired in 1991, he was a production manager at the company's Research Triangle Park facility in Durham, North Carolina. By then, a one-time hobby of collecting antique cameras had by design already evolved into an active sideline business.

Once retired, Powell's Camera Exchange became his full-time focus. His business called for frequent trips to East Coast camera fairs and dealers. But as online computer systems became more universally used, computers and data communications lessened the need for face-to-face meetings as he did increasing business by e-mail and over his own Web page.

Then an unplanned event occurred in 1996, just about the time that he was looking for some more things to do. "I was attending an IBM Quarter Century Club when someone told me that the company was looking for people who enjoyed teaching to

> **"My job is to get people over the fear of computers, and make them feel comfortable with a mouse and keyboard."**

become involved in starting up a computer facility that IBM and Southern Bell were sponsoring. The next thing I knew I was one of the organizers of the SeniorNet Center being set up in Raleigh." Louis simply wanted to be an instructor, but he also became the Center's volunteer manager, a job with about 20 hours of work a week.

The center opened in mid 1996, and during its first two years the team of teachers, including a number of former IBM managers and computer professionals, trained 500 to 600 retirees. The hands-on course is geared to retirees who might otherwise find attending a computer class at a community college with younger students to be somewhat intimidating. The SeniorNet approach is nearly one-on-one. In a room with six computers, two or three instructors are on hand to help students.

For $60, students progress to the point where they feel comfortable with word processing. They also learn how to develop a database, create an address book, run a spread sheet, communicate via e-mail and access Web sites. The intention, Louis says, is not to train people to get jobs, though some might use their new-found skills to return to the workplace.

"They take courses for practical reasons. Some want to use e-mail to write family, friends and grandchildren. Others are interested in genealogy, want to write family histories, keep track of their investments or do some form of research. My job is to get people over the fear of computers and make them feel comfortable with a mouse and a keyboard. When they say they can't type, I show them how I do it with two fingers. By the end of the first day's session, they know how to open a computer file, use the mouse and handle some of the other basics."

Most of the SeniorNet students range in age from 55 to 70. Occasionally, an octogenarian shows up. Many of the students, Louis notes, recently retired and they're looking for things to do. The computer represents a new experience and a new challenge. It's a skill they can share with their children and grandchildren. Some already own computers, and others are planning to buy one. Louis and the other instructors show them how to select a computer to meet their needs.

Louis says that all the students are treated as beginners even though a few have some previous computer experience. At work, they may have used a terminal on dedicated assignments such as inputting or retrieving data. But these repetitious jobs, he says, did not prepare them to use a PC.

As an instructor, he has learned the tricks of the trade. "A number of husbands and wives are students. Naturally, they come together and attend the same class. But I don't let them sit next to each other. I place them in opposite sides of the room to avoid conflict. Otherwise, one would be instructing the other. If I could, I'd put seat belts on them to keep them in their seats."

THERE'S LIFE AFTER IBM

Larry Bumgardner

CORPORATE-TO-SMALL-COMPANY COMPUTER-SOFTWARE DESIGNER

For several years prior to Larry Bumgardner's retirement, IBM was offering early-retirement buyouts, and he was undecided whether he should—stay or go. The dilemmas he faced—deciding if and when he should accept a buyout package, and what to do next—are being faced by countless other managers in the 50-plus set. Larry now admits that he should have accepted an earlier buyout package. But he remained at IBM because he hadn't yet determined the next step in his personal game plan. The factors that were involved in his decision-making are as complex and as typical as those of anyone weighing a buyout offer.

> **Larry sums up the early buyout dilemma: "Taking the IBM package was one thing, but finding something I wanted to do was something else."**

Change for change's sake wasn't in the cards for Larry. Contrary to one of IBM's many nicknames, "I've Been Moved," Larry's career and lifestyle had been rather consistent. "Same company, same location, same house and the same wife. As you can see, I didn't follow the 'grass is always greener' concept."

As a youngster, Larry thought about being a teacher or minister but found that he was better suited for and more interested in science. He received undergraduate and graduate engineering degrees from North Carolina State University and Duke University, joined IBM, and a few months later was activated as an Army Signal Corps officer. Other than two years of military service, Larry's entire life had been spent in North Carolina with IBM. Larry was officially classified as an IBM group leader in charge of designing software for retail-related computer systems. Ironically, as IBM downsized, his division achieved record sales.

Larry found it difficult to realistically consider any form of early retirement. He felt he was much too young, and retirement contradicted his philosophy that work is critical to survival—not in the sense of financial survival, but in usefulness. "I didn't believe in being idle. Taking the IBM package was one thing, but finding something I really wanted to do was something else." Initially, Larry felt that he couldn't leave until he decided on a new pursuit.

Prior to retirement, he was optimistic about life after IBM: "I felt that when I left IBM, there would be a number of options."

Larry had plenty of contacts through his work with retail computer systems and believed he "could join another software company or become an independent contractor and earn the difference between my IBM pension pay-out and my living expenses."

Larry also considered becoming an entrepreneur. He tried to purchase an auto machine shop from owners who wanted to retire. Hardly a newcomer to this field, he first learned how to repair cars from his father, who was a machinist. But the machining business had some serious environmental problems that would be too costly to remedy.

As a trained scientist, Larry considered teaching. "I only wanted to work in urban public schools where I could teach science to city and disadvantaged kids. Teaching in a private or church school didn't interest me. It wasn't where I was needed."

Practicing good works was nothing new to him. Besides his wife and their three children, his family includes several children he adopted from troubled families. He also donates 20 percent of his gross income to charity.

Larry retired officially from IBM in 1997 and has already worked at three different jobs. Consistent with his pre-retirement plan, he became a teacher. Rather than seeking a safer haven in an independent school, he worked for several months at a Durham middle school teaching science and math, but his idealism was shaken by school conditions. Soon after he left teaching, IBM asked him to return as a contract worker, a relationship that lasted slightly less than a year. In early 1998, he joined QVS Software, a small company that produces point-of-purchase software systems, an area that he knows well from his IBM days.

Larry's children are self-supporting. His wife, Nancy, does not work. Like her husband, she is also a community activist involved in leadership positions with several nonprofit groups. "Even if I made less money, we knew that we could live on less," says Larry.

HARDLY A COMPUTER NEWCOMER

Art Lebo

CORPORATE FINANCIAL MANAGER TURNED VOLUNTEER CONSULTANT

Art Lebo is comfortable with computers. There is good reason for his confidence. Over the past 35 years, he has worked with mainframe computers, timesharing systems, and desktop computers. Now retired, Art uses computers wherever possible, as a volunteer in the U.S. and overseas, and in his daily retirement lifestyle.

Like Louis Powell, he was born in Minnesota and graduated from the University of Minnesota. Art spent 25 years in the metropolitan New York area as a financial manager and controller with one company, General Foods, then with the merged General Foods and Kraft Foods operation, which as a result of acquisition subsequently became a Philip Morris subsidiary.

When computers came of age in the 1960s, corporate financial departments became early converts. In the early days before the availability of software applications packages, Art, although a financial manager, designed Cobol and Fortran programs. In the '70s when General Foods switched activities to timesharing systems, Art became a timesharer. During this period, he received an MBA degree, and timesharing was the theme of his thesis. In the '80s, the desktop computer came of age, and once again he migrated to another computer medium and such financial and spreadsheet software packages as Lotus 1-2-3.

> **"A laptop was given to me for the Gdansk assignment. It permitted me to compile and analyze financial information."**

"Nancy and I always knew we wanted to retire at an early age when we were in good health and not wait until we were in our sixties. And we also knew that we wanted to move from New York to another section of the country. But we didn't want to return to Minnesota. It's much too cold in winter."

When they were in their early fifties and still years before they anticipated retiring, the Lebos started to look at possible destination spots in Virginia, Florida and North Carolina. They rated communities for what they offered in terms of culture, sports, weather and continuing education. Health care was not a priority item since they assumed any area they would select would have decent medical facilities. After repeated trips, they selected Fearrington Village near Chapel Hill, North Carolina. In 1990, Art left Kraft Foods and Nancy, also in her mid-fifties, retired as an elementary school teacher. Both would receive pensions, lifetime health-care packages, and in a few years would be eligible to receive social security payments.

To see Art in action is to see a model of

the active retiree. Put aside the occasional paid consulting assignment and an active sports schedule that includes tennis, biking and swimming, or his numerous hobbies. Instead, let's see how Art applies his financial management and computer acumen.

In the mid-1990s, Art joined the Internal Revenue Service's sponsored Volunteers for Tax Assistance. Starting in early January and ending in mid-April, he works two days a week preparing computerized tax returns for elderly and poor people. As a result of a five-year relationship, Art was recruited to help launch the SeniorNet Center in Chapel Hill in 1998.

Nancy and Art are active internationalists. Through Friendship Force, a cross-cultural international organization, they have visited, or had visitors from, Australia, Latvia, Finland, the Czech Republic, Greece and England. "It's a chance to meet different people from different countries and see life as it really is," he says. His financial and computer skills resulted in several volunteer overseas consulting assignments.

"In 1997, I spent one month in Moldova as a mentor and consultant to several small companies. It's important to these companies to learn how to establish and maintain budgets, and to prepare financial plans if they expect to grow. Most of them use homemade bookkeeping systems that few outside the company could understand."

On the assignment in Moldova and his 1988 posting to Gdansk, Poland, transportation, lodging and living expenses were paid for both Art and Nancy by the American sponsors, Citizens Democracy Corporation and the Volunteers for Overseas Cooperative Assistance, organizations funded by the Agency for International Development.

"In Gdansk, I worked with two companies and helped them design financial reporting systems. One company was in construction and the other in the production of point-of-purchase displays. I showed them ways to present financial information in a better format and how to prepare a financial analysis to go with the numbers. In many ways, it was like running a 'finance for non-financial managers' course." Nancy, who joined Art for two of the four weeks in Poland, was given a classroom assignment. She conducted an intensive adult conversational English course for business and professional people.

"A laptop was given to me for the Gdansk assignment. It permitted me to compile and analyze financial information. This way I could review information at the end of the work day and prepare spreadsheets," Art said. He also used the laptop to send e-mail letters home. He even kept up with U.S. news by reading the *New York Times*, *Washington Post*, and *Raleigh News & Observer* on the Internet.

Art's computer saga extends to his personal life. "I spend more time on my computer than watching TV. When my granddaughter learned that she had an injured knee from soccer and lacrosse, I used the Web to find what doctors had to say about the injury."

LUCK IS WHAT YOU MAKE OF IT

Albert Cohen
ANALYTICAL CHEMIST AND CEO TURNED MANAGEMENT CONSULTANT/MUSIC CRITIC

Albert Cohen has two jobs. By day, he's a management consultant a and manager of financial assets. Other times, Al is a music critic and columnist for two daily newspapers, devoting his evenings and weekends to music and journalism, attending concerts and writing his reviews. After he retired early at age 54, Al works seven days a week, having left behind his training as an analytical chemist and a lengthy stint as CEO of a publicly owned high-tech company. His current lifestyle results in large part from having initiated an early-retirement plan—call it setting the stage—and having pursued opportunities as they presented themselves.

A brush with illness compelled Al to take stock of his business life and plan an orderly transition from his chairmanship into early retirement.

Al graduated from Brooklyn College, then received a master's degree in chemistry from New York University. He worked as a chemist for General Cable Co., and then for Curtiss-Wright Corp. Al was interested in getting into sales and, through a series of coincidences, he returned serendipitously to General Cable as a petrochemical salesman.

When the company decided to exit the petrochemical business, Al joined Metex Electronics Corp., a tiny company with 11 employees. As a general manager, he helped build the business in a few years to revenues of $2.5 million and a pretax profit of $1 million. By then, Al had been elected president, and he took Metex public by buying another small public company. The merged company had sales of $5 million. Within several years, sales tripled to $15 million due to Metex's successful penetration of the automotive catalytic converter market.

As Metex grew, events pushed Al to consider early retirement. "It was always my goal to retire by the time I was 65, but in 1982, when I was 49, I learned that I had become a diabetic. I did a full evaluation of my business life and started planning to retire even earlier." As it has for several other people profiled in this book, illness forced Al to rearrange his priorities.

It's one thing to be a corporate employee and have the option to take early retirement, but it is another matter to be the chairman of a public company. There are contractual and stockholder obligations and succession concerns to be considered. In 1984 Al retained a consultant who specialized in the management of small to midsize companies to help him plan an orderly transition that would permit him to retire within ten years, or by the time he reached 60.

"The first thing was to find someone to succeed me as president. I hired an 'heir' and then started looking for a way out." In spite of the best-laid plans, fate sometimes intervenes. Al's answer came earlier than expected when a long-time friend jumped at the chance to buy Al's 9% stockholder share. The following year the company was sold to United Capital Corp. Because the sale was compatible with Al's personal retirement plan, his attitude toward it was positive. He negotiated a long-term employment contract with the new owner but terminated it 18 months later due to management differences.

THE SEEDS OF AVOCATION BEAR FRUIT

Even then Al was not the least bit concerned about how he would keep busy. Despite a heavy corporate and travel schedule at Metex, Al had been freelancing for a small daily newspaper in New Jersey since 1976. He covered the classical music beat and fulfilled a long-term interest. "At college, I minored in music. I don't play an instrument, but I have a good ear and know how to evaluate music." Again, fate intervened. "A friend was the newspaper's regular music and drama critic, but he had an accident and I became his substitute. When he recovered, he continued writing drama reviews and I was named music critic."

Freed from responsibility for managing a growing technology company, Al made music an even more important part of his life. He was hired by the Asbury Park Press as a freelancer to write a Sunday music column, and he extended his ties with the Music Critics association. With his wife, Doris, also a music critic and a concert pianist (they have two Steinway pianos in their living room), the Cohens became the association's paid administrators. In early 1993 Al increased his editorial workload by becoming the music critic for *The Record*, another New Jersey daily.

Al likes to keep his fingers in a number of pies at the same time. At Metex, he personally managed the company's pension plan. The experience provided a natural bridge to becoming an independent money manager. Al passed the Series Six test administered by the National Association of Securities Dealers, became a registered investment adviser and started investing for a friend. Al's name has been passed along to the point that he now manages a $20 million portfolio for 13 clients. "I don't solicit new business. My references come from existing clients. Each client has a personalized portfolio ranging from fixed income to riskier equities, depending on their financial goals." Al manages his clients' investments from an at-home office that is totally computerized. He subscribes to a number of online financial services to help him analyze investments.

Considering his success story at Metex, Al is not wealthy by today's standards, but by his own standards, he's doing fine. Besides pension and deferred compensation from Metex and United Capital Corp., he earns about $20,000 a year from journalism and additional fees from money management. "I didn't plan it that way, but over the past five years, I've made more than during my best years at Metex.

"Once a year, I get writer's block. The computer screen seems blank. Doris and I take a few weeks off, but we usually tie in music with our vacations." They might spend a few weeks in Santa Fe, attending summer chamber music concerts and opera festivals and meeting with musicians, a source of future music columns.

"If anything I'm busier than any time in my life, but I don't want to give anything up. I never thought I'd ever say this, but I don't miss working for Metex or any other company. The secret of retiring is the ability to switch gears and do something that you really like."

START RETIREMENT PLANNING EARLY

Harold Levine
ADVERTISING EXECUTIVE TURNED CONSULTANT/VOLUNTEER

Harold Levine says it straight: "Start planning at 50. Don't wait until you're 65 to make retirement plans. Plan your own exit. Don't wait to die in office or get tossed out." Harold has followed his own advice.

Harold entered the advertising business following service in World War II and attendance at New York University. He worked for 20 years for several small agencies. Then, with two associates, he bought out the owners of the agency where they were working and, with Chet Huntley, renamed it Levine, Huntley, Schmidt & Beaver. (Chet Huntley, half of the former TV network news team, had recently left NBC. His name brought the agency instant identity and recognition, though he died a few years later.) Even as he was launching the agency, Harold, who was the majority shareholder, was making choices that would set the stage for his planned retirement. It was not by chance that Schmidt and Beaver were ten to 15 years younger than Harold, giving him sufficient time to groom them as his successors.

There are three key parts of Harold's life—family, business and community. He had learned a lesson watching his own father's work habits. A traveling salesman, the elder

> **Harold helped build an ad agency. Even as the business was achieving success, he began setting himself up for retirement.**

Levine had spent much of his time away from home. "I saw him struggle until the day he died, and I was determined to work and live differently." As a result, Harold rarely worked on weekends, nor did he bring work home. He preferred to be with his wife, Sue, and their two children. Even with more than two hours' daily commuting from his suburban home in Freeport, Long Island, to his office in New York City, Harold found time to be a community activist—as an elected school board member for 12 years and president for five of them, and as founder of the local arts council and historical society.

By the mid 1980s, LHS&B's future course seemed bright as the agency attracted a number of prestigious accounts. At every opportunity, Harold was turning over a larger portion of the agency's operation to his two partners. Harold became chairman and Bob Schmidt was named president. These changes were critical if Harold was to ensure a smooth succession and retire by age 65. The agency's performance and reputation as a "hot creative shop" was also in its favor. LHS&B's billings were more than $100 million, and its success attracted the attention of larger agencies. The three partners started to explore the possibilities of selling the agency so as to capitalize on their investment.

When Grey Advertising Agency acquired LHS&B in 1985 for an undisclosed amount of cash, Harold had only a few years to go to meet his retirement timetable. He received a five-year contract as part of the buyout agreement. He worked full-time on the transition for the first two years following LHS&B's acquisition. Once the transition was completed, the tempo eased, as did the need for his participation on a daily basis. He worked at the agency only one day a week for the last two years of his tenure there.

After living in Freeport for 25 years, the Levines moved to Westport, Connecticut, in 1978. The move, too, was consistent with Harold's long-term retirement plan. Their two children were grown, and Harold and Sue, an independent public relations consultant, were ready for a change in venue. "The move gave me an opportunity to extricate myself from a number of local organizations, something that is difficult to do when you still live in the community." Even with the move, he intended to continue his involvement with educational and cultural issues. In Freeport, he focused on local groups. Currently Harold is chairman emeritus of the Alvin Ailey Dance Company, president of the New York Alliance for the Public Schools and president of the Westport Education Foundation.

Harold estimates that 80% of his time is spent as a volunteer and the balance as a paid consultant. He conducts an annual advertising management course, one night a week for 16 weeks, for the Institute for Advanced Advertising Studies. He is a paid marketing consultant to small companies, such as the Medical Information Line, a "900" telephone service that enables callers to hear a medically approved discussion of more than 300 health care topics. He uses his advertising expertise to help the company create ads for major consumer magazines. "Sure, I invested in the company. There's some risk, but I expect to get my investment and some profits within the next few years. But more important, I'm having some fun with the company. And what's money for, anyway?" In making this investment, Harold is hardly being imprudent. Unlike some retirees, who unwisely gamble large parts of their portfolios in "get rich" schemes, Harold is assured income from his agency's profit-sharing plan, social security, savings, investments, and consulting fees. His Medical Information Line investment represents only a small slice of his retirement portfolio.

As carefully as he operated his agency and blueprinted a retirement strategy, Harold diligently continues to juggle a range of consulting and volunteer assignments to the point that his granddaughter, Sarah, observed several years ago: "Other grandparents are boring. All they do is watch TV. Mine aren't; they're much too busy."

NO STRANGER TO SETTING HIS OWN COURSE

Hank Baer

LAW FIRM PARTNER TURNED LAW PROFESSOR/INDEPENDENT ATTORNEY

In this era of job and career uncertainty, it is critical to know when and how to take early retirement. At age 55, Henry "Hank" Baer felt it was time to make a change. He negotiated his way out of his law firm from a position of strength, while he had something tangible to offer his partners and they still needed him as much as he needed them. How Hank handled his planned departure could serve as an example to others.

Graduating from Brown University, Hank was commissioned in the Navy. Though he was not a lawyer, he was assigned on a number of occasions as a defense counsel. "From that point on, I wanted to be a lawyer. When I got out of the Navy, I applied to law school at Harvard but was turned down." He went to work first as a sales representative and then as sales manager for ten years with his family's business, Imperial Knife Associated Companies.

"I still wanted to be a lawyer, but I was now married and had two small children. I applied once again to law school. The only person who knew about it was my wife, Ellen. When I was deliberating over my decision, she said, 'Either go to law school or shut up.'" This time Hank was accepted at Harvard.

At 55, Hank chose to give up his partnership and become "of counsel" to his law firm. Held to fewer billable hours, he can indulge his other loves.

The Baers moved to Cambridge and Hank financed his education with the GI Bill, student loans, some savings and Ellen's salary as a hospital nurse. Hank completed law school when he was 36 and went to work for Skadden, Arps, Slate, Meagher & Flom, one of the few corporate law firms that hired middle-age lawyers directly out of law school. It was then a small law firm with only 41 lawyers, all based in New York. Hank was named a partner in 1978, and four years later, as a labor relations specialist, he became chairperson of the firm's labor and employment law practice committee.

Over the years, the firm changed. In 1971 it was "small and collegial, and run like a family business. As it grew, it became increasingly more businesslike and for me less fun." By 1990, its peak year, the firm employed more than 1,000 lawyers, including 225 partners, and a support staff of approximately 2,500 people in its U.S. and overseas offices.

Hank began to consider alternatives, all using his skills as a lawyer and arbitrator. One of his close professional colleagues and his immediate supervisor at the firm was John Feerick, a year younger than

Hank, who had left the firm as a partner in his late forties in 1983 to become the dean of Fordham Law School. Hank, John and a third lawyer, Jonathan Arfa, had jointly written a legal textbook and collaborated on a number of legal articles. Perhaps subliminally, John had set the stage for Hank's departure seven years later.

Two dissimilar events, which occurred almost at the same time, triggered Hank's decision to change his work habits. Ellen's brother died at 47, and Hank and Ellen won an American Express around-the-world sweepstakes. They traveled for 60 days in Australia, New Zealand and Europe. "Until then, I had never been absent from the office for so long a time. I also decided to do things differently than my father, who was literally kicked out of Imperial Knife when he was 85. My brother-in-law's death forced me to face the fact that we're not going to last forever."

RESPONDING TO
HIS WAKE-UP CALLS

It was time to stop putting off things he wanted to do in law and in his personal life—things that could not be readily accomplished in a very demanding law firm practice. "I went to see John Feerick at Fordham and advised him of my plans to step down at the firm," Hank recalls. John told him that when a teaching position opened he would consider him.

In 1990, nearly 19 years after joining Skadden, Arps, Hank resigned as a partner, withdrew his capital investment and became "of counsel." In this new relationship, Hank maintains a professional relationship with the firm but no longer has a partner's vote or shares in the firm's profits. Under the terms of Hank's agreement, he receives an office and administrative support services. Some of-counsel lawyers receive a certain percentage of their legal fees, but Hank is a W-2 employee and is paid a salary. His primary task, besides representing a limited number of clients, is to represent the firm in its relationship with its 3,000 employees worldwide, a job that requires both legal and mediation skills.

"I have an understanding with the firm that was renewed in 1998. My income is less than when I was a partner, but I accepted the change so I could mold my life to my liking—a combination of law, teaching and other interests. I no longer want to bill the required thousands of hours a year and be accountable for the duties of a partner."

Hank was able to save and invest steadily as a partner in what was probably the nation's most profitable law firm during the 1980s, and his down-shifting has not altered his lifestyle. With the money Hank got back from his capital investment in the firm, he and Ellen bought an apartment in Florida and invested the remainder. They remain on Hank's health care plan from Skadden. Their two children are grown, and Ellen, who retired as a professor of nursing at the University of Pennsylvania, now teaches nursing at the University of Miami.

When Hank was asked to teach a labor law course at Fordham, he was once again a fledgling. "I had never taught before. It's different from giving an occasional lecture." Fortunately, Ellen and their son, who also had teaching experience, tutored him on classroom techniques. "Teaching is intellectually stimulating. Students keep me sharp. At first I would spend up to 18 hours preparing for a three-hour lecture. As a result, I have become a better lawyer." Since moving to Florida, he has taught at Nova Southeastern University in Ft. Lauderdale.

Hank's new lifestyle means living in Florida six months a year and the balance of the year in New York and at his summer home on Long Island. He works as a lawyer in Florida and New York. His objective remains constant—to create a balance in his professional life as a lawyer, teacher and arbitrator.

Back to School

THE 50-PLUS SET ARE COLLEGE-BOUND, BUT FOR them education often means more than collecting a degree. No longer do they need to play academic "show and tell." Just visit local four- or two-year colleges. They teem with older students, a few of whom are degree candidates but most of whom are auditing undergraduate courses or participating in a number of noncredit learning alternatives available to older students. Only a small minority of the 50-plus set are getting professional or advanced degrees.

Unlike younger undergraduates, who are scrambling to decide what major to take or career to pursue, or who are grinding away at their studies to earn a grade-point average that will someday look great on their résumé, the 50-plus set are in school for their own reasons. For instance, they might want to:

- **Get a degree** because they didn't have time, couldn't afford to, or weren't interested in obtaining one before
- **Study something they were interested in as youngsters** but didn't pursue because it didn't seem practical at the time.
- **Study in depth** something they became interested in over the years.
- **Challenge themselves intellectually** and broaden their scope of interests.

- **Become "renaissance" people.**
- **Further their understanding of a public issue.** They might even put their new-found knowledge to work on behalf of society or their community.
- **Enjoy the ambiance** associated with a college environment.
- **Search for new meaning** in their lives.
- **Break the shackles** associated with a past career.

Adult-education programs geared to older or retired students often provide more than an intellectual experience. For many students, school is a social experience, a chance to make new friends or an opportunity to learn solely for the sake of learning. Since curricula are so diversified, classes attract birds of a feather—you'll meet others like yourself in whatever course attracts you. Husbands and wives frequently take the same courses. For many, it is the first time in their married lives that they have shared a nonfamily experience. Other students form new friendships to replace workplace relationships lost in retirement.

Those Who Do Seek Degrees

Despite all the scrambling for more education, the 50-plus set still make up only about 2.5% of the total number of students obtaining undergraduate, graduate and professional degrees. And when they get their degrees, says the College Board, a monitor of adult education trends, they "seek degrees that have immediate utility. They deposit their learning into a checking account—not into a savings account—so they can draw on it without delay. To most adults, learning is a liquid resource, not a long-term capital investment."

Return to the Classroom

The U.S. Department of Education points out that nearly 450,000 men and women over age 50 are enrolled in two- and four-year colleges and universities. The majority of these students are not candidates for a degree. About 360,000 are taking courses to enrich their personal lives, to learn new skills to qualify them for a different job or to fulfill a lifetime dream.

And it shouldn't be surprising to learn that twice as many of these over-50 students are women. Consider that many women married, put their husbands through school and, in the process, sacrificed their own undergraduate or graduate education. Now many of these women are deciding that the time has come to obtain a long-delayed degree. As empty-nesters for the first time in 25 years, they typically have the time and resources to start or complete their education, either to embark on a new and more demanding career or to learn for the sake of learning.

POINTS TO REMEMBER

- College extension programs are the prime educational route for the 50-plus set.
- Extension programs are not for everyone; some in the 50-plus set like the discipline of being a matriculated student.
- Master of Arts in Liberal Studies programs appeal to some retirees.
- With Elderhostel, education means a vacation, too.
- Many older students feel more comfortable attending school with their peers than with younger students.
- Older students enjoy the college campus environment.
- Adult education brings families together.

Getting Started

If you're interested in returning to school, start your search with your local community college. More than 1,400 two-year community colleges are located within commuting distance of nearly 95% of the nation's population. Couple this with the 2,200 four-year colleges and it is easy to see that higher-education opportunities exist at your fingertips. And to ease the financial burden for students who to audit courses, more than 40 states presently waive tuition at public-sponsored colleges for students who, depending on the state, are at least age 60 or 65. It's easy to find out whether your state has a tuition-free program. The registrar's office at your community or state four-year college will have the answer.

Even so, many in the 50-plus set feel uneasy in a traditional college setting—not because of the academic requirements, but because they are apprehensive about attending classes with students one-half to one-third their age. For many, it is the first time in school in 30 or more years. Yet age is frequently an asset in the classroom, as many 50-plus students attest.

A Different Kind of Master's Degree

Imagine taking a college course called "Albert Einstein and the World as He Saw It," or "The Foundation of Modern Terrorism," or "Genes, Medicine and Money." These are just some of the courses available to students attending the more than 115 colleges and universities that belong to the Association of Graduate Liberal Arts (AGLS). These schools were started for somewhat older students—men and women over 30 who want to pursue a nontraditional course of study in an academic environment geared to their workday schedules.

The average age of students, says the AGLS, is 37. Hardly a retirement age, although the University of Chicago reports that the average age of its students is 50. And women outnumber men two to one.

The great appeal of these programs is the curriculum, which differs from traditionally structured master of arts programs. The curriculum is interdisciplinary, permitting students to design a personalized course of study. Typical of these programs is Duke University's Master of Arts in Liberal Studies (MALS). Its program provides adult students with "an opportunity to combine varied, perhaps disparate areas of interest into an academic program that satisfies their curiosity and contributes to the achievement of their objectives," according to the MALS program description.

While the association does not maintain demographic records, it notes that 8,000 to 10,000 students are enrolled in member-college programs, with more than 1,000 receiving master's degrees each year. To date, nearly 30,000 students have received master's degrees. The Duke program and others like it are not for everyone, especially those in the 50-plus set who are not degree-oriented. Yet among Duke's MALS students, at least 15% are over age 50, and many of the other schools with MALS programs have a higher percentage of older students.

Rather than base admission totally on past academic record or performance on the Graduate Record Examinations, school officials also consider the applicant's work experiences. Diane Sasson, the director of Duke's program and past president of the Association of Graduate Liberal Arts, points out that "added maturity, recent accomplishments and a determination to succeed may help offset a weak or outdated college transcript."

Students enter the program for intellectual reasons. They are graded, they are challenged by academic discipline and, above all, they are making a commitment—at least three years to acquire a degree for part-time students and usually a year for full-time students. While no thesis is required, students submit an essay based on original research.

> **WHY ADULT EDUCATION?**
>
> • Rekindle the flame of knowledge.
> • Meet other like-minded people.
> • Learn on your own terms.
> • Master a new skill.
> • Study with a particular teacher.
> • Gain an advantage at work.
> • Update skills.

The tuition varies in MALS programs, ranging from the lower fees at public institutions to more costly tuition at private universities. Some students are reimbursed by employers or qualify for financial aid.

FOR MORE INFORMATION. The best way to learn whether a college in your community offers an MALS program is to call the institution's registrar or access the Association's Web site at www.cec.umn.edu.80/mls/aglsp/.

Alternative Learning for the 50-Plus Set

Walk across the Duke campus and you'll find an academic alternative to the MALS program—the Duke Institute for Learning in Retirement (DILR), one of the more than 200 similar college-sponsored adult education programs, with nearly 45,000 enrolled students. Similar dual opportunities—MALS and Institutes for Learning in Retirement—exist on a number of other campuses.

SUGGESTED READING

Aslanian, Carol and Henry Brickell, *How Americans in Transition Study for College Credit* (The College Board, 1988). Though ten years old, it continues to be a sound analysis of the trends in adult education.

Bruno, Frank, *Going Back to School* (Macmillan, 1996). The book's title is also its theme.

The curriculum of the Institute for Learning in Retirement conforms to the academic interests of older students, and it's particularly well-suited to retirees who want to break with the past. An Institute is an ideal place for a retired engineer, for example, to explore a wide-range of nonscientific subjects.

Duke students, like those at Institutes on other campuses, prefer art, music, literature, history and related social science courses. Even with a curriculum of nearly 50 courses ranging from the mathematics of music to a study of Henrik Ibsen as the transformer of the modern theater, Institute for Learning programs at the participating colleges offer few how-to or hobby-related courses. These can be taken at community colleges or through high school adult education programs.

The concept of peer learning is a pivotal part of the Institute programs at most campuses. Students often serve as the faculty, create the curriculum and help operate the institute. Typically, Institute students have little interest in taking courses for credit or being graded on their academic efforts. The tuition and registration fees on most campuses average about $100 to $150 a semester.

Though anyone 50-plus is eligible for Institute for Learning courses, chances are you will find somewhat older students attending them. The average age of Duke students is 69, and it is slightly higher at the New School for Social Research in New York City. Enrollment at Institutes ranges from fewer than 28 students at one school to more than 2,400 at Brooklyn College.

Sara Craven, DILR's director, is candid when talking about her program: "Most of the nearly 650 DILR students do not want to attend class with younger students." Older students have often covered the issues that are new to younger students. DILR students include both high school dropouts and Fulbright scholars.

Institute programs offer more than educational opportunities. They have evolved into a social hub. In Durham, where many of the retirees are newcomers to the area, DILR provides the setting to make new friends. It sponsors duplicate bridge sessions, Sunday afternoon walks, brown-bag lunches and a two-day retreat in the North Carolina mountains.

FOR MORE INFORMATION. To determine whether a college in your community offers an Institute for Learning in Retirement program, call its extension or adult education department. Or, for more information or a referral to Institutes for Learning in your area, contact the Elderhostel Institute Network at 75 Federal St., Boston, MA 02210 (617-426-7788; www.elderhostel.org).

Elderhostel Mixes Travel With Education

Just reading Elderhostel's 285-page U.S. and Canadian catalog and its companion international catalogs is an educational adventure. Elderhostel offers something for everyone with a desire to study and live on campus at one of the 2,000 participating colleges in every state and 70 nations overseas.

The thrust of the Elderhostel program is nontraditional and noncredit education. Don't expect to find conventional college art, political-science or music-appreciation courses. What you will discover, for example, is a course in California on the cave art of prehistoric man, one in Minnesota on American literary humor from Mark Twain to Garrison Keiller, a course in Pennsylvania on birds of prey, and overseas in France on art and artists of Paris and the Riviera.

Approximately 325,000 people enrolled in Elderhostel's U.S./Canada and overseas courses in 1998. Elderhostel students, who are nearly all retired, must be at least 55. A companion can attend as long as he or she is at least 50. Costs are kept to a minimum by living and eating on college campuses. Sometimes the living accommodations are Spartan. Thus, the Elderhostel program tends to attract hardier and healthier 60- and 70-year-olds. Elderhostel's literature emphasizes that "it is important for participants to be realistic about their physical condition and ability to maintain an intensive schedule. Classrooms, dormitories and dining halls are best suited to people who are mobile and able to climb steps and walk distances without difficulty."

The standard cost for a one-week program, excluding transportation in the continental U.S., is $375, slightly more in Hawaii, Alaska and Canada. The fees for the international programs, though less costly than most overseas travel tours, vary depending on air transportation, length of course and the type of accommodations.

FOR MORE INFORMATION. To learn more about Elderhostel, visit your local library, which usually receives both the domestic and international catalogs, or contact Elderhostel at 75 Federal St., Boston, MA 02210 (617-426-8056; www.elderhostel. org).

Who Are These Students?

Here are a few people from the 50-plus set who became students, ranging from candidates for professional degrees to those attending a course for retirees. Each returned to school for a different set of reasons. They all admitted that learning was not as easy as it was 30 to 40 years earlier. For each of these students, college created intellectual challenges as well as new personal and professional opportunities.

LAND MANAGEMENT IS HER LOFTY GOAL

Jean Earnhardt

PUBLIC RELATIONS SPECIALIST TURNED GRADUATE STUDENT & LAND DEVELOPER

Jean Earnhardt has deep roots in North Carolina. They're sunk into 400 acres of property near Chapel Hill that her family has owned for more than 200 years. The farm has called Jean and her family back many times over the years, finally to live there. Jean has created a unique philosophy for herself and her family: to preserve the land and yet arrange things so they work and will have practical meaning in the next century. Jean's creed was incubated during her mid fifties when she became a graduate student.

"When I began at Duke, I had no preconceived idea of what I wanted to study other than wanting to get a degree and having the discipline of attending school on a regular basis. I wanted to explore. At 57, it was my first time in college in 38 years. I was one of the older students, but I found the differences in age to be stimulating. The program captivated my interest and imagination."

Unlike during her undergraduate experience as an English major, this time around she took only one literature course and instead studied physics, oceanography and environmental economics. In contrast to

> **When Jean returned to school at 57, she took an interdisciplinary route, combining subjects that captured her interest and imagination.**

traditional college science courses, those taught in the Master of Arts in Liberal Studies program are interdisciplinary and are not intended to train scientists. "I found that everything meshes together," says Jean. "This differs from undergraduate education, where courses seemed so different from each other. Perhaps being older provides this perspective."

For her master's essay, Jean took the opportunity to explore how her North Carolina heritage relates to the future development of her property. Her subject was land-use options and the environmental concerns relating specifically to the rural parts of Orange County where the property is located. Though Chapel Hill is a highly sophisticated university community, part of the city and the surrounding Orange County are rural. Jean interviewed city people along with rural county residents. "My paper helped me to reach some personal decisions regarding the use and management of our 400 acres, and to understand my role and my relationship to the local environment. The land is a legacy from us to our children. It means maintaining rural values here and relating them to the urban settings in large sections of Chapel Hill."

A FOCAL POINT FROM CHILDHOOD TO RETIREMENT

Jean's relationship with the farm and with North Carolina began early, even though she didn't grow up there. Her father lived and worked most of his professional life outside the state, but each summer the family returned to North Carolina. In the late 1930s, the farm did not have electricity or most modern conveniences. "The days were long. There was not much to do around here except read," says Jean.

She returned to her father's alma mater, the University of North Carolina, for college and her degree in English. "I had no professional training. Women at that time were well educated but usually not trained for careers." An excellent student, she was elected to Phi Beta Kappa. Following graduation, Jean was hired as a researcher with the National Security Agency, in Washington, D.C.

A few years later Jean married John Earnhardt, whom she had met at college, and returned to North Carolina, where John worked as a claims specialist with the Social Security Administration. For the next 20 years, Jean dropped out of the active workforce while she raised two sons. She reentered the job market when she was 41, first as a part-time publicist, then as a full-time staff writer and finally as head of the public relations and development department for the Alamance County Hospital, in Burlington.

In 1978 Jean and her family moved back to the farm and into the home her parents had built in 1965. The house was designed for their retirement by a protégé of Frank Lloyd Wright. By then, both of Jean's sons had completed high school.

Ten years later, John, a year younger than Jean, retired at 55 with a full government pension. Jean was now the family's primary wage earner. About this time, she enrolled in Duke University's Master of Arts in Liberal Studies program, after having toyed with the idea for several years. She could have audited specific courses at several of the area's colleges, but Jean wanted the academic discipline associated with a degree-granting program. She commuted 30 miles each way to her job in Burlington and attended Duke evenings and Saturdays.

Acting as stewards of their property has become a primary challenge for the Earnhardt family, as well as a source of present and future family income. As a retiree, John has little difficulty keeping busy; he describes retirement as the most foreign word in the English language. Until Jean retires, he single-handedly manages the property, including maintaining three pieces of rental property.

Together Jean and John devised a strategic plan geared toward land preservation and accordingly designated about one-third of their land for real estate purposes. To date, they have already sold nine of the 12 available tracts to people who want to build homes on 10- to 12-acre tracts of rural land. The Earnhardts also set up restrictions that state explicitly what homeowners can and cannot do to be consistent with maintaining the property's rural characteristics.

Jean and John are considering developing another 135 acres adjacent to their main property. Their tentative plans focus on building some cluster homes while maintaining a pastoral look on the bulk of the acreage.

In an era when grown children often live long distances from their families, David, their eldest son—a producer-director for North Carolina's public broadcasting system—and his family live in a restored farmhouse a few hundred yards from Jean and John's home. Their other son, Philip, a systems analyst, lives in Colorado.

Jean has begun to consider retiring, but the decision is being delayed until the new Burlington community hospital opens. "When I retire, it will mean that I have more time to manage our property."

FROM "BIG BLUE" TO CAP AND GOWN

Michael Pandich

CORPORATE PUBLIC RELATIONS EXECUTIVE TURNED UNIVERSITY INSTRUCTOR

After 32 years with IBM, Michael Pandich put into practice the advice he regularly gives to others: "When you're thinking about retiring, start preparing in advance. Think of a new career, something you really like to do. Don't be caught off guard by the sudden occurrence of early retirement or downsizing." Mike wasn't.

Part of Mike's preparation called for him to return to college, earn a master's degree and start a new career as a college instructor. "When IBM offered early retirement in April 1990, I took it. My original goal was to retire at 65, but the offer was too good financially to turn down. The following September, I started teaching public relations on a full-time basis at North Carolina State University, so the transition was seamless."

Mike, a native of Binghamton, New York, majored in marketing at Syracuse University. After service with the Army in Korea, he worked for Caterpillar Inc. until he joined IBM in the late 1950s. His career soon evolved from marketing into public relations and public affairs, and he spent some time at Cape Canaveral working on projects related to the use of computers

When IBM offered Mike early retirement, he was ready to roll into a teaching career and related study in Duke's liberal studies program.

on the earliest space launches. When IBM opened a facility in Raleigh–Durham's Research Triangle Park, Mike, then in his mid thirties, was assigned as the public affairs officer for an operation that would eventually employ upward of 10,000 people.

Mike's smooth switchover from corporate to academic life was based on a well-structured plan that began in 1978 when he was named as IBM's representative to the board of the Humanities Foundation at NC State. Part of this appointment required that he be a fundraiser for the foundation. He also served for several years as the foundation's volunteer president. These were among the several activities over a ten-year period that readied him for the change from business to academia.

"I always thought that I might like to teach, and I had done some of it when I was in the Army, Caterpillar and IBM. But I had no formal teacher training," says Mike. He reasoned that teaching at the college level was something he would like to do when he retired.

While an IBM employee, Mike started

to teach a public relations course at NC State's evening school. "I decided to give it a try. The first two semesters, I team-taught with another instructor to learn the ropes."

At the same time that he began teaching, Mike, then 55, also became a student at Duke University's Master of Arts in Liberal Studies program. He sought the challenge of a degree-granting program but, unlike many mid-life corporate managers, he was not interested in a business-related degree. Even so, the Duke program qualified for IBM's tuition reimbursement.

"More important, Duke permitted me to explore a number of different academic areas. When I started, I liked being back in college, and the chance to explore made me feel good." It was an opportunity to synthesize a number of interests that he knew would prove useful in teaching. "I had no particular field of specialty. I was open-ended, but the program gave me a chance to find different topics and tie together courses in politics, public relations and communications."

Mike used an IBM assignment as a substitute for a traditional master's thesis. At IBM, Mike was responsible for government relations. On one assignment, he was the company's representative to the North Carolina Citizens for Business and Industry, a lobbying group that was controlled by the state's traditionally strong industries—farming, textiles and tobacco. "My study investigated whether the lobbying group was actually meeting the needs of North Carolina's emerging industries—computers, pharmaceuticals, electronics and computers."

When Mike retired, he was determined to remain active professionally. He had strong relationships and contacts in North Carolina, he held a master's degree, and by then had been teaching for five years. Mike was lucky. About the time that he left IBM on full retirement with a lifetime benefits package, an opportunity opened at NC State for an instructor to teach its undergraduate public relations courses. He had the qualifications and was available. Without his experience as a part-time instructor, he says, he most likely would not have been offered the full-time teaching assignment.

Mike's salary as an instructor, his income from social security (which is reduced somewhat by his salaried job), and his IBM pension represent the bulk of his retirement income. During the tax season, his wife, Judy, works as a tax consultant. Their children are grown and live independently.

Mike teaches three undergraduate courses and has taught an honors seminar that focused on corporate communications. "It is my way of bringing the students in touch with the corporate world and giving them something tangible to present when they have job interviews. While I don't have a doctorate, my students seem to like my pragmatic approach because I introduce practical communications problems into the classroom. I've learned how to convey my past business experiences to my students.

"Many of my friends feel that they would like to teach when they retire. Some call it a 'nice' thing to do, like a hobby. Teaching is not a hobby to me. I left a full-time IBM job and I now teach full-time. What they don't realize is that it's hard work."

Mike cautions others that teaching differs in many ways from business. Too many corporate executives believe that they can walk into the classroom and apply their business experience in an academic setting. What they don't realize is that they are unqualified to make the changeover. "Sure, they know business, but they don't know how to teach," said Mike. "In the classroom, there's no place for you to hide."

And what about retirement? "I'm definitely not retired. I just changed careers. I don't miss corporate life. Sure, I was nostalgic, but the transition was made easier since I was established at NC State. Anyway, it was time to do something else."

GRANDPA GOES TO COLLEGE

Sol Weiner

INDEPENDENT BUSINESS OWNER TURNED PERPETUAL STUDENT

When Sol Weiner took an unexpectedly early retirement and sold the check-cashing business he'd been running in the Bronx for 25 years, "I was already thinking of doing something else, but my plans rapidly accelerated when I was held up at gunpoint. I put the business on the block immediately."

Where other people his age might ask what's next, Sol had an immediate answer—go to college and fulfill an earlier ambition to be a college graduate, one that life had heretofore precluded. Three years later, he at last had his bachelor of arts degree in economics. Since then, Sol and his wife, Audrey, have also audited numerous college courses in art history, learning about this subject together in their retirement.

Sol grew up in the Bronx and graduated from high school in the late 1930s. College was out of the question at the time, so he got a job as a silk screener. Following four years as an Army Air Corps officer during World War II, Sol, unlike many other veterans, did not attend college under the GI Bill due to family obligations. Instead, he started a silk-screening company. "In the early 1950s, I got out of silk-screening and went to work for Audrey's father and ran his driving school in the Bronx. Then I opened a similar business on Long Island, where we were living. I went back to his business when he got ill, and purchased it from him. I changed it from a driving school to a check-cashing service."

After Sol retired, Audrey, an elementary school teacher in Teaneck, New Jersey, and about seven years younger than her husband, continued to work. Their two children were grown and married. But Sol was not idle. While Audrey taught, Sol became a full-time student at William Paterson College. He took as many as 18 credits a semester, including courses in micro- and macroeconomics, econometrics, and the mathematics of finance. Sol chose to study economics for its academic relationship to business.

He found the learning process more difficult than it was when he was a high school student nearly 50 years earlier. "Just the need to memorize information that would have been a breeze years ago was a challenge," says Sol.

"Some of the students thought I was

> **Sol had to pass up his chance to take advantage of the GI bill. He made up for lost time at 61, earning a degree in the liberal arts.**

the professor, and when my grandchildren attended graduation one of them asked, 'Do all grandpas have to go to college?'"

After graduation, Sol decided to use his college degree to get a job. Though additional income was not imperative, he prepared a résumé and was hired to sell deferred annuities to school teachers. "I left when the company asked me to work evenings and weekends. Enough already!"

Audrey was still teaching and building up a pension from the Teaneck schools. In addition, the couple was assured lifetime health care benefits through Audrey's job. Though Sol was hardly wealthy, he calculated that there was sufficient income generated from the sale of his business, social security, investments and savings, plus the fees he earned for preparing income taxes. What's more, Audrey and Sol were mortgage-free on their suburban home. In late 1993, the Weiners' investments became even more liquid, giving them additional discretionary income, when they sold their home and took their one-time capital gains exclusion, bought a two-bedroom co-op apartment in New Jersey with one-third of the proceeds, and invested the balance.

LEARNING AND TRAVELING TOGETHER

As a liberal-arts student, Sol had taken a required course in art history, leading to a somewhat unexpected twist in his and Audrey's retirement plans. In the past, the couple had enjoyed going to museums and galleries, but they had had limited time to study art. When Audrey, an amateur painter, retired, Sol encouraged her to study art history with him, thus creating a theme for their retirement life together. The Weiners have since taken art courses at William Paterson, and over the past few years they have audited every one of the courses given by one instructor.

Art provides the theme for many of their vacations. Before visiting Egypt and cruising on the Nile River, Sol and Audrey prepared by taking a course on ancient Egypt. On a two-week trip to Florence, their comprehension of Florentine art produced an unexpected effect. Since they had visited Florence before and had studied Italian art, their comments while visiting museums attracted the interests of other English-speaking tourists. Before long, other tourists wanted to tag along with the Weiners to listen to the commentary of two amateur docents.

A SURGEON WITH A PENCHANT FOR THE LAW

Erle Peacock, Jr.

SURGEON & MED SCHOOL PROFESSOR TURNED LAWYER & LAW SCHOOL INSTRUCTOR

"When I was an intern, I promised myself that I would stop doing major surgery when I was 65," recalls Erle Peacock, Jr. Forty years later, Erle kept that vow. He quit performing major surgery, though he continued with medical consultations. He also entered the University of North Carolina School of Law, fulfilling an ambition born of his family heritage and an earlier personal and professional scrape with constitutional law. "By then, the light had started to go out, anyway. It was time to move on and act on the promise I made 40 years earlier. But, even though I wasn't performing surgery, I didn't want to retire completely. Complete retirement is the first step to the grave."

Still, Erle thought he might be too old for school. "When I entered law school, a few students told me that their fathers had been students of mine when I taught at the medical school. And I was older than any of my law-school professors." Age, however, in no way deterred him, and while he was the law school's oldest student, his class had a number of other midlife career-changers.

But there was one hitch if he was to enter law school. Erle had never received an undergraduate degree and was short six academic credits. That's because he had been drafted into the Navy during World War II. So besides taking the law school entry exam, Erle had to make up the six semester hours. He was awarded his bachelor's degree in the spring semester of his first year of law school.

Erle discovered that his goal in seeking education had changed. "When I was in medical school my goal was to be at the top of my class, which I was. In law school, I didn't feel the necessity of being the best student in the class. My objective was simply to graduate from law school and pass the bar exam. My challenge wasn't competing with younger students. It was overcoming ignorance of the law."

As if studying to be a lawyer at any age isn't enough of a challenge, Erle faced an additional and unusual one. He had to learn how to evaluate clients and cases as a lawyer, not as a doctor. Hardly a simple process, that meant breaking past professional habits. A doctor evaluates problems in scientific terms, while a lawyer is trained in the social sciences. "Each pro-

> **Erle finished law school in his late 60s. Then he practiced law five days a week and lectured to doctors on issues relating to medicine and the law.**

fession has different disciplines, and each looks at the same situation differently. Now that I'm a lawyer, I need to think and act like one."

A LONG ROUTE TO
FULFILLING HIS DESTINY

From his upbringing in Chapel Hill, North Carolina, it would seem only natural that Erle would be either a lawyer or a college professor. His father taught accounting at the University of North Carolina, and eight of his uncles were lawyers. "Yet I never remember when I didn't want to be a doctor."

After graduating from Harvard Medical School and completing several surgical residencies, military service and 13 years in a dual career as a plastic surgeon and a professor at the University of North Carolina's medical school, Erle was recruited as the first chairman of the surgical department at the newly opened University of Arizona Medical School in Tucson. Little did he realize when he accepted this position that it would have a decided influence on his decision to become a lawyer 20 years later.

His job was to recruit a faculty and to establish the curriculum to educate surgeons. "It was my goal to start a renaissance in surgical education. The program was to be patterned after those in the great European universities before World War II." Such an educational approach would go far beyond the classical vocational training received by most American surgeons.

Though his program attracted many supporters, it also had its detractors and was abruptly scuttled in 1974 with the arrival of a new group of university administrators. They challenged his theories, then fired him. An eastern medical school wanted him as its dean, but Erle's dander was up, and he decided to stay in Arizona to fight "against overbearing administrators" and for academic freedom and the right of free speech. His case became an education and medical cause célèbre. The federal district court decision supporting the University of Arizona administrators was overruled on four separate occasions on appeal and returned to the district court for a new trial. Erle was supported in his fight for academic freedom by the majority of the surgical faculty and students and by the National Education Association.

Although in the end he was awarded $800,000, the trials were both financially and professionally costly. "But in the process I got interested in constitutional law and my rights as a teacher."

The litigation behind him, Erle left Arizona and joined the Tulane University faculty as a professor of surgery. Five years later, he returned to Chapel Hill and a private surgical practice, until he made the move into law school and his new profession.

A LITTLE OF
EVERYTHING HE LOVES

Graduating these days as a lawyer—at any age—does not necessarily ensure a job. And while some retirees might view another academic degree as a trophy, with little intention of applying their education in a new career, Erle set his sights on an active legal career in private practice as well as teaching health care law. A large number of Erle's classmates have not found suitable jobs or are working outside the legal profession. But Erle was more fortunate. He was hired by Patterson, Dilthey, Clay and Bryson, a 12-lawyer firm in Raleigh that specializes in representing health care providers in malpractice suits.

Besides his five-day-a-week legal practice that provides a regular income, Erle indulges in his first love—teaching. When he has an opportunity, he lectures to doctors on issues relating to both medicine and the law, such as a series of talks to the Florida Medical Society on death and dying or to the Medical College of Virginia on peer review. His payment is usually a small honorarium and expenses. "I provide doctors with some elements of constitutional and contract law so they understand their legal rights," he says.

Erle's pursuit of his law degree and new career was followed closely by his family. His three children are grown and involved in science or medicine. His wife, Mary, reacted to Erle's career change by entering Duke Divinity School the year after Erle started law school. She'll receive her master's degree in religious education.

The irony of Erle's "retirement" hit home his first day on the job when he attended a retirement party for a 62-year old lawyer in the firm. "I asked him about his plans. Did he plan to do what I did but in reverse and now go to medical school? He didn't think so."

ONCE A CLASSICIST, ALWAYS A CLASSICIST

Armando Henriquez, Jr.

HIGH SCHOOL ENGLISH TEACHER TURNED UNIVERSITY INSTRUCTOR

I met Armando Henriquez, Jr. when he was giving a lecture on the classics at a Duke University alumni workshop. His attire, a white toga and sandals, was consistent with the spirit of his talk.

Armando, better known as Mickey to distinguish him from his 89-year-old father, was a high school English teacher in northern Westchester County in New York for 32 years. Born in Tampa, Florida, in a Spanish district, his parents and grandparents were cigar workers, and Mickey learned to speak Spanish before English. Following college and graduate school in Tennessee, Mickey, by then married, moved north and took his first and only teaching job in Katonah, New York.

The toga that he wore at the Duke seminar typifies the classroom style that he used throughout his teaching career. "My job in a course on the Miracles of Greece was to convince high school students how little we all know and that we must come to grips with our own ignorance. I kept students alert by animating and enlivening the class with a bit of histrionics."

> **Mickey finds that teaching retirees is different from teaching teenagers. And it's more than age. "I really have to hold their attention; otherwise they'll walk out on me," he notes.**

Now, as a retiree, Mickey continues to teach and he uses his former high-school classroom style in lecturing to the 50-plus set. When he retired in 1986, family and friends were making book that Mickey wouldn't make it as a retiree, living a retirement lifestyle. Then he remembered that Thoreau said that we have other lives to live. With that in mind, Mickey and his wife, Martha, moved to Durham to be near two of their three children.

"I could have stayed in Katonah and become an elder statesman. I knew everyone in town after working and living there for 33 years. But what good would that do. You become overly critical. Nothing is like the good old days. It was time to leave Katonah and not get into an old age rut." Mickey and Martha sold their house and much to their amazement found that the real estate commission on the sale was more than the cost of the house when it was purchased 30 years earlier. Profits from the sale along with a teacher's pension, savings and social security provide the bulk of their retirement income.

"Martha and I decided not to move to a retirement community. We wanted to live as we did before in an integrated community surrounded by people of all ages and where medical conditions do not dominate the daily conversation. At the time, both my parents were living so we decided to set them up in an apartment near us. Would you believe it? At my age, I'm a member of the sandwich generation."

Mickey differs from other retirees who relocate to North Carolina. He neither plays golf nor tennis. Other than family responsibilities, his world, then and now, focuses on literature and the classroom.

Durham and Duke's Institute for Learning in Retirement became his new stage. Over 13 years, Mickey estimates that he has taught 35 different DILR courses. What he teaches would hardly fall under the heading of light reading: Plato's *Republic*, Ibsen plays and the *Spoon River Anthology* to name a few. "Since most of my audience were in their prime during the 1950s, I used David Halberstam's book, *The Fifties*, as the theme of a recent pre-millennium course." Mickey says the book provided the setting to review events that took place mid-part of the 20th Century.

Mickey finds that teaching retirees differs from teaching teenagers. It's more than age. "In Katonah, I had a captured audience. They needed a good grade to get into college. With older students, I have to really hold their attention; otherwise they'll walk out on me and go visit their grandchildren. And, unlike high school, many of my retired students know more than that I do about the subjects I teach."

As part of the extended sandwich generation, Mickey's responsibilities go further than attending to an aged father. They also extend to his grandchildren. When his grandson's Latin class needed an additional chaperon on a school trip to Italy, "I was recruited. We visited Florence, Pisa and Rome, and for Thanksgiving dinner we had pizza in Pompeii."

Even with a son who is a Duke scientific researcher and a daughter who relocated to Durham and works for IBM, he's a reluctant computer user. Mickey remains a classicist at heart. He recently bought his first computer and is corresponding with some friends by e-mail, but he's still not totally sold on computers, at least in his lifestyle. "I'm not altogether sure whether computers build or weaken the relationships between people."

NEW HOME, NEW LIFE IN THE LIBERAL ARTS

Lorna and Lloyd Johnson
NURSE AND COMPUTER TECHNICIAN TURNED COLLEGE STUDENTS

For 40 years, Lorna and Lloyd Johnson lived in a medical and technical world. When they retired, the couple put their past careers behind them, chose a new city for their retirement home and became devotees of liberal-arts adult education.

Newcomers to adult education, the Johnsons had previously taken only extension courses relating to their careers. For $160 a year, which covers tuition and the annual membership fee in Encore, the North Carolina State University in Raleigh's Institute for Learning in Retirement program, they now attend four courses a semester. A typical course runs about 90 minutes for four to six sessions. "We avoid science and computer courses. In fact, I don't even own a computer, and I haven't read a computer publication since I retired," Lloyd says. "What we like are liberal-arts courses. We didn't take many of them as undergraduates."

A sampling of their selected courses includes "Nathaniel Hawthorne: The Devil in his Inkstand," "Unfinished Revolutions in the Former Soviet Empire," "Current Controversies in American Politics," and "The Many Faces of Christ: An Exercise in Multicultural Theology." The courses are

> **No more technical courses for Lorna and Lloyd. They're indulging in a smorgasbord of courses at the Institute for Retirement.**

taught by faculty members, the students themselves and outside experts—such as a class on ancient Greek history taught by an author and historian. The Johnsons, who live in a wooded area, are also active gardeners and environmentalists, and toward this end they took a course in wildlife rehabilitation and environmental management.

The Johnsons are originally from Kane, Pennsylvania, a small industrial city in the northwestern part of the state. When Lloyd completed his studies at Upsala College in Orange, New Jersey, and Lorna her nursing education at Chestnut Hill Hospital in Philadelphia, they lived all over the U.S. until they settled in McLean, Virginia, a suburb of Washington, D.C.

Lloyd's education in mathematics made him an ideal candidate for a switchover to computers during the late 1950s. In those early days, there were no degrees in computer science and information processing. Computer personnel came from other academic disciplines. After working for Control Data and for Westinghouse, Lloyd took a job in the late 1960s with the U.S. Customs Service in Washington, designing computer and communications network systems.

Lorna, who spent a number of years in general nursing, switched to geriatric nursing about the time that Lloyd went to work for the Customs Service. Her employer for the next 20 years was the Vinson Hospital, a geriatric medical facility in McLean run for retired naval personnel by the Navy Foundation.

"In the mid 1980s, we started to consider places we might want to live when we retired," Lorna says. The Johnsons decided to leave McLean since they found that northern Virginia had become overpopulated. "We had no intention of returning to Pennsylvania. By nature, we like to look ahead. On vacations and long weekends, we would drive to different places." They ruled out the beach communities, Arizona, Florida and any type of planned retirement community. And, because they had no children, moving closer to family members wasn't a consideration.

They settled in Cary, North Carolina, a city adjacent to Raleigh, because "it had the amenities of a larger community and the atmosphere of a small town," Lorna says. "We were fortunate. We found a buyer for our house in McLean the same day we closed on our house in Cary."

They purchased a three-bedroom house in Cary with a master bedroom on the ground level—a plus if either becomes unable to negotiate stairs. The $125,000 tax-free capital-gains windfall from their home sale, together with social security, Lloyd's government pension and their

investments, represents the basis of their retirement income package. Lorna did not have pension coverage in her nursing jobs.

Moving to Cary provided another type of windfall. They liked the area because there were three large universities—Duke, the University of North Carolina and North Carolina State University. Each offers a rich menu of cultural and social events. When they moved to Cary, the Johnsons joined North Carolina State's Friends of the University, and soon afterward, they received a brochure from Encore.

The Johnsons particularly enjoy attending courses with people their own age and in a setting where there are no tests or essays. Encore, like Institute for Learning in Retirement courses on other campuses, is an exercise in learning for the sake of learning. Even though there is a relaxed academic atmosphere, there is a required reading list for most courses.

Sometimes Lorna and Lloyd take courses together. At other times, they go their separate ways. As newcomers to North Carolina, they have made friends with some other Encore members, a typical benefit of many Institute programs on college campuses. "We find that there are two types of people our age—those like ourselves who are naturally curious and others who have decided that they don't want or need to learn anymore," Lorna said.

"Above all, Encore gets us out of the house. It's a commitment, even on cold, rainy winter days."

"THE ONLY AGE GULF IS THE ONE YOU DIG"

Alfred Eisenpreis

RETAIL AND ADVERTISING MANAGER TURNED CONSULTANT AND DOCTORAL STUDENT

Alfred Eisenpreis enjoys keeping a number of balls in the air at the same time. It was his hallmark throughout a 40-year career in retail and advertising management. Still a juggler in retirement, he's busily engaged as a consultant, community activist and doctoral student.

Al deploys his retailing and advertising background as a consultant to newspapers, stores and shopping centers. He is also the editorial director of *Retail Ad Week*, for which he writes a regular column.

He volunteers with City Innovation, a nationwide nonprofit group concerned with improving cities as places to live and work. He directs City Innovation's East Coast operations and he also edits its newsletter.

Consistent with an active retirement lifestyle, Al enrolled as a doctoral student at Cincinnati's Union Institute (which permits students to work off campus) and expected to receive his degree in late 1999.

"Don't worry if you're an older student. The only age gulf is the one you dig. The others students accept you when they know you're also a dedicated student. Going to class is like going to the office. I like the discipline and responsibility." After

> **Al expected to receive his doctoral degree in late '99. "One thing I discovered,"** he declares, **"you don't shut off the brain when you retire."**

completing his thesis (he prefers to withhold the subject), he expects to rewrite it as a consumer history book.

The seeds for Al's retirement strategy were planted early and nurtured throughout his career. Al started out in Wilkes-Barre, Pennsylvania, where his family settled after they fled Austria when he was a teenager. After graduating from St. Thomas College, he worked for 14 years for Pomeroy's, the area's dominant department store and a division of Allied Stores. In 1957, Allied brought him to its New York City headquarters to direct its regional operations.

In 1974, Al was invited by New York City's Mayor Abe Beame to head the city's economic development activities. This was Al's first full-time government appointment, though he had previously served as a consultant on economic stabilization to President Nixon's administration.

With the election in 1977 of Edward Koch as mayor, Al, rather than returning to Allied, became a senior executive of the Newspaper Advertising Bureau, a national trade group that promotes newspaper advertising. His assignment for the next 14 years was to act as a liaison between newspapers and retailers.

Retiring in 1991, Al had little intention of becoming idle. "When you retire, you actually graduate, and you should look to new levels of interests and activities.

"The worst thing for retirees is to stay at home. I even have a small office in midtown Manhattan besides one at home.

"I have computers in both places. The one at home is used to catalog my collection of American political pamphlets and autographs. There's little reason for retirees to be computer-illiterate. If you can work a telephone, why not a computer? You don't need to know how it operates. You go on airplanes, but do you know how they fly?"

Al's retirement philosophy stresses "the importance of not living in the past, particularly the immediate past. It is my way to maintain my perspective. One thing I discovered, you don't shut off the brain when you retire."

COMBINING COLLEGE COURSES AND ELDERHOSTEL

Frederick Levitt
MANUFACTURER TURNED STUDENT

Even in his seventies, Frederick Levitt considers himself a college student. He's not out to obtain another degree or become an academic expert in any field. Rather, Fred finds it challenging to be on a college campus and take courses with students usually one-third his age. When he's not auditing courses, running his part-time business or playing tennis, he's vacationing with his wife and other seekers on an Elderhostel trip.

Fred's current campus is the University of North Carolina in Chapel Hill. But before he moved to North Carolina, he had taken courses for a number of years at several different colleges near his former home on Long Island. He received his only degree, in political science and economics, from Brooklyn College.

As a current college student, Fred is fortunate. Being over 65, he has only to pay a registration fee and get permission of the instructor to audit courses, usually two each semester. "Unless the course is filled, I usually get in. The courses that interest me rarely have a waiting list."

Unlike some retirees who attend Institute for Learning in Retirement courses

In his 70s, Fred brings to class a perspective on issues that comes with age, which many of his instructors and fellow students welcome.

at nearby Duke University, Fred prefers going to class with younger students. "I like the mix; it's half the fun. I avoid taking survey courses because the attendance is too large and there's little interaction with the instructor and the other students. I've yet to find a situation where the students haven't been friendly." Fred brings to class a perspective on issues that comes with age, which many of his instructors and fellow students welcome.

Fred concentrates mainly on courses in the humanities and other topics that interest him. Over the past several years, he has taken a number of religion courses, including studies of the history of the Reformation, Moses and the Exodus, and the New and Old Testaments, as well as a course on Beethoven and another on Alexander the Great and one about the early history of China and Japan.

Even though audit students of any age are not required to take tests or write essays, Fred at times elects, strictly for his own satisfaction, to write a paper or take an exam. Even as an audit student, he's expected to keep up with a demanding reading list. He spends several hours each week reading the required books.

Fred's life since he moved to North Carolina—and what was supposedly retirement with his wife, Claire—has not been limited to academia. A manufacturer of corrugated paper boxes for many years, he sold his business in the 1980s. Now he works from a home office, the equivalent of two days a week, as a broker in the same field. "Most of my customers have been with me for years and are located in the Northeast. Within the past few years, some of these companies have moved South." He services his current customers but rarely seeks new ones. Every few months, he makes a trip to the New York area to visit key customers and suppliers. The rest of the time, a telephone and fax machine are his primary means of communication.

Claire and Fred live eight miles from Chapel Hill in a three-bedroom home in Fearrington Village, a community with a large percentage of retirees. A positive factor in the Levitts' decision to relocate was the proximity to the University of North Carolina and its academic, cultural, and health care facilities.

The Levitts' lifestyle is supported by Fred's income as a box broker, his social security (which is unaffected by his income since he's over 70), investments and savings.

Fred's busy academic routine is not limited to the University of North Carolina. Claire and Fred for the past several years have participated in at least one Elderhostel trip a year. They spent three weeks traveling and studying in Turkey, and at Mars Hill College, in North Carolina, they studied the politics of Latin America and China. On a lighter note, at Peninsula State College, in Washington, they attended an introductory jazz course, and in July 1994 they traveled to Fort Lewis College, in Durango, Colorado, to learn what takes place behind the scenes at a music festival. They attended rehearsals, met with the conductor and members of the orchestra, and were briefed on every facet of festival life. Attending Elderhostel trips is a way of life for the Levitts. It gives them the opportunity to visit other parts of the country and, in a number of instances, to attend nonconventional courses.

Fred's advice to others on adult education: "Age is no barrier to learning." He purchased a computer so he can cruise the information highway. And, in Fred's thirst for knowledge, he looks forward each semester to scanning the UNC course listings to determine what courses he'll audit.

Volunteerism: More Than a Workplace Substitute

WHEN MARVIN LEFFLER EXITED HIS PLUMBING supply business, he was not concerned about how he would occupy his time. He substituted volunteerism for corporate management. What's more, he had already identified the vehicle that could use his talents. Having spent more than 40 years in sales and an equal number of years as an active New York University alumnus, Marvin naturally became involved in the restoration and operation of NYU's Town Hall as one of the city's premier public auditoriums. When Town Hall was spun off from the university as a separate nonprofit organization, Marvin was named president. Though this is a nonpaying job, Marvin works a nearly full-time schedule attending to the things he likes and does best—sales, marketing and getting diverse groups to work together.

Most early retirees, like Marvin, return to their roots when they choose to volunteer. Simply put, a former manager or professional has skills and experience needed by nonprofit groups. A doctor assists in a health clinic, an accountant advises start-up businesses, and an educator teaches nonreaders. One thing is certain: Whatever the assignment, 50-plus managers and professionals usually describe their volunteer work as "payback" time, a form of thanks for a rewarding career.

However, after 30 to 40 years of corporate life, the last thing many managers want to do is serve on a nonprofit organization's board of directors. If they are inclined to be volunteers, they often look for assignments where they can use their skills by working directly with people rather than as members of committees or boards of directors. Not that board work is less important, but many 50-plus managers and professionals want to break from their former corporate lifestyle.

Some in the 50-plus set prefer working in a hands-on capacity teaching handicapped children, delivering meals to the elderly at home, or assisting in a health or legal-aid clinic. But even with a desire for one-on-one work, can you imagine being as adaptable as Mark B., who went from a high-profile publishing job to building homes for the urban poor, or Patricia Lyons, a former advertising manager, who volunteers as a docent in a zoo? Both are among the volunteers profiled later in this chapter.

"Helping others can be surprisingly easy, since there is much that needs to be done." So say Rosalynn and Jimmy Carter in their book *Everything to Gain*. "The hard part comes in choosing what to do and getting started, making the first effort at something different. Once the initiative is taken we often find that we can do things we never thought we could."

President Carter, at 57, was out of work and, like other retirees, he was looking for new relationships. "For us, an involvement in promoting good for others has made a tremendous difference in our lives in recent years. There are serious needs everywhere for volunteers who want to help those who are hungry, homeless, blind, crippled, addicted to drugs or alcohol, illiterate, mentally

---

POINTS TO REMEMBER

- Giving back to the community or society in which one has enjoyed success is one of the primary reasons that the 50-plus set work as volunteers.
- There is no shortage of opportunities to serve as a volunteer.
- There's a volunteer job to fulfill every interest.
- Professional and management skills are always in demand.
- Many managers and professionals prefer hands-on volunteer work—not administrative work.
- You can learn new skills as a volunteer.
- Corporate America is packaging volunteer programs for early retirees.

ill, elderly, imprisoned, or just friendless and lonely. For most of us, learning about these people, who are often our immediate neighbors, can add a profound new dimension to what might otherwise be a time of too much worrying about our own selves."

The Facts Speak for Themselves

Take a look at the demographics of volunteerism. A 1996 Gallup study notes that 71% of men and women, age 55 to 64, are volunteers. They average nearly 5 hours a week as volunteers, making it the most active age group. And those who are 65-plus are hardly slackers; a third of this age group spend 3.6 hours a week as volunteers. The U.S. Department of Labor's Bureau of Labor Statistics points out that people over age 50 spend about 45% of their time as volunteers in church-related work, followed in order of preference by work with civic or political, health care, education, social or welfare, and sport or recreation organizations.

You might think that an even greater percentage of the nation's 50-plus set would be volunteering. The reasons more people do not vary, according to an American Association of Retired Persons survey. Other than sheer disinterest, primary reasons include lack of available time, physical and health limitations and family concerns. AARP finds that retirees with "higher education and those with upper incomes are more likely to volunteer out of a feeling of societal responsibility than older Americans in general."

Help Fill the Volunteer Gap

Nonprofit organizations have an insatiable need for volunteers, one that's more difficult to meet than ever before. That's because the leadership and hands-on work in many volunteer organizations historically was provided by women who are now engaged in the workforce. The management skills required to direct a nonprofit group or head a committee were comparable to those used by their husbands in corporate jobs. But the scenario has changed. Women have entered the workforce, and volunteerism, once a substitute for the job market, has become of secondary importance. In response, some nonprofits have adjusted their operations, offering more flexible options so they can continue to attract working women as volunteers. Others are actively recruiting early retirees and nontraditional volunteers. The point is, if you are interested, someone needs your help.

Remember, whatever your level of volunteer involvement, don't expect it to be a direct replacement of the workplace. It's not and never will be, but it is often the next best thing. Above all, take on a volunteer assignment with a positive attitude. Most times it permits you to continue to hone existing managerial or professional skills, and in many other instances to learn and perfect new ones. And there is always the opportunity to continue peer relationships.

A Nonprofit Sampler

Every base appears to be covered. Some volunteer groups are national organizations with membership in the millions; others are regional with more specific missions. Nearly all need more volunteer help. If you're concerned with homelessness, then Habitat for Humanity offers some practical solutions. Want to use your management skills? Try either Service Corps of Retired Executives Association or the National Executive Service Corps. If you have a particular skill and don't know how to become a volunteer, you can either scan the Yellow Pages for the names of volunteer organizations in your community or contact local volunteer clearinghouses like the Retired Senior Volunteer Program, which brokers volunteers to dozens of community organizations and agencies. Local newspapers and magazines sometimes publish lists of agencies currently in need of volunteers, and public television and radio stations occasionally conduct volunteer sign-up drives. Here are just some of the possibilities.

Elderhostel Offers Community Service

Many organizations have added community service to their basic programs. Elderhostel (discussed in Chapter 3) expanded its programs to offer its members more than the diet of per-

sonal enrichment that they
receive on "learning vacations."
In 1992, it introduced a number of programs in conjunction
with Global Volunteers, the
Oceanic Society and Habitat
for Humanity (discussed later
in this chapter).

In 1997, 3,300 retirees
enrolled in 300 Elderhostel
domestic and overseas projects
at 60 different sites. Some of these projects involve computers.
The Lazarus Foundation, based in Columbia, Maryland, teaches computer repair skills to Elderhostel volunteers who use
these skills to refurbish donated computers. Once repaired,
some of the computers are donated to local nonprofits and
schools; others are taken home by the Eldershostel members to
donate to local organizations.

On another project, Elderhostel has been working for several years with California State University in the San Bernadino
National Park. Volunteers are engaged in reforestation of the
"children's forest," a 3,400-acre tract where children and young
adults can observe firsthand the wonders of the ecosystem. The
project will take ten to 20 years to complete.

Global Volunteers work primarily in rural communities
throughout the world, including China, Poland, Indonesia, and
parts of the U.S. They concentrate on teaching and maintenance
work in poor, rural schools. The Oceanic Society offers a range
of environmentally related research assignments, such as studying humpback whales in Costa Rica or howler monkeys in Belize.

FOR MORE INFORMATION. The all-inclusive fees for the
Elderhostel Service Programs range from approximately $300
for a U.S. project to nearly $1,900 in Belize (including round-
trip airfares). Volunteers live in the community, generally in
quarters comparable in quality to a college dormitory. Before
being accepted in the program, prospective volunteers need to
complete a detailed medical form. For more information, con-

WHY VOLUNTEERS PARTICIPATE

The major reasons volunteers give are:
- For personal enjoyment and fulfillment
- Out of a sense of obligation, duty or responsibility to society
- Because people need help
- To stay active

Source: American Association of Retired Persons

---

tact Elderhostel Service Programs at 75 Federal St., Boston, MA 02110 (617-426-8056; www.elderhostel.org).

Helping Small Business

The Service Corps of Retired Executives Association, better known as SCORE, provides management and professional know-how to potential, start-up and existing small companies. Funded nearly entirely by the Small Business Administration, which is also a source of a large part of its client base, SCORE offers start-ups and small businesses a menu consisting of one-on-one and team counseling, and workshops in sales and marketing, manufacturing, distribution, and record-keeping. In 1997, approximately 13,000 volunteers in 389 local SCORE chapters counseled about 350,000 small-business owners and conducted nearly 5,000 workshops. SCORE seeks volunteers from all levels of corporate life, ranging from managers and professionals to people who ran their own retail, service and manufacturing businesses.

Ann Hopkins, a retail and manufacturing executive for 35 years, is currently a counselor and also the past chairperson of SCORE's New York City office. "By the time I was in my early sixties, I had made enough money to retire. I took a year off—visited the museums and did the things that I hardly had time to do when I worked full-time. Then my children said I was becoming boring—never had anything to talk about. I wanted to do something to occupy my time in a meaningful way, and I didn't want to do volunteer work in a hospital." As SCORE's chairperson, Ann supervised 25 other counselors, worked three days a week, six hours a day. "What I like is helping a client get a loan or serving as a listening post for a company with a problem."

FOR MORE INFORMATION. To learn more about SCORE, call the local office, which you'll find listed in the U.S. Government section of your telephone directory, or contact the National SCORE office at 409 Third St., SW, 4th Floor, Washington, DC 20024 (800-634-0245; www.score.org).

Using Business Skills Overseas

The International Executive Service Corps provides another platform where retired managers and professionals can use their skills.

IESC operates globally, primarily in underdeveloped Latin American, Caribbean, African and Asian nations. Since 1989, IESC has added to its consulting portfolio a number of former Soviet Bloc nations who are making the conversion from a state to a private economy.

IESC volunteer consultants are either corporate managers or entrepreneurs such as the owners of dairies, farms, hardware stores, and smaller manufacturing and service companies. The typical overseas assignment lasts about two months, although some projects run up to a year. Consultants are not required to speak the host nation's language. Even with a multimonth commitment, consultants receive no salary, but IESC provides airfare for the consultant and spouse, insurance and a per diem allowance for living expenses.

> ### WAYS YOU CAN HELP
>
> - Help the poor, homeless or needy
> - Work to help improve your community or neighborhood
> - Work to improve the environment
> - Help provide services to older people through senior centers or other means
> - Help people cope with their problems
> - Tutor schoolchildren, or do other work involving children or youth groups
> - Help out at a hospital, or engage in other health-related work
> - Educate people on specific topics
> - Help foster art, music or other cultural activities
> - Help promote the political process
>
> Source: The American Association of Retired Persons

Over the past ten years, a large number of IESC's projects have been in the former Soviet Union and central and eastern Europe. These projects place a heavy emphasis on defense conversion, industry restructuring and privatization.

Worldwide, about 20% of IESC's projects are in agribusiness, followed by assignments in hotel operations, restaurants, fast food, travel agencies and tourism. IESC finds a growing need for consultants in education, environment, health care, and the judiciary.

IESC volunteers have helped food processing companies in Ghana and Zimbabwe to upgrade their information systems. Consultant Velma Forsythe, working at Astek Fruit Processing in

Ghana, developed a series of computer programs to monitor account receivables on a daily basis. In Zimbabwe, at Cairns Foots Ltd., Robert Mitchell designed a production system, then introduced new technology to computerize the operations and a computer module to replace the manual system used previously in production planning.

One hitch: IESC maintains a database of 13,000 consultants to handle only about 1,100 projects a year. Volunteer opportunities are ruled by supply and demand. Repeat consulting assignments are based on a volunteer's particular skills together with marketplace needs.

FOR MORE INFORMATION. The first step to become a volunteer is to obtain a registration form and information package. Then IESC sets up a personal interview. For a package, contact the IESC at Stamford Harbor Park, Box 10005, Stamford, CT 06904 (800-243-4372; www. iesc.org).

Management Assistance for Nonprofits

The name has a familiar ring, but the National Executive Service Corps differs in mission from the International Executive Service Corps. NESC provides management assistance to nonprofit organizations in the U.S. through affiliates in 44 cities in 24 states and the District of Columbia. In 1997, approximately 5,000 consultants furnished an estimated 220,000 hours of consulting services. NESC seeks individuals with a broad array of management and professional skills.

I am an Executive Service Corps volunteer consultant with the Greater Triangle ESC. Our group started in 1987. We have approximately 45 consultants. During 1977, we worked with approximately 20 different organizations ranging from several large nonprofits to a few mom-and-pop social service agencies. Over the past six years, I've consulted with an AIDS residence group, an historical site and the Durham County Library. One of the by-products is a chance to become associated with different organizations. As a result of my library consultancy, I became a trustee and subsequently chairman of the board.

WAYS TO MAKE A CONNECTION

Besides working through the volunteer clearinghouses discussed beginning on page 100, here are some proven ways of locating volunteer groups that need your help.

- Many newspapers publish "volunteers wanted" listings; TV stations feature them in public service announcements.
- Your library's reference desk may maintain a file of literature from volunteer groups, or the librarians may know of other ways to search the field.
- Scan the Yellow Pages under categories including "Associations," "Political Organizations," "Volunteer Services" or "Social Service Organizations."
- Read bulletin boards in public places.
- To make a quick connection with the organization of your choice, call and ask for the volunteer coordinator.

ESC volunteers average a few weeks to several months advising social service, education, health care, cultural and performing arts, religious and governmental nonprofit agencies on such management fundamentals as how to prepare budgets and financial reports, create long-term strategic plans, recruit board members, improve the relationship between the board and professional staff, formulate fund-raising strategies, and improve personnel policies.

Nearly every assignment starts by matching a volunteer's skills to a nonprofit's specific requirements. When the New York Philharmonic requested NESC's assistance, it asked for someone who understood both music and marketing. William Selden was given the job. Many of Bill's corporate and personal skills were ideal for the assignment. Bill had been employed for almost 40 years by several retail and apparel manufacturing firms. A late 1980s leveraged buyout of the company where he was a principal put him into an earlier-than-expected early retirement.

The Philharmonic was a perfect fit because Bill played the viola and collected antique stringed instruments. His task was to review the orchestra's whole marketing operation and to help it find ways to attract more subscribers. The Philharmonic has

THE SIX SECRETS OF HAPPY VOLUNTEERING

People sometimes talk themselves out of volunteering or give it up for reasons that they actually have control over. They're afraid they will end up doing something that's helpful, but absolutely boring. Or they're afraid the organization will demand more of their time and energy than they want to give up. After all, they just got off the workaday merry-go-round. Before you write off the possibilities, try following these suggestions provided in a pamphlet distributed to volunteers in Minnesota.

• Determine your reasons for volunteering. This chapter will help you define them.

• Determine your time limitations. How much time can you reasonably offer, given your other commitments and your desire for leisure?

• Seek agencies whose work you support. Volunteer clearinghouses, like the one described below, can help you in your quest.

• Communicate your goals and limits clearly. If you plan to be away on vacation for a length of time, the organization should be aware of your limited availability.

• Fulfill your end of the bargain. As in business, if you say you'll head a committee or prepare a report, then do it.

• Ask for an evaluation of your work. It's nice to get a report card to measure your effectiveness.

adopted many of Bill's recommendations, including providing subscribers with more flexible ways to buy concert tickets.

FOR MORE INFORMATION. To learn more about the National Executive Service Corps consult your local telephone directory for the office nearest you, or contact NESC at 120 Wall St., New York, NY 10005 (212-269-1234; www.escus.org).

Mobilizing Professional Talent

The goal of the Emeritus Foundation is to mobilize the time and talents of retirees with professional skills. The foundation, founded in 1979, currently focuses on five principal programs for emeritus professionals including: attorneys; teachers; managers; scientists, mathematicians and engineers; and social workers. The foundation, however, is looking to expand its volunteer base to begin new programs in other fields.

The foundation recruits consultants by tapping the resources of professional organizations. It has approximately 70 active consultants in Washington, D.C., most of whom have been on repeat assignments.

In a typical assignment, former scientists from the U.S. Geological Service, National Institutes of Health or Office of Naval Research bring their practical experiences into the classroom. They perform demonstrations and hands-on experiments, or guide students on field trips to a power-generation plant, science museum or nuclear lab. "The experts," reports one newspaper account, "also dispel the notion that scientists are 'geeky' people who lock themselves in tiny laboratories and wear white coats."

The Teachers Program's 200 retired teachers have provided tutorial services to more than 1,200 students, while Emeritus lawyers have handled sensitive interviews with traumatized refugees seeking political asylum in the U.S.

FOR MORE INFORMATION. To be a volunteer with the Emeritus Foundation, or if you are interested in organizing a local chapter, write to or call the foundation, 1614 20th St., NW, Washington, DC 20009 (202-232-0863).

A Need for Health Care Services

You may think of Hilton Head Island, South Carolina, as a paradise for the island's 30,000 permanent residents and the annual 1.5 million vacationers who visit there. But a real-life problem exists: An estimated 20% of the residents and a large segment of the workers who commute to Hilton Head receive little or no primary health care services. What's more, a significant number of the island's schoolchildren have never been examined by a physician.

Dr. Jack McConnell, a physician and, until his retirement, Johnson & Johnson's corporate director of advanced technology, along with a number of other retired health care professionals living on Hilton Head, recognized the area's medical problems and in 1992 started the Volunteers in Medicine Clinic. The clinic's volunteer staff of retired physicians, nurses, dentists and chiropractors provides free vaccinations, physical examinations, primary health care, pediatric, gynecology, cardiology, eye examinations and dental care to upward of 15,000 patients a year. The clinic also gives retired health professionals a chance to be professionally productive.

SUGGESTED READING

- Hardy, James, *Dynamic Boards* (Essex Press, Erwin, TN, 1990). As a board member, I've enjoyed using this book.
- Flanagan, Joan, *Successful Fundraising* (Contemporary Books, Chicago, 1993)

Before it opened, the clinic managed to get a bill through the South Carolina General Assembly creating a "Special Volunteer License" for physicians who agreed to practice medicine free of charge in a nonprofit clinic and to dispense drugs. In practical terms, the physicians, dentists and other retired health care practitioners are licensed to practice only at the Volunteers in Medicine Clinic. The clinic also obtained unlimited malpractice coverage from the South Carolina Underwriters Association for its staff of health care and lay volunteers for $5,000.

The retired physicians need to apply individually to the State Board of Medical Examiners for the special license. The Board then thoroughly searches the applicant's credentials. The protocol adopted in South Carolina, of course, would vary from state to state for similar types of volunteer clinics.

Some of the retired professionals in Hilton Head have an opportunity to continue in their medical specialties, such as gynecology, ophthalmology, pediatrics and dermatology, while others are assigned as primary-care physicians. A continuing education program is conducted at the clinic on a weekly basis. To many of the participating physicians, the clinic provides a chance to work directly with patients, use skills and be an active player in a medical facility.

According to the Volunteers in Medicine formula, the proper utilization of retired health care professionals should help to control health care costs by relieving hospital emergency rooms of the need to furnish high-cost, primary-care medical services. The Hilton Head clinic has more than 125 volunteer health care professionals, but a volunteer clinic could also operate with only one physician and a nurse.

Hilton Head is the only U.S. town in which everyone who lives there has access to health care, says Dr. McConnell. To date about 1,000 communities have either visited or contacted Volunteers in Medicine Clinic, requesting information or help in replicating a clinic in their community. The Volunteers in Medicine Institute was established to respond to these requests. There are ten other clinics up and running, and another 20 in various stages of development. Dr. McConnell's dream? "There is sufficient retired medical personnel, which if prompted to come out of retirement on a part-time basis, could deliver most of the health care services needed by the 45 million Americans who have been left with little or no access to health care."

FOR MORE INFORMATION. To learn more about Volunteers in Medicine Clinic, write to or call the clinic, box 24126, Hilton Head Island, SC 29925 (803-342-5700).

What About Free Legal Services?

A growing number of retired lawyers, many among the 11,300 members of the Senior Lawyers Division, are providing free legal services to low-income people with everyday legal problems. Arizona, California, Florida, New York and Texas have already adopted pro bono participation programs whereby state bar association dues are waived just as long as the attorney receives no compensation for volunteer legal services. Other states are debating similar types of legislation for retired lawyers. Unlike the open policy in the other states, California does not grant emeritus status to lawyers previously not admitted to practice in the state.

Typically, members of the Senior Lawyers Division, who are age 55-plus, are involved in representing indigent clients in such areas as landlord-tenant and consumer matters, family law, senior citizen issues, public benefits and immigration law. The amount of time devoted to pro bono work varies greatly. As in all professions, there are some lawyers who do no volunteer work while others devote a full week at a time to representing those who are less fortunate. The Division sponsors educational programs dealing with the legal and personal issues of Alzheimer's, social security and comprehensive health care.

FOR MORE INFORMATION. To learn more about the range of pro bono work after retirement, contact the Senior Lawyers Division of the American Bar Association, at 750 North Lake Shore Dr., Chicago, IL 60611 (312-988-5583; www.abanet.org/srlawyers).

Harnessing Corporate Leaders

Finding a volunteer program may be as simple as finding out what programs your company already sponsors. It can be a great way to stay in touch with your fellow retirees and at the same time serve the community. If you haven't been involved before, this may be the time to start. Your company may be able to help you get involved, and if it can't, you may be able to help it get involved. Here's how.

Imagine a volunteer organization that has a client listing that includes 3M, Amoco, Citibank, Heinz, Hewlett-Packard, and Honeywell. The National Retiree Volunteer Coalition has just that and offers a novel twist to volunteerism. Its mission is to help companies mobilize retirees into volunteer groups.

To be sure, some companies go it alone, but others want to avoid reinventing the wheel when it comes to establishing and running a volunteer program for retirees. NRVC offers a high level of know-how and experience. It shows corporate clients how to recruit and train volunteers, meet meaningful goals and objectives, conduct long-range planning, and develop community partnerships. A nonprofit organization, NRVC offers these services to corporations on a fee basis. To date, 96 corporations, hospitals and universities in 37 cities and 19 states in the U.S. and three Canadian provinces, involving about 55,000 retirees, have been organized under NRVC's umbrella.

Why don't retirees volunteer on their own? And why should companies start a new corporate service when they are in the process of reducing overhead expenses? Companies find that many of their retirees want to maintain collegial ties but typically don't have a history of volunteering. Seventy percent of the people recruited by NRVC's participating companies have never before served as volunteers. These companies view community service as a beneficial and practical corporate activity. In short, volunteerism proves to be a sound community relations investment.

Honeywell, NRVC's charter member, reports that its volunteers over the past 16 years have contributed more than three million hours of service, handling a range of projects calling for different management, technical, administrative, professional and blue-collar skills. "[If you] estimate the [value of the] volunteer time," says James Reiner, Honeywell's former CEO, "at a very conservative $12 an hour, that's $50 million worth of value added to the community."

Typical of Honeywell's contribution is the Assistive Technology Project that uses a volunteer core of nearly 60 retired Honeywell engineers, physicists and technicians. They work with 29 non-profit agencies in the Minneapolis area designing and building special equipment for physically and mentally challenged people.

NRVC is currently working with Amoco Corporation to create Retiree Volunteer Programs in 11 communities across America, and in two communities in Canada.

FOR MORE INFORMATION. To see if your employer has a retiree volunteer program or if it's associated with the National Retiree Volunteer Coalition, speak with your company's human resource department, or contact the NRVC at 4914 West 35 St., Minneapolis, MN 55416 (888-733-6782; www.nrvc.org).

Building for the Future

Amateur and skilled carpenters, plumbers and electricians alike are welcome at Habitat for Humanity International. Using a volunteer labor force of youngsters through oldsters in more than 1,700 affiliates throughout the U.S. and overseas in 58 other countries, Habitat for Humanity has built or rehabilitated more than 60,000 homes for people who otherwise couldn't afford decent housing.

Visit downtown Paterson, New Jersey, and you'll see Habitat for

THE GRANDDADDY OF 'EM ALL

The **Telephone Pioneers of America,** as its name indicates, is a pioneer in volunteering. A nationwide group started in 1910, its membership consists of more than 850,000 retired and long-term employees of the U.S. and Canadian telecommunications industry.

The Pioneers, mostly AT&T and regional Bell Operating Co. employees, donate nearly 30 million hours a year to volunteer work. Special attention has been given to projects that help the lonely, disadvantaged and disabled, such as building a 900-foot boardwalk that gives disabled and elderly people easier access to the wooded areas in Flat Rock Brook Nature Center, in Englewood, New Jersey. More recently, the Pioneers have focused on such social problems as illiteracy, homelessness and substance abuse.

Humanity volunteers in action. The area looks like any other construction site—workers in coveralls, hammers pounding and saws buzzing. But on Wednesdays, the scene is somewhat different. The workers, mainly 50-plus retirees, including former managers and craftsmen, have helped to build more than 74 duplex and triplex homes since the Paterson affiliate began in 1984. Some of the volunteers made their living as plumbers and carpenters, others are skilled hobbyists, and some are novices like one retired physician, who said, "When I went to work I just bent nails; now I can 'finish' them and work on my own."

FOR MORE INFORMATION. If you'd like to volunteer with Habitat for Humanity, consult your telephone directory for a local listing, or contact Habitat for Humanity International, at 121 Habitat St., Americus, GA 31709 (800-422-4828, ext. 551 or 552; www.habitat.org).

Volunteer Clearinghouses Help You to Find Your Niche

The American Association of Retired Persons sponsors a number of community-service programs for its 33 million members. For example, in 1979, AARP started 55 Alive/Mature Driving, the first nationwide refresher driving course designed exclusively for people over age 50. The program consists of an eight-hour classroom course with AARP volunteer instructors doing the training.

AARP sponsors a number of other programs, including AARP/VOTE, which educates voters on issues of importance to older Americans and the community at large, and AARP Tax-Aide, which helps low- and moderate-income older persons prepare federal and state tax returns.

AARP also operates a national computerized-matching project that refers volunteers to AARP projects and other nonprofit agencies that are in need of their services.

FOR MORE INFORMATION. To receive information on the AARP-sponsored volunteer programs, consult your telephone directory for the listing of a local AARP office, or contact the AARP, at 601 E Street, N.W., Washington, DC 20049 (www.aarp.org).

A Giant Volunteer Agency

Recognizing that corporate downsizing and early retirement have increased the pool of potential volunteers, the Retired and Senior Volunteer Program has lowered its membership age from 60 to 55. RSVP, a part of the Corporation for National Service, the federal domestic volunteer agency, is a massive broker of people, linking volunteers with organizations and agencies in need of volunteers. RSVP offers nonprofit agencies a base of volunteers with a range of business, education, administrative and blue-collar skills. Its mission is to enhance the lives of the volunteers and the communities in which they live.

Typical of RSVP's 900 U.S. projects is RSVP of Bergen County (N.J.). "One of my problems is to activate potential volunteers who say 'I've never done it before,'" says executive director Bernice Kallet. "I have no problem placing accountants and marketing people. They have skills always in demand. My job is to find ways for others to keep busy in a meaningful way." Bergen County RSVP volunteers help in such areas as child-care centers, libraries, parks, museums, outreach programs and hospitals. It has about 800 volunteers working for 90 county nonprofit agencies, providing about 172,500 hours of work a year. Volunteers contribute from as few as eight hours a month to as many as 40 hours a week.

FOR MORE INFORMATION. For an information kit on how to become a volunteer through the Retired and Senior Volunteer Program, consult your local telephone direction under RSVP, or contact RSVP at 1201 New York Ave., Washington, DC 20525 (800-424-8867; www. seniorcorps.org).

Volunteers in Action

The retirees who are profiled on the following pages devote large blocks if not most of their free time as volunteers. Some were active volunteers throughout their business careers; others became volunteers when they retired. A few had to learn new sets of skills to be volunteers, while others simply used existing skills to do their work. What you'll see are the range of opportunities available to the 50-plus set, including a retired executive-search consultant who gets retirees in their eighties enthused about computers.

SHE LEFT THE LIMELIGHT TO DO A BIT OF GOOD

Katie Kelly
TV PERSONALITY TURNED VOLUNTEER TEACHER

"I would still be at NBC if it wasn't for my December 1988 vacation," said Katie Kelly. "I'd already been around the world—to Cairo, the Middle East and China—so this time I decided to spend a few weeks in Vietnam and see what it was like." It was all part of her vacation checklist, just another place to visit. "I saw the Amerasians and it just destroyed me."

Amerasians are children born of Vietnamese mothers and American military personnel who were stationed in Vietnam. By 1988, Amerasians ranged in age from teenagers to those in their late twenties. Many were homeless, ostracized socially by other Vietnamese due to their mixed parentage. The Amerasians Katie met on the street or in the markets wanted to learn English. Many still had hopes of someday being united with their English-speaking fathers.

"I wanted to do something for them, and there wasn't even a group where I could send a check." She returned to NBC after her "vacation," but the plight of the Amerasian youngsters haunted her. Katie wanted to do something in person. It took time to rearrange her life, but a little more than a year later she left NBC and was back in Vietnam "determined to do the only other thing I knew how to do besides review movies—teach a little English."

After 12 years as a television headliner and even longer in print journalism, Katie Kelly left the TV klieg lights and retired from the paid workforce to begin her new life as a volunteer. Years before, with the encouragement of a teacher and the editor of a small weekly in her hometown in Nebraska, Katie had begun her career with a degree from the University of Missouri's School of Journalism. Her accomplishments included appearing as entertainment critic in New York for WNBC-TV's "Live at Five" program as well as a regular on the Today show and Live with Regis and Kathie Lee, and as a movie critic for Entertainment Tonight. But Katie's experience in Vietnam moved her to leave behind the glamour of network TV and communicate with a new purpose.

Although the Vietnamese and American governments shared no diplomatic relations in 1990, Katie was able to settle in Ho Chi Minh City (formerly Saigon). The Vietnamese government neither encouraged nor discouraged her plan to hold English classes in abandoned buildings, storefronts and

> **Katie's experience with Amerasian children in Vietnam moved her to leave the glamour of network TV and communicate with a new purpose.**

homes. Katie spoke little Vietnamese, but she bridged the language gap with skills acquired while teaching school in the Midwest earlier in her career and in television.

BRINGING HER WORK HOME

After one year, she came back to the U.S. determined to use her communications skills to publicize the Amerasian problem. By this time, Amerasians were emigrating at a greater rate to the U.S. as a result of the open-door policy contained in the Amerasians Homecoming Act passed in the late '80s. Their plight in Vietnam was now transferred to the U.S.

Katie had already written a number of books. It took her one year to write and publish *A Year in Saigon: How I Gave Up the Glitz Job in Television to Have the Time of My Life Teaching Amerasian Kids in Vietnam.* With it, a new phase in her relationships with Amerasians had begun.

She discovered St. Rita's Center in the Bronx, the site of a refugee support group. Soon afterward, she volunteered to teach English four days a week. A typical class has six students, mostly in their twenties to early thirties. They have had little formal education, lack fluency in English and even in their native language, and have problems coping with the American lifestyle. They work in sweatshops and restaurants in low-paying jobs.

Katie's lesson plan and her approach to education are homemade. On January 15, Martin Luther King's birthday, she used a taped TV interview with Coretta Scott King as the basis of her classroom discussion on the need for racial tolerance. Dealing with

students, Katie traded in one form of show business for a different type of performance, this time before a live audience.

Her work with Amerasians notwithstanding, she sometimes misses TV's spotlight. "I loved being famous, people knowing me on the street, and people coming up to me. But that part of my life is behind me. A truck driver will occasionally yell down at me and say, 'What did you think of the Stallone movie?' But there are advantages to not being a film critic. I can walk out of the movie if I don't like it."

Officially, Katie is considered retired, a fact she finds difficult to accept considering she works nearly full-time as a volunteer teacher. "I never know what to fill in the space on the tax form where it asks for occupation.

"Considering how little I know about business, I'm living rather well on my investments. I was paid an obscene amount in TV and I saved. TV had given me enough financial security to be able to give a little back where it was badly needed. It gave me the resources to support myself ever since I left NBC." Katie bought a brownstone house in the Chelsea section on New York's West Side before the area became fashionable, and to reduce costs even further, she rents half her house, sufficient to pay for maintenance and taxes on the property.

Katie is unsure how long she will continue to teach Amerasians, but her contribution is consistent with the summation in her book: "I was so shocked and saddened at the sight of all those Amerasians roaming the streets of Saigon that I wanted to go back and do some little bit of good."

DEVELOPING A VOLUNTEER PHILOSOPHY AT THE ZOO

Patricia Lyons
TRAVEL AGENCY EXECUTIVE TURNED ZOO DOCENT

Patricia Lyons encourages people to look at volunteering with new eyes. "Most people think of volunteer work in traditional terms," she says. "Instead, you need to be creative. Let go."

She should know. As a docent with the Bronx Zoo, Pat has worked as a guide and played hide-and-seek with recuperating baby deer. She has worked on a research project in the bird house tracking an ibis to see how many times an hour the bird ate from a particular tray.

"As a result of my work at the zoo, I've started to collect books at home on animals and zoology. It is amazing I wasn't interested in these subjects in school. If I had to do it all over again, perhaps zoo management would be the basis of a second career."

As it is, Pat worked for years in travel and tourism after graduating with a degree in journalism from Syracuse University. In her early forties, she returned to Syracuse for about a year to work on a master's degree, but she ended up in New York City when she found a job as a copywriter with Grand Circle, then the exclusive travel agency for the American Association for Retired Persons. Seventeen years later, while

> **A takeover soured Pat on corporate employment. After biding her time to retirement, she reinvented herself as a docent at the Bronx Zoo.**

serving as Grand Circle's vice-president for marketing and advertising, Pat's business world fell apart. Grand Circle was sold and moved by its new owners from New York to Boston.

The takeover changed her attitude about future corporate employment. "I had burned out from the pressures of the takeover." Single and too young to collect social security or draw on her IRA, Pat had to earn a living until she was eligible to tap her financial resources. She considered different career options in the travel field, but instead was hired by the Cornell Medical College/ New York Hospital's behavioral research laboratory. "I thought it would be for a brief period until I could get back into the travel field." Instead, she spent six years at Cornell researching and writing grant proposals—uninteresting work that paid.

Pat left Cornell in her early sixties when she became of age to collect social security and draw on her other savings and other retirement benefits. She had no desire to start another career, but wanted to work as a volunteer. An avid gardener in her apartment complex's community gardens, Pat had a proven affinity for working outdoors.

She had read about the Bronx Zoo's docent program. "I took things in my own hands. I called the zoo to see if they could use my services. I was interviewed. They liked my views on animals and conservation, and I was accepted as a docent."

DOCENTS GIVE AS GOOD AS THEY GET

Docents are volunteers who work in museums, zoos and historical sites, leading tours and providing backup to the professional staff. To become a docent, as Pat discovered, one need not be an expert or skilled in the work. Many organizations, like the Bronx Zoo, sponsor in-depth programs to train docents.

Pat, along with 40 other volunteers, went to the zoo once a week for three months of classroom and on-the-job training. She was told that the program is the equivalent of a semester's worth of study in zoology. When Pat completed training, she was assigned as a docent and is expected to work at least one full day a week conducting tours or doing research. Pat is sometimes assigned to the "biocart," a mobile workstation used to exhibit various specimens from the zoo's collection. Her job is to tell visitors about the items on display.

Pat enjoys the esprit de corps that is fostered among the several hundred active docents. "The zoo sponsors an active social program for docents where there's an opportunity to meet other business and professional people your age who are interested in animals and the environment."

Pat has taken on additional volunteer responsibilities. From time to time she writes advertising copy for use in the zoo's public service advertisements to attract more volunteers. "Even with this extra work, I'll never give up being a docent. That's where the fun is.

"People need to take the initiative. Don't wait for them to call you. Often smaller organizations have a desperate need for volunteers because they're not as well known. You can volunteer in any field you want. It's no different than business—you create a job for yourself."

"JUST CALL ME BUTTERCUP"

Michael Turk

COMMUNICATIONS COMPANY EXECUTIVE TURNED CLOWN

When he was a vice-president at AT&T, few people ever thought of calling Michael Turk a clown. He was an expert in manufacturing electronics and computer chips. During a 31-year career with AT&T, he managed production facilities in California, Illinois, New Jersey and Pennsylvania. But following his retirement, Mike traded in his business suit for a clown suit and joined his wife, Sue, in clowning with a mission.

In a typical month, the Turks perform for children in New Jersey hospitals who have been diagnosed with cancer, work as clowns in a juvenile diabetes walkathon and entertain at a program for children with AIDS. They also perform with the Mental Health Players of New Jersey, a group that entertains in jails, hospitals, high schools and senior citizens centers. And, for each of the past five summers, Mike and Sue have spent one week at a summer camp where they train about 30 cancer patients or survivors, ages 17 to 20, to be junior counselors. Mike's volunteer work has given him a chance to help youngsters with problems far more extreme than being a retired executive.

In 1988, Mike, took early retirement—the first time since college that he had been

> **Consulting and recreation failed to fill the gap for Mike, who, at age 51, was unprepared for retirement. Clowning for sick kids made the difference.**

unemployed. Mike, who graduated from Newark College of Engineering and has an MBA from New York University, was known as a hands-on production manager. He enjoyed line rather than staff assignments, especially the years when he was general manager of an AT&T semiconductor plant in Reading, Pennsylvania. In this capacity, he was actively involved as AT&T's representative with a number of local community organizations.

His accomplishments in Pennsylvania resulted in a promotion to vice-president at AT&T headquarters in New Jersey, where he supervised the operations of 13 manufacturing plants worldwide and 20,000 employees. "Even with the promotion, I missed the Reading job. I believe in and practice participatory management. I had introduced the concept in Reading, and it got results." By comparison, his promotion to the 9-to-5 staff job brought additional pressure and less satisfaction.

Then AT&T made him an attractive retirement offer. "When I was younger, I considered 65 as the normal time to retire. My timetable changed with the years, and I lowered the age to 60." At 51, it certainly wasn't what Mike had originally planned. AT&T's

offer included incentive payments, an excellent pension and lifetime benefits. Along with investments and savings, that package would offer the Turks a secure income. But Mike was not otherwise prepared for retirement. He was unemployed, with no specific plans but lots of energy. He had an urge to find a job relating to people yet had no direction for starting a new career. And after holding challenging positions at AT&T, he found most other jobs uninviting.

"A search firm could have easily placed me in another job, but the AT&T package made it too financially attractive to look at work alternatives. I traveled, took golf lessons, played tennis and fished."

Over the next two years, Mike served as a consultant at no pay for a start-up software firm owned by a friend. While the owner concentrated on software development, Mike ran the business, working 30 hours a week. Then another friend hired him to run a manufacturing plant. He served as its manager until it moved to Pennsylvania. Mike had no intention of relocating.

CLOWNING PROVIDES AN ANSWER

Then began the Mike—and Sue—Turk story. It was Sue's volunteer involvement with clowning that added a new and fulfilling dimension to Mike's somewhat unstructured retirement lifestyle. Sue began clowning in 1982, while Mike was still managing AT&T's Reading plant. She joined the Pioneers, the AT&T community service group (see page 100). An audiologist and speech pathologist, Sue had had a long-time interest in the theater. One of the Pioneers' projects was clowning, entertaining and putting on shows at no charge for local charities.

When the Turks returned to New Jersey, Sue didn't affiliate with the local Pioneers group but instead became a clown for the Valerie Fund, a source of medical help and personal counseling to children with cancer and blood disorders. Sue, a diabetic since age 26, personally related to people with chronic medical problems.

Sue, who is known theatrically as Sweet Pea, got Mike involved as her clowning partner "Buttercup" after he had left AT&T. She makes their costumes and creates their routines. During the fall and holiday season, they often work three to five times a week. "In our act, we sometimes make fun of doctors. Doctors enjoy it. Children and their parents learn to relax," says Mike. "In one skit, I clown as a doctor. My stethoscope is a plunger. I even use participatory management techniques, when I let kids hit me over the head with a plastic mallet."

While Mike is still considering some possible business ventures, he also serves as the volunteer treasurer of the local synagogue. He spends a few days a week there working on its financial records, getting financial information ready for the independent audit, signing checks, and handling the administrative duties of a chief financial officer.

As for his clowning, former AT&T associates are hardly surprised about it. It parallels in many ways his business career as a corporate maverick, a person who did things differently within the organizational structure yet was still an achiever.

SHE SPEAKS FOR THOSE WHO NEED HER

Mary Pat Toups
TRIAL LAWYER TURNED ADVOCATE FOR THE POOR

Many women in the 50-plus set have much in common with Mary Pat Toups and her mid-life career as a lawyer, which she has parlayed into a nearly full-time volunteer commitment in retirement. She specializes in serving the elderly poor and actively recruits other senior lawyers to the effort.

Mary Pat was married by the time she graduated from the University of California in Los Angeles, then for 20 years she was a homemaker, a civic volunteer and an elected school board member. Seeing the influence of lawyers in the governmental process, Mary Pat decided when she was in her early forties to become a lawyer. She was one of ten women in a class of 100 at Pepperdine University School of Law.

"My work as an elected school board official prepared me for law school by making me conscious of issues facing children, parents, the poor and the elderly. When I passed the California bar examination, I became a sole practitioner, taking any case that walked in the door." She also liked the independence of being her own boss.

When her husband, a civil engineer (from whom she was divorced in the early 1980s),

> **Mary Pat is a pro bono lawyer with a mission: "I want to empower senior citizens so they better understand the laws that impact on their lives."**

was transferred to Washington, D.C., in 1978, Mary Pat decided to concentrate on a few legal specialties that personally interested her. "I first specialized in representing abused and neglected children, and then in 1984, I started to specialize in elder law." By then, Mary Pat had recognized that poorer elderly people received inadequate legal assistance.

As a practicing Washington attorney, Mary Pat never had a formal business office. "For $50 a year, my office was the library in the courthouse. All my child-abuse cases were assigned by the District of Columbia Superior Court. It was mostly trial work, which is like the theater. Both require acting and dramatic skill."

When Mary Pat turned 63, she decided to return to Southern California to be nearer her sons and daughters and grandchildren, though she fully intended to continue practicing law.

Leaving Washington meant selling her Watergate apartment and severing her ties with the Washington community, especially the Kennedy Center for the Performing Arts. As a drama and music fan, she had performed as supernumerary and had had non-singing, walk-on roles in several operas—*Tosca, La Boheme, Manot,* and the Royal Ballet's performance of *The Prince of the Pagodas.* "I'd be in court all day, then rehearse until midnight. We were paid a $70 honorarium and had to agree that we would only 'mouth' words, never sing them."

In California, she bought a two-bedroom home in an adult community in Laguna Hills, near Los Angeles. For more than a year, she commuted from the East Coast, living and working in both areas as she severed her professional and personal ties in Washington. Mary Pat financed her move and her "retirement" with profits from the sale of her home and income from investments, social security, and payments from writing and teaching. "In short, I'll never go hungry."

SHE PRACTICES
MULTIFACETED ADVOCACY

Her legal practice is now totally voluntary. "I wouldn't consider it a good week unless I spend two days at the Legal Aid Society office in Santa Ana. I no longer accept fees. I only take clients on a consultation basis, referring them to other lawyers if necessary for additional legal help.

"I want to empower senior citizens so they better understand the laws that impact on their lives." This she accomplishes through her writing, teaching and active participation in the American Bar Association's Senior Lawyers Division. Mary Pat has started to teach a how-to law course for the elderly at a local community college, and she is writing a book on elder law.

Mary Pat is an advocate in the broadest sense, recruiting older and retired lawyers to work as volunteers with the elderly poor. Her goal is to convince them that, as retired lawyers, they can use their skills to help the elderly understand their legal rights. It might be difficult for some lawyers who formerly had large, well-paying practices to work at this level, but volunteering with groups like the Legal Aid Society represents one way for them to continue being active, practicing lawyers. Mary Pat provides a model.

SPREADING THE WORD ABOUT COMPUTERS

Herbert Halbrecht

EXECUTIVE RECRUITER TURNED COMPUTER LITERACY INSTRUCTOR FOR SENIORS AND KIDS

Herbert Halbrecht spent 30 years in the information technology field. He was neither a techie nor an information specialist. Herb was the founder and principal of Halbrecht Associates in Stamford, Connecticut, an executive search firm that recruited top-level managers in the information technology and telecommunications fields. Herb describes his forte as a "layman who understood the dynamics of the field." His industry experience enabled him to be one of the founders and a president of the Society of Information Management.

Now retired, Herb continues to apply his understanding of technology in a different setting—helping retirees, many in their eighties, to go online, or teaching school children their computer ABCs.

After Herb sold his business and his house in Connecticut, he relocated to Durham, North Carolina, and started a personal mission to make more folks computer literate. "Before retiring, I had never used a computer even though I was involved in the high-tech worlds of information, telecomunications and assorted exotica. I took several brief courses on computer usage at Duke, but I don't consider myself the typical user. I do very little word processing. I'm not a real computernik. I'm mostly interest-

> **A former entrepreneur, Herb continues to convey the enthusiasm of the workplace in his approach to volunteerism.**

ed in e-mail and the Internet. What I do doesn't call for a computer techie."

Wanting to help the elderly learn how to use computers, he talked with gerontologists at Duke University. They convinced him that older people often suffer from severe loneliness and the related health problems that loneliness produces, namely depression and physical illnesses. To test this theory, he became involved with the Methodist Retirement Home in Durham. His goal was to get elderly residents to use computers.

A former entrepreneur, Herb continues to convey the enthusiasm of the workplace in his approach to volunteerism. To launch the project, he donated three computers to the Methodist Home. The 310 residents were asked to enroll in the computer course; 18 people signed up, 16 actually took the training, and 14 of them completed the six hours of training. Currently 35 residents at the Methodist Home are computer users. "One resident who is 69 met a 71-year-old in Texas on the Internet. When I last saw them they were engaged. Some residents use the chat rooms to exchange ideas on hobbies, or they play bridge over the Internet. Another resident sends e-mail letters to a son in Denver who rarely writes or calls her."

Herb feels that computers scare older people. Even so, they can enjoy many of the advantages of networking with new devices such as Web TV. Toward that end a program was initiated in Durham with the Jewish Family Service. "We installed Web TV in the homes of five shut-ins to help them decrease their loneliness. One of the five users was middle-aged but she was wheel-chair bound while the four others were in their late sixties and seventies."

At the other end of the age spectrum, Herb also works with elementary-school children. "I'm obsessed with education. It was my way up. For the past eight years, even when I was living in Connecticut, I've been an elementary-school tutor." Herb's interest goes beyond teaching youngsters to read. He works with students to make them computer literate. "If I can learn how to operate a computer then they can, too.

We can teach almost any fourth or fifth grade student the basics of the Internet in 30 minutes; third grade students take a little longer.

"In Connecticut, I tutored second grade kids. In Durham, I've been a reading tutor at a local magnet school. Originally, I was working and assisting a reading-recovery teacher for three years, and two years ago I started teaching third to fifth graders how to use the Internet, how to access certain Web sites and how to use search engines. Then I helped to initiate a program that sets up training tutorials for the teachers to essentially 'demystify' the Internet."

As a low-tech computer user, Herb is guided by a single principle in working with retirees and school children. "When older people say to me that they never could use a computer because they don't know how it works, I ask: Do you know how your car's engine works? Who cares? You just drive."

THE LIFETIME VOLUNTEER

Iris-Rose Ruffing

GIRL SCOUT EXECUTIVE TURNED CONSULTANT TO NONPROFITS

When Iris-Rose Ruffing graduated from Meredith College, she went to work for the Girl Scouts where, then and now, there was no gender discrimination. By the time she retired in the late 1980s, she had spent 26 years as a Girl Scouts paid professional and a score of additional years as a volunteer, with time off for marriage and raising two daughters. After a lifetime of either being a volunteer or supervising them as a Girl Scouts executive, she signed up as a volunteer with the Executive Service Corps.

As a former employee, her partiality to the Girl Scouts is based on the way the organization operates. "The Scouts are unique. There never was a glass ceiling since the organization is run by women. This has enabled women to fill leadership positions that were not open to women in industry until recently."

Widowed at an early age, Iris-Rose, a North Carolina native, was living at the time in Greensboro, North Carolina. When she went back to work, she was named director of the regional council serving that community.

"After my council was merged with another council, I was no longer in charge. I was given a new job in the merged council but frankly my nose was out of joint. I liked

> **"You soon discover the importance of volunteers. Without them a nonprofit organization can't exist."**

running my own show. I promised myself that I would stay in Greensboro until my youngest daughter went to college. When that took place, I was transferred to the Chicago area to head a council comprising 18 Chicago communities. I intended to stay for six years and I ended up staying 18 years until I retired."

With a paid staff of 14, along with a cadre of volunteers, Iris-Rose learned most of the tricks of the nonprofit world from the Scouts. "You soon discover the importance of volunteers. Without them, a nonprofit organization can't exist. I had a board of 25 people who represented the economic and racial diversity of the 18 communities that we served. I had to learn how to work effectively with all of them if I was to be successful in my job."

About a year before she planned to retire, she started preparing for her departure. She reached out to the Chicago affiliate of the Executive Service Corps to help her in the transition and to ready her board. "When I left the Scouts, I was not altogether sure whether I'd stay in Chicago or return to North Carolina. I liked Chicago and its cultural life," she says.

Following her retirement and still debating whether to move or stay put, Iris-Rose joined the Chicago ESC as a consultant, applying her know-how about the workings of nonprofit organizations and volunteerism in a series of consulting assignments.

In 1990, she left Chicago and returned to North Carolina. This was "home," even though her two married daughters with two daughters of their own lived in Florida and Georgia.

As an expert on effective management of nonprofit organizations, Iris-Rose's talents were soon put to work by the ESC affiliate serving central North Carolina. "This is a natural thing for me to do. It means sharing my past skills and my experiences that I learned as a Girl Scouts executive.

"Volunteering should mean more to retired executives than payback time, a way they can say 'thanks' for a successful career. More important, it is a way that retirees can feel useful by applying what they know best to help others," she says.

VOLUNTEERING IN THE BUSINESS OF SHOW BUSINESS

Ira Wheeler

MANAGEMENT EXECUTIVE TURNED ACTOR AND CONSULTANT TO NONPROFITS

Ira Wheeler looks the part of a successful retired corporate manager, a role he knows all too well after spending 35 years as a senior executive in the chemical and plastics industry. He puts his look to work as a film actor. And, as a volunteer consultant with the National Executive Service Corps, he has applied his management skills to solving business problems for nonprofit organizations.

Anticipating the advice later given to Benjamin Braddock in The Graduate— "I just want to say one word to you: plastics!"—Ira launched his business career in the emerging plastics industry. In 1946, that was a natural move for a guy with a chemistry degree from Princeton and four years as a commissioned Coast Guard officer under his belt. Ira worked for several companies in research and development, and sales and marketing, ultimately landing with Celanese, now Hoescht Celanese. He spent the next 20 years moving up the corporate ladder, ending his career there as vice-president for corporate planning. As a result of a corporate reorganization, Ira left Celanese at 62.

In retirement, Ira received a golden parachute and a pension. In addition he gets social security and income from invest-

Ira's corporate background and love of theater made him a natural for nonprofit consulting with the National Executive Service Corps.

ments. Ira's wife, Mary, who is somewhat younger, is a full-time executive search consultant in New York. It's a third marriage for him and a second for her, and their children from previous marriages are all grown.

Ira's a long-time amateur actor and a member of the Blue Hill Troupe, which performs Gilbert & Sullivan operettas. About the time he was leaving Celanese, he learned from a troupe newsletter that film director Alan Pakula was looking for actors to play corporate executives in his next film, *Rollover.* Lean, gray-haired and distinguished, Ira looked the part. He applied, auditioned and was signed by Pakula. It was Ira's first step in making the change from amateur to professional status.

Over the past decade, Ira has had speaking roles in 18 films, including nine Woody Allen productions and *The Killing Fields,* for which he spent five weeks on location in Thailand. "When I'm working, I earn about $750 a day plus residuals. I'm not as busy acting as I would like, since New York has lost a number of jobs due to higher costs."

Ira's business background made him a great catch when he volunteered to become a consultant with the National

Executive Service Corps. NESC tries to match volunteers as nearly as possible to its client needs. Given Ira's theatrical background, he was assigned as a consultant to the Actors' Fund of America, which operates social service programs for entertainment professionals in New York City and a nursing and retirement home for actors in Englewood, New Jersey—a perfect match. Ira spent a year preparing a long-term strategic study to determine how the fund should operate in the future. The report recommended ways that the fund could benefit from installing a planning system, broadening its funding sources, and making its retirement and nursing home financially self-sufficient. Based on his report, the fund asked him to help implement a number of his recommendations.

Ira's NESC involvement continues and includes other assignments, such as a modern-dance group for which he developed a financial "disaster plan to help stop the blood flow," an independent school where he helped get the books in order, and community-based social service organizations in need of improved management systems.

Ira's secret to success in nonprofit consulting is rather basic. "I apply the same methodology to problem-solving for a non-profit group as I would have used at Celanese. I get immersed in an organization, learn what they do and work with them to find ways to manage their programs better."

As much as he enjoys volunteer assignments, Ira misses day-to-day corporate involvement. "Sometimes I'm not as organized as I would like to be. At Celanese, I had a job and a place to go." He compensates for this loss with film acting and volunteer projects where there are deadlines and schedules to meet. "Even though I'd like to be even busier, I feel fortunate in having these activities to focus on. I don't want to sit on the terrace of a condo in Florida watching the golf balls fly by."

FROM THREE-PIECE SUITS TO COVERALLS

Mark B.

PUBLISHING EXECUTIVE TURNED HOME BUILDER FOR THE POOR

"At 57, I was literally reorganized out of my company." That's how Mark B. frankly refers to his leave-taking in 1989 as president of several departments in a major publishing company. Mark received job offers, but he didn't want to return to work. His immediate response to being "downsized" was to play.

Why not? Because of his employer's excellent retirement and benefits program, he could afford to continue his present lifestyle. There was little need to work to pay the bills. He lived the life other would-be retirees can only fantasize about. He scuba dived, sailed and played tennis. He biked in France, skied during the winter, and in the summer vacationed at his Cape Cod home.

Two years later, Mark was still living the life of Riley. It was enjoyable, but by his own standards he was, for the most part, idle and increasingly dissatisfied. Right after he returned from a summer vacation, his wife suggested that he broaden his interests beyond being a director of the local YMCA, singing in a local choral group and sailing. She wanted to know how he expected to spend his time. Knowing that Mark was a skilled home craftsman and do-it-your-selfer, she suggested Habitat for Humanity. "I called, and in two days they had me at work," he says.

Becoming part of a local Habitat for Humanity has furnished Mark with a vehicle for his various skills and interests. As a member of a Habitat construction crew, he enjoys working with his hands building small one-family homes in northern New Jersey. At first, Mark was satisfied to be just another Habitat worker, spending several days a week as a builder. After a corporate career that emphasized administration, office work, and obligatory meetings and conferences, he was glad to be doing hands-on work. But Mark couldn't totally escape his management roots, and he was elected to the affiliate's board of directors and served as chairman of its building committee. In his new role, he helped to systematize a number of procedures, including scheduling of construction materials so that they are delivered to the appropriate site when needed.

Construction had been a recurring theme, one way or the other, throughout Mark's work life. He grew up in suburban

> **After his company downsized, Mark was, for the most part, idle and increasingly dissatisfied. Then he picked up a hammer for Habitat for Humanity.**

New Jersey, and he worked part-time in college on some construction projects. Mark attended Wagner College with the intention of becoming a Lutheran minister, but his career goals changed. Following graduation, he joined the Army and was trained as a Russian-language specialist. After the Army, he sold real estate, got married and, after a two-year stint at New York Telephone, was hired by a construction company where he was directly involved in supervising building projects. Little did he realize that 30 years later this experience would provide the thrust of his retirement lifestyle. The business, however, did not succeed and was dissolved.

As a married man, Mark needed steadier work. He landed at a major publishing company, where his varied experience led to a job selling advertising space in magazines. Promotions came rapidly, and by the time he left the company 26 years later, Mark had headed nearly every operation, from information systems to books and publications, including several professional and news magazines.

His downsizing from the company resulted in a two-year odyssey. "I had lots of time to reflect on current corporate conditions. With what's going on in business today, this is a wonderful time to be out of corporate life, since so much of a manager's time involves downsizing both programs and people. It is not a very creative experience."

Mark is long gone from the corporate roller coaster, and he's found the fulfilling outlets he needed in retirement. From the several days a week he spends on Habitat construction and board assignments, he has discovered that "there's nothing like seeing a neighborhood change and giving people the chance to live in their own home."

Despite Mark's immediate attraction to Habitat work, he feels other retirees might take longer to reach the point where they feel that they're making a real contribution as a volunteer. He suggests that they join several groups before they decide on the direction they want to go. "Experiment. Look around and you'll find your niche."

GIVING BACK TO NONPROFITS

Marjorie Hart
CORPORATE STRATEGIC PLANNER TURNED PLANNER FOR NONPROFITS

Marjorie Hart has always been a doer, as befits one of only two women in her early-1950s class to graduate with a degree in chemical engineering from Cornell University. When Marjorie retired, she was not ready to call it quits. She created an early-retirement lifestyle that combined various interests—business consulting and nonprofit work—into a patchwork lifestyle. Keeping active, being pertinent, and using her skills were Marjorie's prime objectives.

For a number of years following her retirement, Marjorie was a paid independent consultant in the fuel industry, but has since has shifted to volunteer consulting on a pro-bono basis. Unlike some corporate retirees who find little satisfaction as volunteers, Marjorie learned that her corporate planning skills were readily adaptable to nonprofit organizations. "This is part of my 'give back' philosophy of using some of my energies to directly help community organizations."

Marjorie's first job after Cornell was at the Esso (now Exxon) Research & Engineering facility in Bayway, New Jersey, as a staff engineer analyzing high-octane fuel. This training served as a bridge into a cor-

> **Marjorie gave up the frustrations of consulting in retirement for hands-on volunteer work. She lends her strategic planning skills to the community.**

porate career in strategic planning, during which she received a couple of plum overseas assignments—several years in Japan on a liquefied petroleum gas project and a posting in England. During the '70s, she received her most challenging assignment, to study the world's energy supplies.

Marjorie took early retirement in 1983 after "Exxon sweetened the pie with incentives that were too good to refuse. I was then in my early fifties with 30 years of service and no immediate plans to leave Exxon. But I decided I might as well retire. If I wanted to be promoted within the company, it would require taking a field job outside of New York and I had little desire to move."

Until then, Marjorie had set age 60 as a possible target retirement date. Even though her departure was seven years earlier than expected, she was not concerned about the next step. She knew that her corporate experience would be invaluable as a consultant. She actively networked among Exxon alumni, including a number of former colleagues who had left the company to go into their own businesses. One former Exxon vice-president put her in touch with a new fuel research company, which retained Marjorie for her strategic planning know-how and her knowledge of emission-control products. Other consulting projects followed. She affiliated and worked several years with Supply Planning Associates, a consultancy that is staffed entirely by retired engineers and managers with fuel-industry expertise (see the profile beginning on page 215).

No longer an Exxon executive, Marjorie began to understand some of the frustrations that accompany corporate retirement. "The longer you're away from the corporate community, the rustier your business skills become. You also lose your networking capabilities as former associates leave, are promoted or retire." As a result, Marjorie had to develop new contacts to obtain consulting assignments. Some of these contacts were renewed, reinforced or formed when she was elected to be a Cornell University trustee, and to the board of Scenic Hudson, a group interested in protecting the Hudson River shoreline.

THE COMMUNITY'S GAIN

Since Marjorie stopped taking paid consulting jobs, she's been using her capabilities as a volunteer. "I find that the real work of most nonprofits is done by the staff, and board members, more often than not, are expected to be fundraisers or advisers. I prefer hands-on volunteer assignments where I can see the direct results of my work."

She has worked an average of two days a week reorganizing many of the managerial functions at the Institute for Life Coping Skills, a project administered by Columbia University's Teachers College to help disadvantaged people get back into the workforce.

She also spends one or two days a week with the YWCA, where she has been a director and member of the executive committee for many years. Marjorie was asked to join the Y's board after receiving one of the Y's business achievement awards several years earlier. Once again, she's a hands-on worker, chairing the YWCA's Academy of Women Achievers, a group that encourages women executives to help each other.

IT'S NEVER TOO LATE TO MAKE A DIFFERENCE

A. Judson Wells

RESEARCH CHEMIST TURNED ANTI-SMOKING ADVOCATE

A. Judson Wells knows firsthand that you can't wait for the telephone to ring in retirement. If you want to be a volunteer, then take the initiative. Develop a plan that harnesses your different skills and interests, then market it to possible users. That's the approach that Judson used when he retired from Du Pont.

Rather than ending a distinguished career as a Du Pont research chemist and division director, his retirement was the opening round in a new career as a volunteer player in the war against cigarette smoking. "I had a reasonably good pension, I didn't need additional income, and my six children were all grown. I looked for something useful to do where I could apply my various skills, and I also wanted to avoid any type of administrative job or be responsible for managing other people. I had had that at Du Pont. And I had some personal experience when it came to cigarette smoking. Four close friends, all smokers, died of lung cancer, including one who died in my arms."

Judson's plan to get involved was direct and creative. He approached the American Lung Association with the proposition that he would work as a part-time staff person on their anti-smoking programs for the

After four friends died of lung cancer, retired chemist A. Judson Wells heard his call to action. He volunteered to research the effects of passive smoking.

equivalent of two and a half days a week at no pay. All he asked was for reimbursement of his expenses. Even more important, Judson, a Harvard-trained PhD chemist, is using the skills he honed in industrial research to alert Americans to the dangers of passive cigarette smoke. His work has been primarily educational and informational, helping to develop programs that local lung associations could use to combat smoking in their communities. "In this work, I could afford to be independent and innovative. I wasn't looking for money. I had no ties with tobacco companies, nor was I a paid researcher depending on grants to support my research."

His work also caught the attention of the Environmental Protection Agency where, as an unpaid consultant, he was involved in preparing parts of the agency's 1992 landmark study on respiratory effects of passive smoke. Though the EPA can't officially honor outsiders, his co-workers gave him a small medal for his contribution to the study. "It's the first medal I've received since high school," said Judson.

In a postretirement volunteer career that includes testifying before Congress on the mortality effects of passive smoking, consulting assignments from the Occupational Safety and Health Administration on smoking in the workplace, and publishing several articles in medical publications, Judson is not yet ready to call it quits.

"I have friends around the world due to my work," Judson says. "I might phase out in the next few years, but I'm now developing an interest in studying the effects of passive smoke on breast cancer."

Hobbies:
The Pleasure Is All Yours

SAUL "SONNY" MARTIN IS A RELATIVE NEWCOMER TO his hobby. Sonny was a mechanical engineer until he retired in his mid fifties. "I was brought up in an apartment and never built anything as a boy, though as an engineer I did some work with my hands." When Sonny retired, he considered a number of hobbies, tried some and found little satisfaction. Then, thanks to being the father of three daughters and the grandfather of several more girls, he started building dollhouses. "Over the past few years, I've built several to-scale models for my granddaughters, and I have some more in my house." Sonny has become totally immersed as a hobbyist and craftsman. He visits hobby and dollhouse shows and museums to increase his knowledge of the field and to find new design concepts.

As many 50-plusers have learned, there is no fixed limit to the parameters of a hobby. A hobby is simply defined as "a pursuit outside one's occupation." It can be manual, intellectual or creative, or all of these.

The listing of possible hobbies is nearly unlimited, ranging from active sports such as tennis or skiing to something more leisurely such as gardening or cooking; cerebral pursuits such as learning Greek or mastering Chaucer; dexterous skills like sculpting, piano playing, weaving or rebuilding colonial furniture; or sedentary pastimes such as calligraphy, reading or collecting 19th century apothecary jars.

Some hobbies are costly, requiring special equipment and training. Though books, craft hobbies and travel rank high in expenditures by the 50-plus set, other hobbies cost nothing but the effort of imagination. Hobbies can be done individually, in a group, or both. Many are very time-consuming; others take only a few minutes a day.

Some hobbies fit best into the lifestyle of 30-to-40-year-olds, while the ones of interest to the greatest number of retirees can be pursued over a lifetime. You're more likely to find retirees walking than running regularly, and gardening than bungee-jumping. Even so, it seems that nearly everyone knows someone who's defying the odds—a 77-year-old who plays tennis regularly five times a week or an 82-year-old downhill skier. Witness also the success of the Senior Olympics sponsored for those 55 and over. Whether they are competitive athletes or just doing it for fun, chances are many of these athletes learned and perfected their sports skills long before retirement.

POINTS TO REMEMBER

- Hobbies can be demanding, absorbing large blocks of time.
- Some people need several hobbies.
- Hobbies are leisure-time activities, but some retirees convert their hobby into a new career.
- Don't be disappointed if you never build the same enthusiasm for a hobby as you did for your job.
- If you don't already have one, it might take a couple of false starts before you find a suitable hobby.
- There's no shortage of opportunities to explore a new hobby.
- Schools conduct courses to help hobbyists learn and perfect their skills.

Countless numbers of retirees call travel a hobby. Even so, many members of the 50-plus set find that travel is only one part of a much larger leisure-time pattern that goes beyond cruises, overseas travel odysseys and other once-in-a-lifetime travel events. In some instances, retirees combine walking and hiking, or explore different areas by car and camper. Opportunities also exist to travel and study on an Elderhostel trip in the U.S. or overseas, or to build homes for Habitat for Humanity in a third-world nation. Besides affinity groups sponsored by college and university alumni associations, you'll find more about travel with an educational or humanitarian purpose in mind in Chapters 3 and 4.

In short, a hobby is whatever you decide you want to make of it.

Women as Hobbyists

The Hobby Industry Association has a vested interested in hobbies. HIA members produce and sell craft supplies such as art supplies, needlecrafts and floral crafts. In its most recent industry analysis, the Association noted that one or more persons has a craft or hobby in 84% of American households.

It also reported that crafting remains a popular leisure-time activity for women throughout their lives. Nearly one-half of women age 55 to 64, half of whom also work, completed a crafting project during the past six months and about the same number anticipate starting one within the next six months.

And interest in crafting does not decline with age. Forty percent of women 75-plus expect to continue crafting. The only thing that stops them is poor health, especially bad eyesight. The crafts with the highest level of interest are floral arranging, crossstitching or embroidery, cake decorating or candy making, wreath making or floral accessorizing, crocheting and creating scrapbooks. More people of all ages would do crafting if the instructions were easier and the projects less time consuming.

Barbara Brabec, a former publisher of Barbara Brabec's Self Employment Survival Letter, gave up newsletter publishing to concentrate on writing business self-help books for craft people who want to be self-employed and also work at home. Her titles include *Creative Cash—How to Profit from Your Special Artistry, Creativity, Hands Skills and Related Know-How; Handmade for Profit—Hundreds of Secrets to Success in Selling Arts & Crafts,* and *The Crafts Business Answer Book.*

Want to know more about these books? Call Brabec at 630-717-4188 or access her Web site at www.crafter.com/brabec.

Getting Started

Getting involved in a hobby is as simple as visiting a local library or bookstore, or attending an adult-education workshop given by community colleges, high schools or hobby organizations. As a first step, obtain the course listings from your local community college and high school extension programs. Hobbyists have their own "birds of a feather" groups, and they, too, sponsor workshops to attract and train new enthusiasts.

Hobby- and craft-supply shops, as well as other retail outlets catering to the clothing, equipment and literature needs of all kinds of enthusiasts, usually post notices of related classes, meetings and outings. If you're lucky, you might enjoy a productive chat with a knowledgeable clerk—also likely to be an enthusiast—in such a store.

"How-to" books and magazines abound in nearly every field, appealing to both novices and advanced hobbyists. To test this theory, visit your neighborhood bookstores. You'll find that easily one-third to one-half of the nonfiction books in stock are in hobby-related fields, including gardening, cooking, collecting, woodworking, crafting and painting. Such publications contain plenty of leads to hobby organizations and other prospective contacts for more information.

> ## SOURCES OF IDEAS
>
> - Browse through the Yellow Pages of the phone book.
> - Visit the library. Read books and magazines about an activity. Ask the reference librarian at your public library to help you find the names of associations, clubs and organizations in your field of interest, or consult directories such as the *Encyclopedia of Associations*.
> - Contact local recreation departments for information about their programs and schedules.
> - Talk to retailers who sell hobby and recreational equipment.
> - Learn as much in advance as you can about the required initial investment and ongoing costs.
>
> Source: New York University Center for Career and Life Planning

Selecting a new hobby depends to some extent on your income, aptitude and personality. Some hobbies, due to more costly equipment and training, naturally attract fewer people. But don't let expenses deter you. If your goal is to make pottery, for example, you can get instruction and access to wheels and kilns on a shared basis through community and extension schools and hobby-related clubs. This same cooperative spirit aids flying enthusiasts who individually can't afford the cost of buying and maintaining a plane.

There's no reason to limit yourself to one hobby. Why not enjoy several, with each selected to fit different moods and interests?

Or how about finding new ways to expand the scope of your current hobby? For example, bird watchers do more than track birds. They lead hikes, attend workshops and join environmental groups. A hobby can also broaden you, as Iris S., a retired New York City high school English teacher, has discovered. Iris grows African violets in her apartment, and is an officer in a group that meets regularly to discuss and show their plants. For those wanting to take the next step, she points out, there is a worldwide society devoted to African violets, which publishes a quarterly magazine and conducts regional, national and international meetings.

If you've been pursuing an avocation for years and have developed some expertise, maybe it's time to begin teaching others.

One admonition, however: How far you're willing to go with a new interest may be limited by your tolerance for "risk," and not necessarily in the life-or-death sense. "A man at 65 doesn't suddenly pick up a camera and revive himself with a second career as a photographer," Gail Sheehy noted in her book, *Passages*. "Whether one has a natural talent or not, any learning period requires the willingness to suffer uncertainty and embarrassment. Even in the fifties, one is apt to be too self-conscious to wait out such a period of trial."

A Hobby Probably Won't Take the Place of Work

Some hobbyists personify perfection in their dual roles as professionals at work and hobbyists at home, with equal devotion to both throughout their lives. Others balance what they often consider lackluster or uninteresting careers with more spectacular extracurricular lives. Whereas a 9-to-5 job provides income, a hobby is the real focal point of their lives. Retirement offers an opportunity to put their priorities in order. But members of either group value their hobbies as a creative outlet that differs radically from day-to-day workplace challenges. Still others show more interest in hobbies in retirement than they showed in their workday lives. Even among the upper echelons of corporate managers, you'll find these differences.

Most assuredly, Alan "Ace" Greenberg, chairman of Bear Stearns & Co., and Norio Ohga, former president and current chairman and CEO of Sony, will have little trouble keeping busy once they retire. Both fit the description of a dedicated executive and hobbyist to a T.

Besides being a principal in one of Wall Street's largest and most successful investment-banking firms, Ace Greenberg, a magician since he was 9, performs at fundraisers and charitable events, and is a member of the Society of American Magicians. For a change of pace, Ace plays bridge with similar vigor, having won a national bridge championship in the late 1970s.

Norio Ohga, whom *The New Yorker* profiled as responsible for making Sony "emblematic of Japan's technical and economic domination," is a classically trained singer. He piloted his Falcon jet from Tokyo to New York, where he conducted an orchestra performing Beethoven's Seventh Symphony and Schubert's Unfinished Symphony in a fundraiser for Lincoln Center.

Top executives typically do not have hobbies, observed Jeffrey Sonnenfeld of Emory University in his book, *The Hero's Farewell*, a study on the retirement habits of CEOs of major corporations. "Their greatest gratification was generally in the job they left and not in deferred recreation or outside organizations." The executives interviewed by Sonnenfeld frequently asked, not at all rhetorically, "How much tennis can you play before you look for something bigger to do?"

A hobby has its limitations even for the most enthusiastic fans. As much as Russ Larson, publisher of *Model Railroader*, enjoys writing about model railroad hobbyists, he does not advocate "spending 40 hours a week on a hobby after retiring. I suspect that for most people a mix of more serious pursuits along with hobbies and games would be the most satisfying."

When you're working full-time, a career and a hobby are often in conflict. The late Jules Willing, who was employed as a human resources executive with Revlon, candidly wrote about the problems of trying to substitute a hobby for a lost job in his book, *The Reality of Retirement*:

"When work no longer provides activity, interests and hobbies are substituted. Early in retirement, there is a carry-over of attitudes—you tend to approach your hobbies as you did your work: intensively. The hobby gets the highest priority, the most time, the greatest energy, the extensive investment. . . . In retirement, hobbies are not pursued at all in a leisurely way, but more as a matter of job replacement than of pleasure, the anxious need to fill an unendurable void."

Willing was quick to point out that successful managers normally find hobbies "unsatisfying as major preoccupations. Hobbies do not generate the kind of psychic satisfaction your work did. They may entertain or amuse and occupy, but they rarely make the adrenaline flow the way winning a budget battle did. With a hobby you generally have nothing to risk."

> ## SUGGESTED READING
>
> How CEOs and up-and-coming entrepreneurs spend their free time is a topic that Marilyn Wellemeyer covered for ten years as a *Fortune* editor and then chronicled in *The Fortune Guide to Executive Leisure* (Little Brown, 1987). Her book spotlights a potpourri of hobbies and leisure-time activities from ballooning to barbershop quartet singing. Some of the executives she profiled pursued relatively inexpensive hobbies; others used their larger-than-average incomes to invest in costly photographic equipment, elaborate greenhouses or valuable antique pieces. The book is a great source of ideas and inspiration if you need them, and it is still the only book that chronicles how managers relax and enjoy themselves.

As a hobbyist myself, I understand the relationship between a hobby and work. I average about 12 to 15 hours a week on my hobbies—cooking, gardening, reading, playing the piano and tennis. Yet I don't feel that I could ever find total satisfaction from these leisure-time activities. Work and work-related activities are still my main focus. I still have the mind-set that a hobby is something to be sandwiched into evenings, weekends and vacations; it is part of my lifestyle but hardly an end unto itself.

Many of you may view hobbies as a form of leisure-time smorgasbord, something layered between more important functions—somewhere between sleeping and working. That's a trait from a time when occupational tunnel vision was the order of the day. Your first priority was to the workplace, a habit that you may find difficult to break.

Only you can decide to what extent one or more hobbies can

FAVORITE SPORTS OF THE 50-PLUS SET

In order of preference:
- Exercise walking
- Exercising with equipment
- Swimming
- Bike riding
- Fishing

- Camping
- Golf
- Bowling
- Billiards/pool
- Aerobic exercising

Source: National Sporting Goods Association

replace the demands and satisfaction of the workplace, and how much of your time in retirement you want it to fill. At the least, a hobby can be one part of your total portfolio of activities.

The Hobbyist in Action

Bottom line, there is no such thing as a bad hobby. The worst scenario is that it does nothing more than fill a time gap in one's daily schedule or serve as a casual pastime. At best, hobbies can be vibrant activities, forming the basis of a new lifestyle or even providing the incentive to launch another career. Be aware that if your hobby should become your new career you run the risk of a wonderful hobby becoming a terrible new career—as much of a taskmaster as your employment of old.

Hobbies for some avid practitioners started as casual recreation and then flowered from there. Some hobbies call for intellectual and physical energy once reserved for a demanding career. The people you are about to meet have hobbies that serve as the cornerstone in their 50-plus-set lifestyle.

Chances are you will not become a consummate hobbyist like these folks but you'll see how their hobbies have helped shape their lives and retirement.

LEARNING A NEW SPORT

Bruce Berckmans
CORPORATE EXECUTIVE TURNED COMPETITIVE ROWER

When Bruce Berckmans attended Princeton University, his mother discouraged him from trying out for crew. Though he had no health problems, she feared that rowing might do bad things to his heart. Ironically, Bruce suffered a massive heart attack about 40 years later, and rowing became an integral part of his cardiac recovery program.

Bruce points out that rowing has a comparatively small following among the 50-plus set, perhaps only 30% among the U.S. Rowing Association's 16,000 members who row at least three times a week. Unlike Bruce, most are veteran rowers, dating back, in most instances, to college.

Bruce played tennis and boxed in college, but later on became the "the typical weekend athlete," he says. After graduating from Princeton, Bruce joined the Marine Corps and ten years later received a medical disability due to injury. Several years later he returned to government service, this time doing classified work overseas. In 1975, Bruce was back in the U.S. as vice-president for international operations for Wackenhut Corporation, a guard and security company based in Coral Gables, Florida, and about ten years later he joined Cordis Corp., makers of high-tech medical

> **Unlike most 50-plus rowers, who were collegiate competitors, Bruce took up the sport to rehabilitate his heart. It has become a way of life.**

equipment, as security director. He was working there in July 1987 when he had a heart attack.

"I came close to dying. Fortunately I got emergency balloon angioplasty, which relieved the blockage." While he was recuperating, a friend gave him a copy of David Halberstam's book *The Amateurs,* an account of four young men who competed to represent the U.S. in the 1984 Olympics. The book became a turning point in his recovery. "Maybe [the message] was subliminal," he says.

Another friend suggested that he try rowing as part of his rehabilitation and offered the use of his rowing shell. Bruce followed his friend's advice, but first he checked with his cardiologist, Ted Feldman, who he discovered had rowed on Harvard's freshman crew. "Ted knew what rowing was all about. He thought it would be a good aerobic conditioner. It would provide exercise for the entire body yet involve no physical impact." Within a few months of his attack, Bruce started to row. Even with positive heart tests, he still feared that rowing might lead to another heart attack, and he also realized that he had too much to learn about rowing to tackle it alone. To acquire the basics, he enrolled in a four-day program at the Florida Rowing Center in West Palm Beach.

During his early recovery period, Bruce returned briefly to Cordis. But because he wanted more time and independence, he left the company and started Corporate Support Services, a consultant group that helps clients protect trade secrets and proprietary information.

During his recuperation, Bruce and Ted Feldman started the Cardiac Rehabilitation Rowing Project with a small grant from the U.S. Rowing Association to study the beneficial effects of rowing on recovering cardiac patients. They developed some health protocols and an odometer for cardiac stress testing.

At first Bruce rowed for aerobic exercise, but in mid 1988 he started to compete in the 50-plus age bracket in Florida and in such races as the Head of the Broad, in Charleston, South Carolina, and the Head of the Charles, in Boston, the nation's largest rowing regatta. Of the several thousand participants of all ages competing in the three-mile Head of the Charles, about 40 of the entrants were 50-plus and nearly all long-time rowers. Within a few years, Bruce was entering six sprint races (less than a mile) in the spring and an equal number of three-mile races in the fall.

"There is more to rowing than racing," says Bruce. "It's relaxing. Most waterways are physically attractive, and it's a chance to be outdoors. I average about ten hours a week rowing or working out on a machine or lifting weights." Bruce finds that rowing has given him new self-respect and a sense of accomplishment. "It's hard work, but exercise is a critical requirement for people recovering from most serious illnesses. You don't have to compete in races to enjoy it. I do because it matches my personality."

Rowing soon became a family event. Bruce's wife, Lee, enjoyed watching her husband compete, and the couple donated trophies for college competitions. The Head of the Charles regatta became an annual family reunion for Lee and their five grown children. Then, in 1993, Lee was diagnosed with terminal cancer, and rowing took a back seat in Bruce's life. "I gave up rowing and much of my consulting work when she became ill, so we could spend as much time as possible together." Lee died several months later. Bruce returned to competitive rowing in late 1994 in a number of East Coast cities.

Bruce looks forward to many years of rowing and racing. "There's no reason I can't row for at least another 15 to 20 years."

Charles Hansen

CONSTRUCTION INDUSTRY CONSULTANT TURNED ANTIQUE-TOY COLLECTOR AND AUTHOR

In June 1988, Charles Hansen, then nearly 50, realized that he had a case of career burnout, and he left his job with a consulting firm where he estimated costs of construction jobs for architects and builders. "I told Lucy, my wife, that I didn't want to do anything for the next few months. But within a couple of weeks I got the idea of doing a book. I had the time, and my hobby was a way to relax. I'm always reading books on history, so the idea of writing one myself was not too strange." He wrote an outline and found a publisher that specialized in hobby-related books. Charles Hansen's fire engines had literally come to his rescue.

That was the beginning of what may someday be a whole series of books by Charles Hansen on subjects near and dear to his heart and hobbies.

Ever since Charles and his family moved to Tenafly, New Jersey, in the mid '60s, he has been collecting antiques, starting as a generalist in Americana and then, during the early 1980s, concentrating on antique toy fire apparatus. Now his collection of several hundred firefighting toys, mostly of American origin, occupies several rooms in his home. The toys range in size from handheld items to model engines designed to be pulled by a pony. Charles buys his toys at auctions, shows and estate sales. "Toys represent another view of American history. They reflect real life and help you better understand history and the times. Washington, Revere and Lincoln were firefighters," Charles says.

> *A collector's passion for firefighting toys, cowboy gear and toy race cars has opened the door to a life of research, writing and travel.*

For security reasons, Charles never reveals the monetary value of the collection. At this time, he has little intention of selling it, but says, "I'm sure if that day ever comes I'll get my money and more so from it."

Following his several months of "leave" in 1988, Charles found a job as an estimator with another company. But he continued to write his book on antique firefighting toys at nights and on weekends. After six months of writing, Charles published his first book, *The History of American Firefighting Toys,* with Greenberg Publishing Co., a publisher of hobby-related books.

At $50 a copy, Charles's illustrated book is hardly an impulse item, though a few thousand copies have been sold. After the book was published, Greenberg was acquired by a larger company with far greater distribution, thus making the book available to bookstore browsers. "If nothing more, I can now tell my friends they can find my book in their favorite bookstore. I still get royalty checks every six months." Charles, however, doubts that the income will ever compensate for his research costs.

Four years after taking his new job, Charles was laid off when his employer downsized. As a skilled cost estimator, he decided to give up salaried employment in favor of independent consulting in the same field, which he still pursues. As expected, his antique fire-engine collection and other hobbies continue to dominate his leisure time. He considers that his hobby is collecting; writing is just an offshoot. Even so, he finds the research and writing very absorbing, requiring that he use different skills than the technical ones he uses at work.

Lucy, a hobbyist herself and a well-known quilter, fully understands and appreciates her husband's hobbies. Their son, Eric, is a computer consultant in San Francisco. "Lucy and Eric seem to enjoy the collection as much as I do. Even though Lucy never read a word of my book until it was published, she helped with some of the research."

RETURN TO A
CHILDHOOD PASSION

Despite his avid interest today, as a boy Charles never wanted to be a firefighter. When he was growing up in eastern Washington state's sagebrush and scrub country, cowboys were his idols. He rode horses as a youngster, and over the past few years he has begun to ride again. Now, along with his firefighting toys, he collects saddles, holsters, and other western and cowboy gear.

From this interest in cowboys came the theme of another book—the old hotels and saloons found in the cattle-drive country. "I drove through western Kansas to do part of my research. I visited Dodge City, followed the route of the Chisholm Trail and explored parts of Oklahoma." On another vacation, Charles took a three-week solo trip through Montana, Nebraska and the Dakotas, collecting data and visiting sites. This time he brought a computer "notebook" to prepare notes for his home computer, thus blending the western lore of the 19th century with the technology of the late 20th century.

And when he finishes that book, there's another one in the wings: a history of American toy race cars, reflecting the period about 20 years ago when Charles traveled the East Coast circuit racing cars professionally in his free time.

Sometime in the early part of the 21st century—or whenever he decides to retire as a consultant—Charles will undoubtedly have little trouble keeping busy writing historical books about his collections. Meanwhile, Charles and Lucy expect to turn Charles's fascination with the West into a major lifestyle change, when they move to Cody, Wyoming.

MEET THE CYCLING BERLFEINS

Harold Berlfein

CERTIFIED PUBLIC ACCOUNTANT TURNED BIKING ENTHUSIAST

To Jean and Harold Berlfein, bicycling is a part of everyday life. They bike in Los Angeles, where they have lived since they got married just after World War II. They also take an annual bike trip, often in conjunction with attending an Elderhostel course. Though both are in their seventies, neither finds it remarkable that they not only bicycle but also hike, swim and ski. It fits with their goal of staying physically strong, one they recommend for other retirees— though plenty of them have already gotten the message. The Berlfeins are part of a growing number of older bicyclists who take to their wheels regularly. Nearly 2.7 million cyclists are age 55 to 64 and another 2.9 million are over 65.

Biking is a Berlfein family tradition. Harold, a certified public accountant, biked from his home to Berlfein & Co., a midsize accounting firm, for more than 30 years. His company, which employed more than 50 professionals, was merged in 1980 with a predecessor of Ernst & Young, one of the world's largest accounting firms. A few years later, Harold retired. Biking, then and now, has been an important part of his lifestyle, whether as transportation to the golf course or as a means of running errands.

Harold was inspired to bike when, during a trip to London in the mid '60s, he noticed people there cycling to work. He began bike commuting, and then he and Jean took various biking holidays as a couple and with their four daughters. In succeeding years, they have toured numerous countries and more than half of the states, including tracing the 1863 route taken by the Union Army from Washington to Gettysburg.

Jean and Harold usually bike by themselves but at times join another couple. "Our goals are usually the same," says Harold. "We're out to enjoy the outdoors and get some exercise. We are never in a hurry. We stop along the way to speak with people, and we have little interest in how fast or how far we go on any particular day."

Biking also ties in with their participation in Elderhostel study programs. One summer they biked in Minnesota around the headwaters of the Mississippi River, then attended a one-week poetry and

> **This couple's philosophy? "We're out to enjoy the outdoors and get some exercise. We are never in a hurry. We stop along the way to speak with people."**

nature workshop near Grand Rapids, Minnesota. Another time they took a bike tour of the Olympic Peninsula in northwestern Washington, followed by an Elderhostel stopover. Depending on location, the Berlfeins either bring, rent, borrow or even buy their bikes.

HARDLY ONE-DIMENSIONAL

The Berlfeins' activities aren't limited to sports. Harold conducts seminars to show retirees how to find new options and things to do in retirement, and he recruits retired accountants to provide financial advisory assistance on a volunteer basis to local community groups.

In 1993, Harold and Jean became members of an Elderhostel-sponsored Habitat for Humanity team that was building homes in Cohoma, a town in rural Mississippi. The Berlfeins' previous home-construction experience was limited to building a sum-

mer cabin 45 years earlier with Jean's two brothers on Lake Arrowhead in California.

In two weeks, the 21 women and men in the Habitat group completed a single-family home. Harold handled the electrical work, using his experience in the Signal Corps during World War II. Jean, who makes early-childhood-development videos and filmstrips as a freelancer, was assigned by the Habitat for Humanity team leader to hold boards and paint shutters. "Finally, after a brief demonstration, I got the courage of my convictions. I picked up a power saw and cut boards.

"It was an emotional experience when we turned over the house to the mother and her four children," says Jean. "After years of entertaining ourselves on vacation, we had found the time to give something back."

(For more on Elderhostel, see Chapter 3, and on Habitat for Humanity, see Chapter 4.)

VAN GOGH IN VERMONT

Stanley Gilbert
DRUG COMPANY EXECUTIVE TURNED PAINTER

At 50, an age when most managers are still looking for yet another business or corporate challenge, personal events in Stanley Gilbert's life forced him to exchange management for art.

Stan is a full-time painter. He works seven to eight hours a day, about the same number of hours he did in his business career. Painting has become his primary focus. He has studied under a master painter, and he's done abstracts, portraits and landscapes. He has made several trips to Mexico to study and paint. The Gilberts added studio space to their home to accommodate his creative endeavors.

> **Faced with health problems and new management, Stanley gave up chemical engineering for painting, a full-time passion.**

As a new painter, he struggled, particularly with watercolors. "When I switched from watercolors to oils, I felt more comfortable and I was on my way.

"One teacher suggested that I work in three dimensions, so I took a course in sculpturing." Besides painting, Stan now enjoys sculpting in a variety of media, including limestone, marble, fiberglass and terra cotta.

What a switch from his first career! Stan and his wife, Ruth, went to high school together. Stan graduated as a chemical engineer from Newark College of Engineering, then worked for several different chemical companies. By the time the Gilberts were 35 and the parents of two young children, both Stan and Ruth wanted to move to New England.

Stan landed a job as the general manager of a small drug-manufacturing company in Rupert, a farming community of 600 people in southwestern Vermont—a town so tiny that their children attended a one-room schoolhouse. Ruth worked as a librarian. Stan managed the plant for 15 years until the owner died and the new management decided to make changes, including downgrading some of Stan's responsibilities.

At the same time, Stan was troubled by various health problems. He had had several heart operations and was also diagnosed with a mild form of multiple sclerosis. "I was now 50 and I didn't want to relocate." He was an avid fly fisherman, who enjoyed the outdoors and the rural lifestyle.

"While tourists might find Vermont expensive, living costs are rather low for residents. We owned our home, we had saved money, and our investments were profitable. We decided to stay in Vermont. Ruth had a good job and it boiled down to the simple truth that I wanted to do the things I wanted to do with my life. Besides, I liked the lifestyle in Vermont."

Their two children were grown and on their own, and the Gilberts' expenses were under control. In addition to Ruth's salary, Stan receives some disability coverage, and the Gilberts draw on their investments and savings.

Before Stan's illness, the Gilberts spent several summer vacations in Maine in an area that attracted a number of artists. "I enjoyed looking at art, but I never painted. I felt I had little artistic talent. The artists challenged me to paint. I spent two weeks painting during one vacation and got hooked on it." Within the year, Stan's business career ended. But by that time, deciding what to do was not a problem.

Since then, Stan's paintings and sculptures have been shown locally, and a few have already been sold.

THE DOCTORS CALL IT QUITS

Rose Ruth and Arthur Ellison

UNIVERSITY MEDICAL RESEARCHERS TURNED MUSICIAN AND PAINTER

Meet Rose Ruth Ellison and her husband, Arthur. When the Ellisons retired as Columbia University medical researchers, they turned their creative energies to a number of different hobbies, some of which they do jointly and others independently. "We didn't need a definitive retirement plan [of activity] since we had so many interests," said Arthur. "We were itching for the opportunity. We were fortunate. We feel as busy today as we did when we worked.

"I'd advise other prospective retirees to carefully consider in advance what they'll do when they retire. If you have no hobbies or no other interests or you think you'll be bored, then don't retire."

The Ellisons met while they were in high school and married after Arthur had finished dental school at Columbia and when Rose Ruth was a third-year medical-school student there. Like Arthur, who has a doctorate in microbiology in addition to his dental degree, she was never interested in having a private practice. Both spent their work lives engaged in medical and dental research with various well-known institutions before returning to Columbia. Their two children are grown and live in Chicago and Colorado.

> **For Rose Ruth and Arthur, retirement made sense when the frustrations of grant applications and bureaucracy outweighed the satisfaction of work.**

Arthur decided to retire when he started to "tire of the frustrations in academia. I no longer wanted to write grant applications. [Except for that,] if I could do it all over again, I'd actually change very little. I would still be a researcher." The day he left Columbia as a tenured researcher with a joint appointment to the faculty of Columbia University's School of Physicians and Surgeons and its Dental School, he literally dumped all his scientific files in the wastebasket.

"I took a week off to go skiing and then came back to the viola. I've been playing the viola as far back as high school, and as an amateur musician ever since. I never had any thoughts about being a professional musician. I always wanted to be a scientist."

Over the years, he played with different amateur musical groups, but since he has retired, Arthur takes private lessons from a violist retired from the New York Philharmonic Orchestra and practices his instrument at least one to two hours a day, five days a week. Though he has no interest in giving concerts or becoming a member of an orchestra, his goal is to become even more musically proficient and to follow his teacher's advice: "Remember, it's supposed to be fun."

The year after Arthur retired, Rose Ruth also left Columbia, where she was a professor of medicine and chief of medical oncology. She had been one of the first women to be named to head a Columbia medical division and to be elected president of the American Society of Clinical Oncology. Even though there were no pressures to leave, she decided to retire when she found that the hospital and medical bureaucracies were making it more complicated to get things done. Even after more than 40 demanding years of medical research in oncology, specializing in acute leukemia, she, too, made a smooth transition into retirement. Like her husband, she credits the ease of passage to the fact that she had a number of nonprofessional interests.

Rose Ruth has been a painter since her youth. As a high school student, she attended classes at the Art Students League in New York City. In retirement, she looked forward to having more time to paint. Rose Ruth has become a prolific painter of what she calls abstract, "hard edge"—that is, geometric—paintings. Her paintings use angles, curves and parallel lines to tell their stories.

Her works have been in many shows.

In addition to their solo hobbies, the Ellisons are jointly interested in artifacts, particularly those related to American Indian culture. They have gone on a number of archeological digs in the U.S., some with Elderhostel. On a non-Elderhostel dig along the San Juan River in Utah, they looked for images painted on rock, better known as rock art.

Arthur's interest in Indian artifacts arose early. Growing up in New York City, he lived near the Museum of the American Indian. Sixty years later, he returned to the museum as a volunteer researcher, reviewing parts of the collection and writing papers on the jewelry.

In the time they have left over, the Ellisons attend concerts, the opera and art galleries. They enjoy the pleasant lifestyle made possible by two retirement incomes supplemented by social security benefits. They contributed regularly to a retirement fund while they worked. "Now we let TIAA [Teachers Insurance and Annuity Association] do the worrying. They manage our portfolio."

But whatever the pursuit—music, painting, or art and cultural history—"we are both students and researchers, and we can't just turn it off," says Arthur.

THE REBIRTH OF A HOMEMAKER

Betty Neese

WOMEN'S APPAREL SALESPERSON TURNED CLOTHING DESIGNER AND NEEDLECRAFTER

On some of the overseas vacation trips Betty Neese shares with her husband, Perry, she carries one suitcase for clothes—and several empty ones to hold the unusual fabric and wool that she collects. Retirement has given Betty the ability to do the things she literally had neither the money nor the time for as a young divorced mother and for many years thereafter.

"I always liked to sew but it was usually out of economic necessity. With three boys I made all my own clothes and theirs as well." Sewing has since changed from a household chore to an active hobby. Besides spending several hours a day designing clothing, based primarily on modifying patterns or copying items she sees in catalogs and magazines, Betty sews clothes for her grandchildren. She also works two days a week in a local fabric store, not because she needs the money but to learn more about fabrics. Betty is also a quilter, and in her loft studio, she uses a computerized sewing machine and expansive work space to design, sew and assemble quilts.

"While Perry continues to be involved as a director of several nonprofit groups, I enjoy being by myself, doing the many things that I never had time to do when I was younger. Being a divorced mother, I sewed and

> **"I enjoy being by myself, doing the many things I never had time to do when I was younger.**

cooked out of need. This is no longer the case. Now I can enjoy something as simple as making my own raspberry and strawberry jam. After all my years of working and saving, I enjoy a hobby based on domesticity. Making jam and clothes for my grandchildren is one way to be a super-granny."

Her life in retirement is a far cry from her earlier days in Indiana. Betty grew up there and went to work for Indiana Bell as a customer service representative at age 17. She was so young she needed working papers, issued by the local health department to minors to permit them to work. In her early forties, after an unfortunate management incident, Betty found herself demoted from a managerial to a staff position.

"Looking back, my downgrading at Indiana Bell proved to be one of the best things that ever happened." It made her examine her life and consider what she really wanted to do. For the next few years, she stayed at the company and planned the next step. By now, her sons were self-supporting, and Betty knew she was self-sufficient and willing to take a risk. Like many women her age who have worked and raised children alone, Betty had an instinct for survival.

Pursuing her long-time dream of living in New York City, Betty asked for a transfer from Indianapolis and Indiana Bell to New York and the company's then corporate parent, AT&T. By working for AT&T, she would at least continue to be part of the AT&T employee-benefits plan, including its pension program. It was not a high-level job, but she was soon promoted to district manager of a department that prepared employee manuals and related personnel materials. "It was a hollow victory after what happened at Indiana Bell," she says. But the move to New York more than compensated for that.

A long way from Indiana, Betty became the consummate New Yorker. On her larger salary, she bought an apartment in a brownstone building. "I found life in New York exciting—with Lincoln Center, the art museums, the stores and parks."

LIFE AFTER AT&T

Then came the company's divestiture in the early 1980s, in which AT&T split up into seven regional operating companies. The company offered early retirement and at 53, after 32 years' service, Betty left with a package that included one year's salary, pension, lifetime health care benefits and a goodly amount of AT&T stock bought as part of the employee purchasing plan.

"The first six months I did nothing but travel and enjoy myself in New York." Then, to keep busy and supplement her income, Betty found a job as a salesperson at Saks Fifth Avenue. She was soon promoted to the store's couture department selling high-fashion women's apparel.

In the late 1980s, Betty married Perry Colwell, a senior executive at AT&T. Even after Perry was transferred to AT&T's new corporate offices in central New Jersey and the couple moved, Betty continued to commute two days a week to New York and her Saks job. "I could have worked in one of Saks' suburban stores, but it was not the same thing as working on Fifth Avenue. I also found another part-time job doing word processing. It's easy to find part-time work if you're not too particular."

When Perry retired in the early 1990s, they decided to relocate. Their combined retirement incomes eliminated any need for future paid employment. They looked at Arizona and New Mexico but ruled out settling there. "We wanted to live in a college town for its cultural activities yet be convenient to my three sons and four grandchildren in Indiana, and Perry's family in Philadelphia and Baltimore. Perry preferred a climate warmer than northern New Jersey, and I wanted a home within walking distance of the stores, craft outlets and post office." Perry, also a hobbyist, owns and operates several motorcycles. He needed space to maintain and house his motorcycles, and to build an English sports car. His need for a garage and work space eliminated an urban home. They chose central North Carolina.

In her approach to many of life's problems, Betty has demonstrated a willingness to learn and do new things. She sees no difference when it comes to acquiring a new hobby. She advises others to simply "learn it and do it."

HIS FAMILY SPARKED HIS INTEREST IN PAINTING

Kemp Anderson
PUBLISHING EXECUTIVE TURNED ARTIST

You can take the boy out of West Texas but you can't ever take West Texas out of the boy—and you're likely to find that spirit in many of his paintings, too. That's the case with Kemp Anderson, who prior to taking early retirement as a vice-president of McGraw-Hill was a career journalist, fulfilling his teenage dreams and his professional ambitions. Now he aspires to achieve a style resembling the great western painter Frederic Remington, with his western landscapes, horses and cowboys.

Kemp characterizes himself as a rapid painter, working nearly exclusively in oils on both large and small canvases. He exhibits his paintings only at fundraisers for his church and local civic groups. "I usually give my paintings away to friends, but when they wanted to buy them at the show I asked that the money be donated to the church to pay for a new organ." To Kemp, painting is a creative challenge, not a source of income. Just as important, painting complements his lifestyle: "I'm not the type of person who can sit around on my hands all day."

Painting gives him a chance to get out and do something. Now that he's retired,

Corporate restructuring sapped Kemp's energy. Painting— engaging in "the process of creation"— has given it back and more.

longer visits with family members in Texas and with his five grown children in other sections of the country give Kemp additional opportunities to paint. On nearly every vacation trip, he tries to paint as much as possible. He prefers to paint on site, a change from his working days and briefer vacation trips when he painted at home from photographs taken on location. He has done landscapes in northern New Jersey as well as in other parts of the U.S. and Hawaii while on vacation.

Born in Texas, the son of a Methodist minister, Kemp was captivated by journalism as a youngster. After graduating from Oklahoma State University, he followed a traditional journalism career route, starting with a small daily and working up to the *Dallas Times-Herald*. Recruited by a friend to McGraw-Hill's Dallas bureau, Kemp worked his way up and eventually became the first non-engineer to be named as *Electronics* magazine's chief editor. "I was a little familiar with the technology, but I did know how to cover the news." By the late '70s, Kemp was promoted, this time to vice-president of McGraw-Hill's magazine division supervising the development and installation of the publisher's first computerized editorial system.

Then and now, Kemp's hobby was amateur photography, a pursuit dating back to his newspaper days, when reporters on smaller papers wrote the story and took the photos. As a photographer, he knows how to frame the subject of a picture and how to use light to the best advantage—both factors he would learn were important to painting.

Kemp was introduced to art by one of his children, who was attending an art course. Kemp was soon taking Saturday classes at the Ridgewood (New Jersey) Art Institute. He found that painting gave him a way to express himself and engaged him in the process of creation. It was a change of pace from the editorial and corporate world. Frequent business trips gave him an opportunity to photograph scenes that he would copy at home on canvas. "At the time, I enjoyed art but didn't worry too much about its quality. But in the back of my mind, I knew that art would play a strong part in my retirement plans."

AN EFFORTLESS SEGUE INTO RETIREMENT

Thirty-two years with McGraw-Hill came to an end. Kemp was a senior-vice president in McGraw-Hill's corporate offices responsible for the development of future computerized systems. While under no pressure to leave, he started to tire of the restructuring taking place throughout the company, and he looked forward to spending more time painting. Kemp worked out a favorable buy-out package that permitted him to retire at 64 rather than 65. His retirement portfolio, which—no surprise—he manages on a computer, includes a pension, investments, savings and social security. His retirement package included health insurance benefits.

Retirement has changed Kemp's attitude toward his painting as he works to perfect his style. He continues to take lessons at the Art Institute and to go on painting field trips.

Kemp retired with confidence. When people ask him about retirement, his answer is direct: "Find something you like to do and plan ahead. Start doing it before you retire, so you have something to look forward to doing."

BACK TO THE FAMILY FARM

William McGoldrick
BANKING EXECUTIVE TURNED FARMER

William McGoldrick has returned to his roots, literally. He bears all the accouterments of a senior bank officer, with degrees from Harvard College and Harvard Law School and 30-some years of work with Morgan Guaranty. But his heart and handiwork are down home, on 160 acres of a working family farm in Litchfield County, in the northwest corner of Connecticut.

Bill's father ran the farm as a dairy operation until he died in 1970. Since then, the farm has switched to raising cattle and alfalfa due to market conditions. Life has changed in other ways around Sherman, Connecticut. When Bill was a boy, there were 30 other farms near Sherman, which have since been replaced by residential and commercial developments. Now only the McGoldrick farm remains. And compared with other farms in New England, the McGoldrick farm is rather large.

Bill owns 60 acres of the farm. The balance of the property is owned by his youngest brother, who never left Sherman and has farmed his entire adult life. Their other brother, who has little interest in farming, is a corporate retiree and lives in Denver. Bill gives his proceeds from the sale of cattle

> **William happily left the prestige and perks of corporate life with Morgan Guaranty to bale hay, repair fences, and worry about the weather.**

and alfalfa to his youngest brother out of personal obligation for his running the farm during the years when Bill was a banker and a weekend farmer.

Depending on the season, Bill and his wife, Phyllis, spend a minimum of three to five days a week at the farm, managing and working it. "I get up at six, have an early breakfast and then, other than a lunch break, I work in the fields until early evening. In the winter, when farm life is somewhat slower, I go into the woodlands and cut lumber. I'm also a frustrated lumberjack."

Mechanization and automation have reduced the drudgery of farm work and eliminated the need for full-time hired hands. "I still bale hay, build and repair barns and fences, and like most farmers I worry when there is too much or too little rain." When there's extra work to be done, Bill hires day workers.

The eldest of the three sons, Bill went to a one-room grade school before going to a central high school and Harvard. "Though I graduated from law school, I never really liked the law. I only finished to get the degree."

Following service in the Navy, he was hired by J.P. Morgan, which merged several years later with Morgan Bank. Thirty-one years later, Bill retired from the Morgan Guaranty Trust Company as a senior vice-president.

His career was hardly humdrum by banking standards. His first assignment was in the corporate trust department, where he worked for 16 years, eventually becoming head of the department. He was transferred to the custody department, where he supervised a staff of 1,000, then moved to the bank's trust and investment division, which managed more than $80 billion in individual and personal trust accounts. Being department head had its perks, including the chance to travel overseas regularly to supervise branch offices in London and Geneva.

IN HIS HEART, HE
NEVER REALLY LEFT

Nonetheless, throughout his banking career, Bill retained his interest in farming. Whenever possible, he and Phyllis would return to the farm on weekends and holidays. "All my years at banking, I never gave up my love for and interest in farming." Unlike many retirees, Bill didn't need an activities plan for retirement. He knew what he would do and where he would do it.

"I could have retired with full benefits at 60, but I decided to leave when I was almost 59. I decided to follow a friend's advice on early retirement: You need to consider the time gained to do the things you want versus the money you could have made."

Even with a slight loss in the annual payout he would have received if he had stayed another year, Bill still has an excellent pension, social security, a 401(k) plan, full benefits, and savings. All told, his retirement income is just about the same as when he was working. Bill and Phyllis's son is out on his own. Trained as an investment banker, he left Wall Street after three years to work for a Dutch record company.

For occasional New York getaways, Bill still keeps the Brooklyn Heights apartment that he and Phyllis bought in 1968. Bill is a director of a U.S. subsidiary of a Japanese bank and a limited partner in a film production company. "At least once a month, I dust off a necktie to attend a board meeting."

Otherwise, he's a dedicated, hands-on—not merely gentleman—farmer. "I hope to continue working the farm for as long as possible, at least ten years or more." The McGoldricks are in the process of renovating the original family homestead. It was Bill's mother's home until she died in 1992 at age 95, and Bill looks forward to living there for many years to come.

While Bill himself is now a full-time farmer, he cautions the uninitiated about pursuing a similar venture in retirement. "Unless you hire workers, it's hard physical work, and if you don't have farming experience, it would be suicidal."

NO MORE NOM DE PLUME

James Duffy
CORPORATE ATTORNEY TURNED MYSTERY WRITER

For several years before his early retirement, James Duffy lived two lives. By day, Jim was a corporate attorney and a partner in Cravath, Swaine and Moore, one of New York City's premier law firms. By night and at other times, Jim was Haughton Murphy (Haughton is a family friend and Murphy is the maiden name of his late wife Martha), author of the popular Reuben Frost mystery series.

Like many novelists, Jim draws heavily on personal experiences in developing the series. He definitely writes about what he knows. "I admit that most of the characters are composites of people I've met."

His principal character, Reuben Frost, is a 77-year-old retired Wall Street lawyer and one-time senior partner in a large firm. Senior citizen Frost is a good vehicle because he gets around, circulates in a legal environment and is intimate with New York City's professional, social and cultural worlds, an environment that Jim has known for more than 30 years. Frost's wife in the series, Cynthia, is a former ballet dancer who works for a nonprofit foundation that supports the arts.

Jim has a long-time interest in the ballet and modern dance, having been a member of the Mayor's Advisory Commission for Cultural Affairs and chairman of a committee advising New York's mayor on his annual awards to individuals in the arts.

When Jim moved the setting to Venice, Italy, for his seventh (though first offshore) Reuben Frost mystery, A Very Venetian Murder, he once again drew on personal experiences. Jim and his wife vacationed in Venice for many years.

Reuben also gives Jim an opportunity to express some opinions about retirement. In Murder Keeps a Secret, Reuben is asked whether he still practices law:

> "Not really, I go down to my little cubbyhole now and then, but for all intents and purposes I'm retired."
>
> "Do you miss it?"
>
> "Of course. You don't just erase 50 busy years from your memory."
>
> "I'm interested. Barton died with his boots on, of course, and vowed he'd never retire."
>
> "Most lawyers are like that."

Though, of course, neither Jim nor Reuben is.

While most creative people tend to do their creative work in an at-home office or studio, Jim likes to separate his home life

> **Jim set himself up for a fulfilling early retirement by following the advice so often given to authors: Write about what you know.**

from his writing. He maintains a one-room office a few blocks from his midtown New York apartment to do his writing and much of his research.

While bar association and corporate meetings were once essential in his professional life, Jim, under his Haughton Murphy persona, now speaks at conferences of the Crime Writers Association of the United Kingdom and the Mystery Writers of America.

HIS CAREER WAS RESEARCH

Until Jim started to write mysteries, his career focused mostly on corporate law. In textbook fashion, he graduated from Princeton University and three years later from Harvard Law School. Following military service, he joined Cravath in the early 1960s and was named a partner in 1968. A specialist in corporate and financial law, he represented a range of domestic and international clients, including, in one transaction or another, nearly all the nation's major banks.

Jim's interest in writing dates back to Princeton, where he wrote for the literary and humor magazines. At the time, he considered a career in journalism but instead became a lawyer. His first writing jaunt outside the realm of corporate law came in 1978, when he wrote a book analyzing some of the current issues in American politics. His publisher, Simon & Schuster, would in future years publish the hardback editions of his mysteries.

Eight years later he wrote his first mystery. "I started to write strictly as a hobby, not in anticipation of retirement." He

selected mysteries rather than straight fiction because they are more structured and they permit the author to feature one or more central characters in multiple books. While he reads a lot of mysteries as background, Jim does not consider himself a "mystery-book junkie." He thought at first that he would collaborate with his wife. They soon discovered, as many long-time married couples do, that collaboration of this sort would not work.

"From the start, I found that I could easily mix law and writing. I never let my books invade my professional life. I wrote on weekends and vacations, and I worked under different names to provide further separation of my two lives."

In 1988, when Jim was 54, he retired from Cravath, about six to eight years earlier than most partners normally elect to leave the firm. His goal was to write full-time. "When I left, I didn't know what life would be like. Other than writing, I had no specific goals in mind. If nothing more, writing would keep me busy." While Jim hoped to make money from his writing, he hardly needed the money for survival. He was assured his income as a retired Cravath partner along with income from his investments and his wife's earnings as a senior editor on *Time* magazine.

Once Jim left Cravath, he was no longer concerned with compromising his relationship there. Retirement gave him not only more time to read, research and write but also the opportunity to drop his pseudonym. He finally gave it up when a *Wall Street Journal* review revealed his identity. "Even so, about half the people I know call me Haughton."

LIVING ON A SAILBOAT

Jerome Zukosky
MAGAZINE EXECUTIVE TURNED SAILOR

Jerome Zukosky is living his dream. He has become a full-time sailor with plans to spend several years cruising New England waters, the Caribbean and perhaps even beyond. Living this lifestyle is the fulfillment of years of preparing for the day that he and his companion, Judith Sloan, would make their 38-foot sailboat, the *Herman Melville*, a retirement home.

Jerome was in his mid fifties and *Business Week's* deputy chief in charge of the magazine's network of U.S. news bureaus when he started to formulate a new lifestyle as a dedicated sailor. Until then, Jerome, a graduate of the University of Rochester and Columbia University Graduate School of Journalism, had been a newspaper and magazine reporter and editor throughout his professional career.

In 1987, while many of his contemporaries were investing in second homes as their retirement retreats, Jerome bought his sailboat. He began to learn how to join that small world of full-time cruising couples who are serious year-round sailors.

Jerome first took an interest in sailing as a youngster at summer camp, where he learned the basics in a canoe outfitted with a sail. When he and his former wife were raising their two children in New York City during the 1960s and 1970s, the Zukoskys owned a small sailboat. "It was our summer home. Each weekend and on vacations we would take the subway to our boat, which was docked on the Long Island Sound in the Bronx.

"I never took a sailing lesson. I learned by doing it. I'm constantly reading how-to books and magazines on sailing. Before you're ready to make a boat your home, there are many skills to be learned, from astronomy to do-it-yourself equipment repair."

In 1991, he knew that his 15-year *Business Week* career was nearing an end, perhaps a few years earlier than he had hoped for. McGraw-Hill, the magazine's owner, was downsizing. Jerome accepted an early-retirement package that included an enhanced pension, a lump-sum severance payment and health benefits.

Next, he began to put into place an intricate plan involving his sailboat and another job as a journalist. There were some restrictions. He would only work where he could live year-round on his sailboat, thus eliminating jobs inland and in most northern cities.

> **For Jerome, early retirement was a chance for a complete change of lifestyle— location, job, home. Now it's full-time cruising.**

While he worked for *Business Week* in New York, Jerome had dry-docked the *Herman Melville* for the winter in Annapolis, Maryland. Now Jerome familiarized himself with a number of the larger ports on or near the Chesapeake Bay, especially those with daily newspapers. His search ended with a job in Newport News, Virginia, at the *Daily Press*.

"I got a job working three days a week on the metropolitan news desk, editing copy, tutoring young reporters and consulting with the metro editors on their big news 'take-outs' and other projects." He also taught writing at Christopher Newport University as a part-time instructor and acted as faculty adviser to the student newspaper. For almost three years he lived aboard the *Herman Melville*—moored at a marina on the James River about 200 yards from the newspaper. Here he experienced what it would be like to make the boat his year-round home.

As much as he enjoyed newspaper editing, Jerome had little intention of being permanently tied to the job. It paid the bills as he learned more about shipboard living. Then in 1994, Jerome left Newport, sailed to New York and planned the next step—three to four years of long-distance cruising.

For the first time in his adult life, Jerome is out of the workforce. Retired, he's living on his pension, social security payments and savings. Living on a boat is much like living in any community, and some marinas are more expensive than others. But other than boat fixtures and maintenance and travel expenses, he does not incur many of the day-to-day operating costs faced by traditional homeowners.

"I have only one regret—that I wasn't able to become a full-time sailor years ago. I always envied retirees from the military who had the time and the income to indulge themselves when they were in their early fifties. But I'm better off than others who spend their old age wishing they had been able to live their dream."

Staying Put,
but Not the Same

IN ADVISING OWNERS AND MANAGERS OF SMALLER companies how they can stay put, management consultant William Buxton Jr. likes to cite an example in his immediate family. "My father, William Buxton Sr.—or 'Mr. B,' as he is called—was president and major stockholder in the Peoples Trust & Savings Bank, founded by my grandfather in Indianola, Iowa. Mr. B planned to step down as president and let my brother run the bank. But unfortunately my brother died, and Mr. B, then 75, was once again president. Soon afterward he sold the bank to Iowa National Bank in Waterloo."

Instead of stripping Mr. B of his lifelong career, the new owners gave him a small office in the bank. While no longer an officer or on the payroll, he goes to the bank two to three hours a day. As the bank's volunteer goodwill ambassador, one of his unofficial duties is compiling a newsletter called *Words of Wit and Wisdom,* which the bank mails to customers throughout the region. "The bank is more than my father's career, it is also his hobby," notes Bill Buxton Jr., who specializes in family-owned businesses as president of Alpha Partners, in Chapel Hill, North Carolina.

By and large, Mr. B is the kind of person you'll find profiled in this chapter: Self-described "old workhorses" who can't imagine being turned out to pasture and for whom work is their abiding passion. These are the people who can't fathom retiring in any traditional sense. For them, hobbies and other recreation, volunteer work, going back to school and spending more time with family—are pale alternatives to the invigoration of the workplace. The motivation is the same for the chairman of a multibillion-dollar company, the owner of a hardware store, the partner in a law firm or the corporate manager—to stay involved, responsible and challenged.

In his book, *The Hero's Farewell*, author Jeffrey Sonnenfeld describes one group of CEOs who exemplify this attitude: "Monarchs do not retire, but wear their crown until the end....These monarchs led their enterprises for lengthy reigns that ranged from 20 to 60 years. They were often in office until the last day they breathed." Sonnenfeld portrays Justin Dart, who built United-Rexall Drugs into a national drug chain and proclaimed at 72 that "I want my death and my retirement to be simultaneous." Three years later, Dart got his wish. He died after merging United-Rexall with Kraft.

Or consider Dr. Armand Hammer, who literally "died with his boots on" at age 92 while still chairman of Occidental Petroleum. He had taken control of the then-unprofitable company some 30 years before and was still in charge until the day he died in 1990.

Then again, not everyone hangs on by choice. Some do it out of financial necessity. They can't or don't want to maintain their current standard of living from pensions, savings and investments alone. Perhaps a large part of their retirement nest egg is tied up in a business that they haven't yet been able to sell.

For others, continuing to work has additional benefits, including being able to take advantage of tax deductions on entertainment and travel, or enjoying the fellowship that comes with being an active member of the business or professional community.

POINTS TO REMEMBER

- Many in the 50-plus set want to continue working.
- Additional income is only one of many reasons for working.
- You can work without being a work horse.
- There are ways to continue to work on your terms.
- Flexible work patterns are one answer.
- You may want to pass along your business—or you may not, or
- You may want to stay involved, but take on a different role.

For many old workhorses, staying on in the workplace is simply a matter of "not whether you win or lose but how long you play the game."

The Risks They Run

One of the privileges enjoyed by an Armand Hammer—or just about anybody who is self-employed—is the greater likelihood of staying put, adapting their role at work to their needs, and continuing to work if they want to. Why retire? Chances are they have more control over their fate than most corporate employees do. But even they may encounter inhibiting forces.

Even if they continue on by choice, some old workhorses may encounter resistance to their decision by a board of directors that maintains the company needs new blood and new direction. Other times, there is an heir apparent who's champing at the bit.

Although their lives, souls and egos may be wrapped up in the business, many workhorses remain in family-owned businesses and professional services at a cost to the firm. More often than not, the operation is reduced in scope, size and quality of service as the owner gets older and less aggressive.

Retirement-age professionals who want to stay on in midsize to larger firms have little choice but to produce. They're allowed to remain with the firm just as long as they are "rainmakers," bringing in new business. The logic goes that the day-to-day professional work can be done by younger partners for less money.

But in the small wholesale enterprise or the one- or two-person professional firm, there may be no one looking out for the best interest of the business—say, if it fails to update and install the latest in computer or manufacturing equipment, or if it continues to operate with outdated methods.

Many professions recognize the danger of getting into a rut and have instituted educational programs to improve quality performance among all members, not just the 50-plus set. The accounting profession, for example, requires that certified public accountants enroll in continuing education each year to maintain their professional credentials. But, in effect, the requirement particularly affects some older professionals who might have a tendency to let ongoing education take a back seat.

Ideally, the sole proprietorship or professional firm can take steps to assure continuity and to provide an opportunity for the owner to work past "normal" retirement age: Bring in a younger associate. Share responsibilities. Agree to take home less money in return for working fewer hours each week. Sounds good, but more often than not it doesn't work. Egos get in the way. After years of running the business, the owner still wants to be boss even though he's working less. Too many times, the associate ends up leaving because the owner was not totally committed to changing his work habits or to sharing the profits or ownership.

Some "die with your boots on" advocates face this possibility and take a more realistic approach. By design rather than attrition, they reduce the size of their operation and run a truncated law or accounting practice, or choose to operate a small and usually not too dynamic retail or service business.

ONE MAN'S STORY. Harold T. maintains nearly total control of an $11-million industrial-testing company that he started about two decades ago. Harold prefers to remain anonymous since it would hardly be in his best interest to tip off competitors on his corporate strategy. "Not a month goes by when I don't get a call from someone who might like to buy the company. We've even had some serious talks with two companies. Sure, I would get

SOME RULES FOR SCALING DOWN YOUR BUSINESS

- Start off with a business plan.
- Maintain a core of dedicated customers.
- Make sure you're running your business on at least a break-even basis. It doesn't make sense to sap your financial resources with a dying enterprise.
- If you can, move your business to your home, or at least to less expensive office space.
- Invest in good office equipment. Chances are you won't have a staff to do routine office work.
- Don't downscale your business at the risk of being bored.

some money and stock, but they would want me to remain with the company after the takeover. I'd end up working harder than ever for the new owners so I could collect more money if my company increases sales and doubles profits. It would mean changing the friendly yet effective way we run the company. As you see, I'm not too interested in retiring and selling out." Harold feels that time is on his side. His father, a Nebraska farmer, retired when he was 75.

> ### SUGGESTED READING
>
> - Davidow, William and Michael Malone, *The Virtual Corporation* (Harper Business, 1993). Slightly futuristic, but gives readers a peek at some important workplace trends.
> - Hammer, Michael and James Champy, *Reengineeering the Corporation* (Harper Business, 1996). This bestseller helps you look at the same old problems differently.

But Harold is also a realist, and he's concerned about the company and its future. His two sons are young teenagers and he estimates that even if they were to become interested, it would take at least ten years before they would be ready to enter the company. By then he would be in his late sixties. Harold's hedging his bets. He's setting up an employee stock ownership plan that permits his 50 full-time employees to buy some of his holdings. "At least this way, the ownership will be shared by our people."

It's Harder for the Corporate Workhorse

Corporate or government managers, and partners in professional-services businesses normally don't have the options that are available to the self-employed or owners of smaller businesses. Employment contracts may force them to leave. Or they are forced out by downsizing or lured out by early-retirement packages. They can be pushed out by diminished rewards, unwelcome transfers, or work rules that make any sort of flexible or creative approach to retirement impossible. It might be nothing you could call age discrimination per se, but the message is still clear.

That's unfortunate when you consider that, given the option, those in the 50-plus set prefer to work, an observation confirmed by the Commonwealth Fund, a nonprofit group that studies social issues. More than half of workers between age 50 and 64 would extend their careers if their employers provided training for a different job, continued pension contributions past age 65, or offered a position with less pay but fewer hours and responsibilities as a transition to full retirement.

According to Betty Friedan, most 65-plus men who continue to work are either at the "top or the bottom of the occupational ladder." It's mandatory for some men to hang on just to pay the bills, though she noted in her book, *The Fountains of Age*, "The increased availability of pensions has decreased the proportion of older men who work simply because they need additional income." More people at the top of the ladder would work after age 65 if they could find a position commensurate with their ability.

The possibility of staying in the corporate workforce would be enhanced if both employer and employee accepted such practices as flexible work schedules, telecommuting and job sharing. But the pros and cons of flexible staffing and scheduling notwithstanding, these corporate programs usually don't extend to most mid- to higher-level managers and professionals. At best, we hear the occasional anecdote about, say, a 62-year-old executive who wants to continue working but would like to avoid commuting three hours a day to and from work. To keep him in the work force, new arrangements are made so that the executive can work three days a week at home and commute the rest of the week.

Those Who Are Keeping On

Professionals and self-employed people have many options if they want to continue working. They can go at full throttle or at a reduced pace. Above all, they find work to be a stimulant, more uplifting and challenging than retirement. The people you are about to meet have fashioned a lifestyle in which their work continues to be pivotal.

HE CONTINUES TO NETWORK

Peter Cott
PUBLIC RELATIONS CONSULTANT

We all have our dreams and our fantasies. In one of Peter Cott's dreams, he wins the New York lottery. "Then I'll be able to work less, preferably at home, and at a less hectic pace." In the meantime, he says, "In theory you are supposed to take it easy, but I'm busier than ever."

Peter is a facilitator who enjoys getting things done. It has been his hallmark throughout his diverse career, one that enhances his current work as a self-employed public relations consultant. Peter's profession is still a pivotal part of his life—so much so that whereas ten years ago he might have charged every client a hefty fee, nowadays he's willing to compromise on fee size if the client and its mission interests him.

Peter's client base and public service work, past and present, reflect his social and community interests, including the Northside Center for Child Development, EDGE (Educational Designs that Generate Excellence), the National Awareness Foundation, and the High School of Economics and Finance. He also serves on the board of the New York Youth Symphony, the New York Chamber Ensemble and the New York City Community Board, which

Peter, self-employed in public relations, won't retire as long as work is "fun." He can take on clients for less if they and their mission interest him.

serves Chelsea, the neighborhood where Peter makes his home.

Single, Peter supports his needs with income from his business, social security and investments. What's more, he lives mortgage-free in a townhouse that he owns. "I even make a modicum of income by renting out a few apartments in the house."

Growing up in a Long Island suburb, Peter came of age just in time to serve in World War II. He went to New York University for three years but left to join the Army Air Corps, where he flew two-engine transports. "I returned to NYU, quit and enrolled instead at the Dramatic Workshop run by the New School [for Social Research]."

This led to a series of theater-related jobs, starting as the manager of the newly formed American Shakespeare Festival in Stratford, Connecticut, which is patterned after the Royal Shakespeare in Stratford, England, and the Hedgerow Theatre, a repertory theatre. Peter then moved on to become director of public relations for the New York Chapter of the National Academy of Television Arts and Sciences, the presenters of the Emmy Awards, and for the next

13 years he was the National Academy's executive director.

"I resigned in 1969. I was in my mid forties, and I considered the possibility of a career change, either to teach or to be a lawyer." Instead, Peter changed the thrust of his work. He became executive director of Westbeth, an apartment house for actors, artists and their families. The position permitted him to use his various theatrical, public relations and management skills.

Several years later Peter was hired as executive director of the Population Institute. "My job was to get the message on the world's population explosion to the media and entertainment industry." He left in the late 1970s as the movement started to lose its momentum.

At a time when others start thinking about taking it easy or possibly retiring, Peter started a new career in public relations. He began by working for a few years for a small firm where he learned the mechanics of the business. Wanting more professional independence and greater control over how he worked, he launched Peter Cott Associates in his home. The following year he formed a partnership that lasted two years, until he realized he'd be happier in his own shop. Back again to Peter Cott Associates, this time with offices on New York's Madison Avenue.

Shortly after turning 70, Peter made more changes in how he worked, somewhat counter to his lottery dream. Instead of moving his business into his home, as he once intended, he affiliated with Diana Stark, another veteran public relations consultant, and shares his office space with her in Manhattan, only a few blocks from his home. In this relationship, Diana provides backup services on some of Peter's accounts.

Peter's open-ended attitude toward his work is not a case of "like father, like son." His father retired at 65. The company he owned was passed along to Peter's older brother, who several years ago also retired at 65 and sold the company to its employees. In contrast, Peter says, "As long as the work is fun, why retire?"

SHE'S NOW A MUSICAL INSTITUTION

Olga Bloom
MUSICIAN AND IMPRESARIO

Chamber music performed on a barge? On the East River in New York City, just opposite Wall Street? Despite the unlikely setting, Olga Bloom had a dream that she made come true.

But as rewarding as a Bargemusic concert is, part of the joy in attending the year-round, twice-weekly performances is watching Olga in action. Olga, who started the concerts in 1977, is Bargemusic's lifeblood. As its president, she is actively involved in management, taking on fundraising and public relations duties. But she also attends to the details. She sells and collects tickets, positions folding chairs in the auditorium, serves refreshments and personally greets the 130 or so people who attend a typical performance. Olga plans to stay put and has no intention of retiring anytime soon. But she is making sure that others will be able to take over for her once she's out of the picture.

"It takes as much energy doing things in retirement as it does to work. Going dancing or playing golf takes energy. If you like your work, why retire?" Her own schedule gives testimony to her words. She works six days a week, from 8 in the morning to 4 in the afternoon. She takes off Saturdays to do her personal chores.

> **Music—playing and sharing it—has dominated Olga's life, exemplified through her creation and eventual legacy, the Bargemusic concert series.**

"I still don't have a job description. When I clean floors, I'm the floor cleaner; when I'm raising funds, I'm a fundraiser. Other than music, I have few interests. My life is identified with the barge."

Even with her hectic schedule, Olga is still a performing musician. About once a month in a concert not open to the public, she invites three other musicians to join her on the barge in an evening of chamber music.

Olga never expected to get rich from her music or from Bargemusic. She admits to living rather simply on less than $40,000 a year, her income from Bargemusic. She lives by herself in a small house that she owns in Brooklyn—an improvement over the late 1970s, when she lived on the barge. If she ever does bother to retire, she will collect her social security, as well as her own and her deceased husband's pension payments.

Born in Boston, Olga attended Boston University to study music. "I left when my mother got sick. This was deep in the Depression years. I played in WPA [the Works Projects Administration, a federal agency supporting the arts during the 1930s] concerts, and in chamber music groups—first the viola and then the violin."

She moved to New York in 1943. "I decided it was time to stop being a student and to work as a musician. I met my first husband, who was then a violinist in an Army band. He had more noble purposes and did not want to spend the war years as a musician. He switched into the air corps and was killed in action in the South Pacific."

For the next 30 years, Olga played wherever she could, from symphony and ballet orchestras to chamber music. During this time, she recalls, "my philosophy about music was developing."

SPREADING THE WEALTH OF MUSIC

One of her observations was that music as a profession was being restricted to the wealthy, who could afford to buy costly instruments. She knew this firsthand. Her second husband, Toby, a violinist in Arturo Toscanini's National Broadcasting Company Symphony Orchestra, mortgaged most of his possessions to buy more-expensive violins.

Olga and Toby were living on Barnum Island, off the south shore of Long Island. They gave chamber-music recitals at their home for friends, and at these informal concerts Olga began to explore the relationship between music, water and the environment. Toby encouraged her to pursue the idea that would eventually become Bargemusic.

After Toby's death, Olga read in a newspaper ad that a barge was for sale. That seemed like an answer to everything—a concert hall on water. The first two barges that she bought had acoustical problems due to heavy planking that absorbed sound. On her third try, she found a 102-foot, 80-year-old steel barge, lined with cherry wood, that made the difference. A year later, in 1977, it was refurbished and towed to its current mooring in Brooklyn. The location, a few hundred feet south of the Brooklyn Bridge and directly across the East River from Wall Street, proved ideal. Getting a mooring in Brooklyn was no easy task. But Olga by then had a number of influential supporters and the ability to attract "friends in high office who could look after us."

Her intention in the late 1970s was to present concerts by students from New York's leading conservatories. That changed when violinist Ik-Hwan Bae was named as Bargemusic's artistic director. He convinced Olga that they should not rely exclusively on students for the level of performance that sophisticated New York audiences demand. Nowadays the pool of nearly 100 musicians are all professionals. But the program is still consistent with Olga's original concept that Bargemusic concerts should, above all, further a young musician's career. "When musicians finish their studies, they need a place to perform. There are more good musicians than we can absorb. The barge is my answer."

The barge also counters what Olga finds is the "sameness" in society. "Compared with most concerts, Bargemusic is not 'yuppie-ish.' It is not a glitzy place to go."

In the late 1980s, Olga began to think about ways to operate Bargemusic more efficiently. She appointed a board of overseers consisting of professional musicians, a board of directors drawn from community leaders and a business manager to administer the organization, all calculated to leave Olga with more time for fundraising. The scheme partially fell apart when a number of board members resigned as their plans to institute managerial systems came into conflict with Olga's impresario style. After the rift, friends and patrons who consider Bargemusic synonymous with Olga Bloom, contributed $30,000 at a dinner and concert on the barge to help pay off debt and meet expenses.

Olga's dreams extend beyond her Brooklyn Bargemusic concerts. She would like to see other cities with waterside locations and a source of talented professional musicians develop similar chamber-music concerts on the water.

THE MIND IS IN HIS EYE

William Normand
PSYCHIATRIST

When William Normand talked about his 50th college reunion, the natural response was, "You're putting me on, Bill—you're much too young." But Bill did attend his Harvard College reunion. And unlike nearly all his classmates, who had fully retired, Bill carries a full workload that includes both a private psychiatric practice and a part-time position in a New York City hospital.

Practicing psychiatrists Bill's age aren't rare. Within the medical profession, psychiatrists as a group continue to practice many years longer than other medical specialists. Psychiatry is less demanding physically than, say, surgery. And, as Bill puts it, "perhaps psychiatrists—like good wine—improve with age." Nonetheless, Bill's private practice has shrunk in recent years. "Perhaps I'm not getting as many referrals as before. Some of the doctors who used to send me patients have retired. Some patients come in for a preliminary consultation and never return. People who are considering long-term psychotherapy may be uncomfortable in starting with an older psychiatrist, who may desert them because of illness or death."

Bill likes the balance in his professional life. At Bronx Lebanon, a hospital affiliated with Albert Einstein College of Medicine, he teaches psychiatric residents and third-year medical students and manages the grand rounds program in which guest speakers present lectures on various psychiatric topics.

"Since I finished my training, I have had a half-time job teaching and managing out-placement clinics, and a private practice. I like the mix and I enjoy teaching."

The practice of psychiatry has changed since Bill completed his residency. At that time, nearly all psychiatrists were trained in psychoanalysis. Nowadays the approach is more chemically and biologically oriented, and most psychiatrists emphasize short-term psychotherapy, biological methods and shock treatment. Over the years, depending on the patient, Bill has changed his approach to psychiatry to include both biological and psychoanalytic treatment.

Bill grew up in Missouri and entered Harvard prior to World War II, intending to become a writer. He graduated in 1943, but the last semester was cut short when he joined the Army. Bill was assigned to the Army Specialized Training Program, spent

> **Bill enjoys a mixed bag of private practice, teaching and outpatient-clinic management. But some things do change with the years.**

nine months learning to speak Chinese and was trained in cryptoanalysis. At the end of the war, he entered Columbia University to continue studying Chinese.

"At the same time, I started to take an interest in my own neuroses, and I considered becoming either a psychiatrist or a psychologist." A trusted friend from Harvard, who had been exempt from military service, was already a physician and he advised Bill to become a doctor, too. Bill dropped the Chinese program and took the basic science courses needed to apply to medical school. At that time, medical schools were swamped with applicants because of the GI bill. Bill entered the University of Kansas, where he received an MA in physiology and an MD. He returned to New York City for his residency and the start of a lifelong association with the Albert Einstein College of Medicine and its affiliated hospitals.

Bill, who married when he was in his late thirties, has three grown children. His wife, Marjorie, a lawyer, is ten years younger, a factor that has favorably influenced his youthful professional and personal demeanor. She became a lawyer in her early forties and thus has practiced law for only 20 years. What's more, many of Bill's friends are near Marjorie's age, encouraging him to think and act younger. He plays tennis year-round and skis regularly during the winter.

"As for retirement, it never crossed my mind or Marjorie's. Our friends have not retired, so why should we? And, anyway, we like our work."

CONTENT WITH A SMALLER WORKLOAD

Dorsey Whitestone
POINT-OF-PURCHASE ADVERTISING SPECIALIST

"How long will I work? Perhaps a few more years or as long as I stay well," says Dorsey Whitestone. "But we have little control over this. I look at it this way: Man proposes, but God disposes." Still, Dorsey has exerted a fair amount of control over his fate.

Dorsey is a point-of-purchase advertising specialist, a field in which he has worked for nearly 50 years. Compared with the hectic earlier years when he was building the business, he has intentionally trimmed the scope of his operation over the past several years, running Dorsey Display Corp. on a reduced basis from an at-home office. "All I need these days is a fax, copier, answering machine and a part-time bookkeeper. If there's some typing, I do it myself.

"I work no more than 20 hours a week, sometimes even less, but I visit my customers regularly. I give them what they want. At my age, I have an advantage. I do what customers want me to do, and I don't do what I cannot deliver. There's a wonderful word in the English language, called 'no.'" Using it has proven to be an ideal way to stay in business on his terms.

"What with people being downsized from the workforce, the best thing for younger workers is to get skills so they can be their own boss," Dorsey suggests. "There's nothing like self-employment as you get older."

Besides income from the business, Dorsey has investments, savings and, because he is over 70, social security with no strings attached. (Social security recipients under 70 sacrifice some benefits if they earn more than certain income limits. For more information, see page 272.)

Dorsey graduated from Yale University and went to work for the display advertising firm that his father had started in 1915, when this form of advertising was in its infancy. Exempt from World War II military service, Dorsey nonetheless felt an obligation to support the war effort and worked for Curtiss-Wright Corp., a producer of fighter aircraft. After the war, he returned to the family business, and worked with his father in the design and sale of display materials used at the point of purchase. He arranged with his father to succeed him in the business, if and when his father retired. In 1960, his father, then in his early seventies, retired reluctantly as a result of pressure from Dorsey's mother, and the agreement he had with Dorsey took effect.

> **Dorsey now works at his own pace, knows how to say no and has opted for the natural demise of his business.**

Point-of-purchase is a highly competitive field where clients make buying decisions based on both price and the creativity of the sales effort. Dorsey Display creates and designs the displays, using subcontractors to build them. This technique allows the company to operate with comparatively few employees and control overhead costs, yet fulfill contracts with large consumer-goods companies. In the long run, this approach—coordinating subcontracting to get the job done—eased the transition to Dorsey's semi-retirement lifestyle.

In the early 1970s, Dorsey moved the company from its office in New York City to a new space in Westchester County, so he could be nearer to his suburban home. When Dorsey approached age 70, he closed the office, which by then consisted of only a secretary-bookkeeper and himself, and took a series of steps to ensure that he could run the business on a reduced basis for about as long as he wanted. His new approach was, "I no longer solicit new business. When business dries up, I'm out of business." Dorsey's four children have gone into different careers, so preserving the business for them wasn't an issue.

"I met with a number of long-time customers. I told them of my plans and that I was moving to New Haven and the business would be located in my home. I think I was more concerned about the change than they were, since I had never worked from home before. They didn't care where I worked just as long as I could assure them of quality work, personal service and a good price."

Moving to New Haven provided other advantages besides those related to his business plan. Living ten minutes from Yale, he and Patricia, his wife, audit courses, and regularly attend athletic and cultural events. "One day I presented myself at the Yale library and told the curator of my collection of musical recordings and my interest in the musical theater. Yale, like all colleges, is short of staff and money. They put me to work as an unpaid consultant." Among other things, Dorsey spends a day a week helping to catalog the library's music collection, including the complete works of Yale alumnus Cole Porter.

CONTINUES AS A PART-TIME PHYSICIAN

Tom Sawyer
OPHTHALMOLOGIST

Tom Sawyer is considering retiring as an ophthalmologist in 2000; he'll be 72. But retirement does not mean that Tom plans to reduce his workload. It will simply mean shifting gears.

A University of Michigan medical school graduate, he practiced for nearly 30 years in Milwaukee until 1985, when he moved to Pinehurst, North Carolina "I was 58, and my office lease was not going to be renewed. I could easily have found a new office but I didn't want to start investing in leasehold improvements. I made an offer to my associate to buy me out, which he accepted."

Even so, Tom wasn't ready to retire. He still enjoyed practicing medicine, and he had no loss of manual dexterity, which is critical in his specialty. Serendipity stepped in. Tom saw a classified advertisement in *JAMA*, the *Journal of the American Medical Association*. A multi-office ophthalmology practice in south central North Carolina was looking for a board-certified specialist to join its staff. It was the first time in his professional career that Tom responded to an employment ad. He applied, was hired and joined the staff of the Carolina Eye Associations, which operates offices in more than 15 communities.

Tom and his wife, Marilyn, moved to Pinehurst, bought a house and he went to work. By the early 1990s, Tom was ready for another change. This was not a signal that he intended to retire. Hardly so. He would continue to work but at a slower rate, two days rather than four days a week. His views met with the approval of Carolina Eye Associates, which reassigned him to a smaller office that is open twice a week. By this time, he had already decided to restrict his medical work to eye examinations and other medical routines.

> **Tom wasn't ready to retire. He had no loss of manual dexterity, which is crucial in his specialty.**

"This is a great relationship since I have no administrative or business responsibilities. The firm handles personnel, billings, insurance forms and bookkeeping. I just practice medicine. I'm paid a salary, plus I receive a percentage of the gross above a certain level." Now that he's turned 70, Tom is officially a double dipper, collecting both social security and his salary without paying a penalty for exceeding the allowed level on earnings.

Tom still has mixed emotions about retiring from medicine. He maintains the enthusiasm of a medical school student. What's more, he's under no pressure from his employer to stop working. Don't for a moment think that Tom's a grind who's devoid of any outside interests.

After he moved from Pinehurst to the

Chapel Hill area in 1994, he returned to college as a University of North Carolina student. He's taking full advantage of the ruling that permits residents over 65 to take courses at state universities at no charge.

Once again, Tom is unusual. Rather than audit a course, he takes tests, does laboratory work and writes papers. "Why not? I want to do the full course and 'duke' it out with the kids.

"Most of the students in my class have no idea that I'm a doctor. I don't volunteer this information. To most, I'm just another old guy in class with them." He likes attending class with younger students and listening to them talk about careers in science and medicine. When this occurs, he breaks silence and serves as an official mentor to a student interested in a medical career.

Compared with the time he was a college student, Tom notes that he has more passion for the things he's learning. Over the past four years, he's taken ten different courses ranging from molecular biology, ecology and population genetics to astronomy. A number of these courses weren't given in his college days, and the lab equipment currently taken for granted wasn't even invented 50 years ago.

Tom says that doctors of his generation weren't trained to use computers. "When I moved to North Carolina, I wanted to learn about computers, so I took some courses at a local community college. But my computer needs are simple. I use the computer as a word processor to prepare spreadsheets for my reports. I sometimes log onto Medline, but I'd rather go to the UNC medical library and read the papers. I guess it's the way I was trained."

If he actually retires from active medical practice, it won't mean the end of Tom's dreams. His goal is to become a high school laboratory assistant, and use his science training and nearly 50 years as a physician to help students.

ONCE A JOURNALIST, ALWAYS A JOURNALIST

Pete Johnston
UNIVERSITY PROFESSOR

No sooner had Donald "Pete" Johnston retired from the faculty of the Columbia University Graduate School of Journalism than he walked across campus and joined the faculty of another Columbia graduate school. Teaching is Pete's forte, and his love, and he doesn't see giving it up just because he's in his seventies.

Pete's approach to college teaching has stayed constant over the years. Despite the way that computer technology has changed the processing of data, it hasn't much changed how a journalist reports and writes. "I spend a lot of time with the students, criticizing their work and helping them reach decisions relative to their careers. I have always let a job expand beyond its normal dimensions," says Pete.

> Pete knows that tools may change, but the essentials of his craft are enduring. He anticipates teaching them indefinitely—wherever.

As an adjunct faculty member, Pete officially works half-time, but keeping to official working hours has never been his strong suit. Pete enjoys helping students improve their basic communications skills, something he does in his "off" hours in one-on-one sessions. "Ever since I've been a teacher, I have felt I'm contributing something very useful in motivating my students."

For a change of pace, he serves as the volunteer editor of the Columbia Journalism School's alumni newspaper.

Born in Buffalo, Pete served in the Air Force during World War II. He graduated in 1949 from Cornell University and the following year from Columbia's journalism school. He worked as a reporter with the United Press International bureau in Buffalo for several years, then was transferred to the foreign desk in New York, where he covered the UN. *The New York Times* then hired him for its Sunday "Week in Review" section to report on national and international events and on trends in social issues.

"I always wanted to be a journalist. Little has changed. When I worked for UPI and the *Times,* I commuted from Westchester. The other commuters, who made more money than I did, sounded disgruntled with their work and their pay. They couldn't wait until the weekends. I never felt that way toward work."

While at the *Times,* Pete taught journalism part-time at one of the colleges in the New York City university system. The experience encouraged him to apply to Columbia Journalism School as a full-time faculty member.

Pete found his true challenge as a

teacher and mentor. "I like people, I like the Columbia environment, and I particularly like working with younger people—they make you feel younger." Students enjoyed his enthusiasm. He gave more time to the job than was required. His comments on their writings were both critical and helpful. None of that changed over the years.

During the mid 1980s, Pete, then an associate professor, was promoted to associate dean for academic affairs as well as director of admissions. When a new dean was named, Pete was replaced as an administrator, and he returned to teaching. His effectiveness as an instructor aside, Pete had an academic problem: He had neglected scholarly research, a critical factor in receiving tenure. Years earlier, he had been denied tenure but his faculty position wasn't jeopardized because he was also serving as associate dean, a position protected by university regulations. When he reached age 65 and lacked tenure, it appeared his teaching career was at checkmate. This time he would have to leave the journalism school, with lifetime health care benefits and a pension based on 15 years' service.

At that point, Pete knew one thing. He did not want to stop working, unlike his older brother who worked as a sportswriter for 40 years, retired to Florida and has not written a word since. "He is content to play tennis, walk, read, ride his bike and watch TV. I'm not ready for that yet."

Fortunately, Pete's teaching credentials did not go unnoticed. As an associate dean, he knew other Columbia administrators, including those in the Graduate School of International and Public Affairs. They asked him to join the faculty as an adjunct professor, teaching basic journalism courses and working part-time as director of the school's International Media and Communications Program. So long as Pete works no more than half-time, he can earn income and continue to collect his pension.

Pete's experience with an apparently seamless switch from one faculty to another on the same campus has carryover value for many managers and executives exiting the corporate workplace. Rather than retire, perhaps they, too, can find another department within the same organization that can use their skills.

Pete's five children are all grown. His wife, Jane, a former high school English teacher, is a published writer of murder mysteries. Jane brings in a small pension, social security benefits and some book royalties. And now that Pete's past 70, there are no income limitations placed on his social security payments.

Several years ago, Pete thought that at 70 he would leave Columbia and he and Jane would move to their summer home on Cape Cod. Jane spent about six months a year there, and Pete lived there during the summer months. But any decision on Cape Cod as a full-time home has been tabled. Consistent with Pete's desired lifestyle, the Johnstons have rented an apartment within walking distance of the Columbia campus. "Jane likes living in New York and I just can't see myself retiring. And even if we were to move to Cape Cod, I'd be freelancing, and I'm sure I'll teach journalism part-time at some college."

PASSING ALONG THE KNOW-HOW

Laura and Sandy Sanborn
CAMP OWNERS

Meet the "happy campers." Laura and Roger (Sandy) Sanborn are the founders of Sanborn Western Camps, in Florissant, Colorado, a dot on the map 35 miles west of Colorado Springs, with a view of Pikes Peak. Sanborn Western Camps is also a diversified family business that has made an orderly transition in management to the next generation. That doesn't mean that Laura and Sandy have totally bowed out. Instead, they've structured a new, yet informal, managerial role for themselves. Says Sandy: "It's kind of like being grandparents; we have fun with the kids, go home, and let others do the real work and cleanup."

> **For Laura and Sandy, "It's kind of like being grandparents; we have fun with the kids, go home, and let others do the real work and cleanup."**

Unlike most camps, which operate only during the summer, Sanborn is a year-round facility with a full-time staff of 30 educators and support personnel. "What we do is run an educational experience for children and adults alike. We're more than fun and games," says Sandy.

In the late 1970s, the Sanborns opened a conference center to accommodate small groups of managers and professionals who spend a week meeting on their field of specialty while also participating in a nature pro-gram. Sanborn also serves as a learning center for the Colorado Springs school system. An estimated 100,000 youngsters have spent one-week sessions learning and living outdoors. And to give even more authenticity to the nature program, Sanborn Western Camps started Pikes Peak Research Center.

What else would you expect from two former teachers? Laura and Sandy met in Colorado, where he was stationed as an officer in the ski troops during World War II. They married in 1944, and when the war ended, Sandy began his civilian career as a teacher.

"We decided that we would make something of our lives, even in a minor way, by staying in Colorado and eventually starting a summer camp," Sandy recalls. "We had little money but were able to borrow $7,500 and buy 480 acres in Florissant. And I figured if I was going to be a Westerner, I'd better start learning something about it, so I went to Colorado State University on the G.I. Bill. Laura, who had graduated from the University of Colorado, taught school while I earned my degree in animal husbandry."

Sandy's next job was as principal and superintendent in a sparsely populated rural school district where he and Laura were the entire faculty for a one-room junior and senior high school system. The Sanborns taught in Florissant for several years until they officially opened their camp for its first season in 1948.

MAKING WAY FOR THEIR KIDS

As a family business, Sanborn Western Camps was eventually concerned with succession. Laura and Sandy found the answer within their family. The process of passing camp management to their son, Rick, and daughter-in-law, Jane, began in the mid 1980s when they, rather than Laura and Sandy, made the annual month-long sales trip to promote the camp in 15 or more metropolitan centers. Their daughter, Jan, and her husband, Rein, a teacher, live in Colorado Springs, and during the summer months and weekends they, too, work at the camp.

The transition was eased by Laura and Sandy's willingness to accept change. "Most camps are family businesses," Sandy says. "I had watched a lot of people in this field work past their time. They got too old and their camps failed. I've also seen a number of guys in this business let go by selling out to a real estate developer."

Sanborn Western Camps was more fortunate. It had a second generation of family members who had grown up at the camp. They had been campers and counselors, done about every job at the camp during summers, and became full-time workers after graduating from college. Rick and Jane had also been involved in developing additional camping services that

could be offered to youngsters and adults alike on a year-round basis. In short, as in many family-owned businesses, the next generation of owners learned the business from the ground up, by being involved and watching their parents.

When there is a mature relationship between the parents and children, the baton-passing appears effortless. What's more, there is little need for family members to attend business-school seminars on how to affect an orderly transition within the business. At its best, the change is handled instinctively and with a spirit of good will. That was the case at Sanborn Western Camps. With Laura and Sandy there never was any question or hesitation that their children were prepared to take over.

"So far our children have not resented our presence," says Sandy. "Rather, they have encouraged us to continue our ties with the camp. But when I become overbearing, they tell me to keep quiet and sit down." And he does.

Laura and Sandy still enjoy camp life. Both help train new counselors and staff members, and participate in many of the conferences held at the camp.

Now that the camp attracts the children and grandchildren of former campers, Laura and Sandy also provide a new role. They send newsletters and birthday cards to all former campers. "In our emeritus role, we know that we are still needed. Camping is a very personal business, and in our case we've been doing it for over 40 years. About half the campers are the children, and even grandchildren, of former campers. The 'alums' know Laura and me, and when they visit the camp to look it over, they want to talk with us. In a way we're the link with their past."

As an experienced outdoorsman, Sandy is now blending that skill with a newly acquired one. He's become computer literate, and he's using his new know-how to help catalog animal and plant species found at the camp.

Though Sandy is no longer CEO and admits that he no longer has a formal job, he continues to receive a salary. "We expect to work indefinitely. Retirement is out of the question. We're lucky to live here. When your business has been your home and your home has been your business, you don't necessarily want to give it up."

TURNING OVER LEADERSHIP

Southgate Jones Jr.
INSURANCE COMPANY OWNER

If you're looking for continuity in a family-owned business, then J. Southgate & Son has few peers. The Durham-based firm, founded in 1872, is North Carolina's oldest insurance agency. Southgate Jones Jr., now in his mid seventies, gracefully shifted control of the business to his son, Southgate Jones III, who is the president and co-CEO of Asura, a company that represents a merger of several independent firms, including J. Southgate & Son. Unlike so many other heads of family businesses, Southgate was not the least bit apprehensive about helping his son obtain a majority share in the 123-year-old company. And, despite the changes in role and control, he still gets up every morning and goes to work, with relish.

Southgate never really expected to lead the family business, and now he doesn't really expect to leave it—though the day-to-day worries fall to his son.

"I still have no plans to retire. In fact, I deplore the concept of having to retire at a specific age. Most of my friends no longer work. They're always asking me to play golf at 8:30 but I need to remind them that at 8:30 I'm getting ready for work."

Southgate Jones Jr. represents the fourth generation of the family in the agency. But when he graduated from Davidson College in 1942 he had little interest in the insurance business. Southgate's father was a banker, and there was no expectation within his immediate family that he would join the agency. Besides, fate took care of his immediate employment needs. "When I graduated, there were two ceremonies. First, I got my degree, then I took off my cap and gown, put on my uniform jacket and was sworn in as a second lieutenant in the Army." After infantry training, Southgate served as a combat officer in Europe. "When the war was over, I was a major, and I debated whether to apply for a regular Army commission or to stay in Europe to paint and write music."

He returned home in February 1946 when his father was hospitalized. Needing a job, he took an entry-level position with J. Southgate & Son. "I was in my mid twenties. I was married. The pay was less than I had made in the Army." A few years later, Thomas Southgate, the grandson of the founder, died, and Southgate Jones Jr. was named president.

Southgate Jr. joined the agency during a period when central North Carolina was attracting new industry. But growth also meant more competition for the agency. He set the standards that blended the old with the new, as noted in a company brochure: "J. Southgate & Son every day proves it has aged only in experience and wisdom. [We're] still nurturing the zest and freshness of modern insurance ideas which five generation of clients have appreciated most."

A TRADITION OF CURRENCY

Southgate never looks back. Though he is not a computer user, he began to automate agency operations in the 1970s with the installation of the first in a series of specialty software packages. As far back as 1978, he helped establish a group of users of Agency Management Services, the largest vendor of insurance automation systems, with software packages installed in more than 7,000 insurance agencies. Southgate is a member of the group's executive committee, which means attending meetings with AMS management to discuss such technical matters as transactional filing and downloading and uploading of software packages.

Until he was in his late fifties, Southgate was mostly unconcerned with succession. "I knew one thing. I didn't want to be an old guy who has to be dragged out. I wanted to be first to realize that I'm no longer mentally and physically able to do my work." Fortunately, things never went that far.

Before the early 1980s, succession within his immediate family was a rather moot question. His three daughters and their husbands were not interested in the business, and Southgate III, the youngest child, had not yet graduated from college.

"When my son was in college, he was interested in a business career, but not with our firm or in insurance. He worked for other people on summer vacations. In his senior year, he came to work for us in anticipation of going to graduate business school. When he did not get into the school of his choice, he became a J. Southgate & Son employee.

"Let me assure you, as proud as I am of my family's part in the business, I put absolutely no pressure on my son. That's a bad way to hire a new employee. As I've told friends who own businesses, no family business should be a home for inept relatives, and certainly family members shouldn't be brought kicking and screaming into the business."

When Southgate III joined the company, his training and responsibilities were the same as any other new employee's. His job was to learn the insurance business from the bottom up. By the time that he was ready to succeed his father as CEO, Southgate Jr. was assured that Southgate III had the respect of the staff, nearly all of whom were older and more experienced in the insurance business.

The switch began in 1988, when Southgate gave 50 percent of his stock to his son. Four years later, when Eleanor Bolich, daughter of Thomas Southgate, retired as the agency's chief operating officer, she sold her share to Southgate III, making him president, CEO and majority shareholder. "Sure, I could have sold him my shares, but what's the sense?" says Southgate Jr. "If I had, I would have gotten the money. It would have gone into my estate, and he and his sisters would have gotten it back years later when I die." He feels his approach was simpler and a far better way to assure continuity of the agency.

"Giving Southgate half of my stock was strictly voluntary on my part. It was a way to show him my confidence without any murmur from him that he wanted some ownership.

"My son has been positioning the company for the 21st century. We've upgraded our computer systems, and we expect to move to larger office space in Durham. And I'm pleased to say that he's a much better manager than I ever was.

"Besides having my name, my son is a natural salesman and manager. Since he has become president, we have lost none of our other senior people who might have felt they had been bypassed by a younger person.

"He conducts Monday morning staff meetings that I attend like everybody else here. My son is the boss. He knows it and I know it."

While Southgate will not discuss it specifically, it's apparent that he has been a role model for his son. Both are deeply involved in community activities, though they are members of different organizations—not by design, but due to their individual interests and priorities.

NEW TRICKS FOR AN OLD HORSE
While Southgate III was assuming greater responsibility within the agency, Southgate Jr. used his new freedom to take on some additional insurance industry projects. Having a 14-person professional staff gave him the freedom to spend five years in the late 1980s as an officer and then president of the Independent Insurance Agents of

America, a group that represents about 240,000 independent agents and their employers. During his presidency, he divided his time between association work and J. Southgate & Son. "I made almost 120 trips from the Raleigh-Durham Airport on association business in two years. This wouldn't have been possible without a staff and a changeover in management."

Southgate's work habits have changed in other ways. He spends less time on day-to-day operations. He's shifted his focus to the Alliance for Productive Technology, a trade group he helped start. Using his industry contacts, he travels to independent insurance agencies throughout the U.S. to convince their management of the need to use uniform computer software.

If he stopped working tomorrow, Southgate wouldn't be too concerned about paying the bills. As a retired colonel in the Army reserves, he receives retirement pay, plus he gets social security and has income from investments and savings. He no longer takes commissions on insurance sales because others in the agency are most likely servicing the accounts. Instead, he receives a "realistic" salary that is consistent with his contribution and the agency's operating budget.

Staying in the workforce doesn't reflect a lack of other interests. Besides boating, hunting and golf, Southgate paints and writes music, mostly religious anthems and prayer responses. "But I now realize that if I had lived my dream and stayed in Paris, I would still be an unknown professional painter and musician."

Starting Over

YOU'RE 50- OR 60-SOMETHING AND YOU'VE JUST been pink-slipped. You definitely don't want to retire. Business is your lifeblood. What's the next step—do you look for another job (the subject of Chapter 8), buy an existing business, start your own, purchase a franchise, begin a new career, become a consultant?

Chances are the 50-plus set won't find a friendly welcome mat at most Fortune 500 companies. Many employers, while respecting your credentials, assume that you've been overpaid, that your work skills have plateaued or that you're no longer as aggressive as a 42-year-old.

Now's the time to downplay the traditional job market and consider some form of self-employment or career change, an idea that fictional Rabbi David Small contemplated in *The Day the Rabbi Resigned*. "Because I'm 53, it occurred to me that in a few years I'd be too old to be considered for a teaching job. Maybe I'm too old now, but I'd like to give it a shot."

The rabbi's not alone. According to the Small Business Administration, about 10% of workers of all ages are self-employed, but by the time workers reach age 65 and over, the rate climbs to 25%. Perhaps one reason for this spurt is that owning a business has become a prime way to remain employed.

That does not mean that all older entrepreneurs are putting in a 60-hour work week. Some operate seasonal businesses; others are consultants who work two or three days a week.

Do You Want to Own Your Own Business?

You've probably daydreamed about owning your own business. But before taking the plunge, be hard-nosed. Starting a business calls for enormous amounts of energy and endurance, a tough hurdle for anyone but more so for new business owners who are 50-plus, and especially so for those past 60. Above all, it means risking capital—rather little for an at-home consultancy but much more for buying or starting other types of businesses. Surely, your lawyer or accountant will point out the pitfalls of jeopardizing retirement-related resources on any new business venture.

Is it a risk worth taking for the 50-plus set or, in fact, for would-be entrepreneurs of any age? It probably depends on whether you're an optimist or a pessimist. The SBA has found that 53% of all businesses are terminated within four years of inception and 71% within eight years. Yet when each of these businesses started out, the owner was convinced it was a sure-fire winner. Dun & Bradstreet notes that the failure rate for businesses has declined from its high in the early 1990s. D&B, however, does not chart business failures by the size of the company.

At age 54, 60 or 65, you hardly want to gamble a life's savings on a new business. Of course, there may be exceptions: a former executive with capital to spare as the result of a golden handshake, or the seller of one business who is in a favorable cash position to invest in another. Or how about retired high-income CEOs like Chrysler's Lee Iacocca, who started ventures including a food and wine company? Or Marvin Traub, past chairman of Bloomingdale's, who formed his own consulting firm, Marvin Traub and Associates? Or Dow Jones's former chairman, Warren Phillips, who with his wife founded Bridge Works, a book-publishing company. Occasionally you will find people such as research engineer Harry Wayne, who was employed for more

THE LEGAL STRUCTURE OF YOUR BUSINESS

Before you're really in business for yourself, you'll have to decide what legal form your business should take. Should it be a sole proprietorship, partnership, a general partnership or a corporation? The answer can affect your potential legal liabilities, the kind of government paperwork and tax forms you'll have to fill out, the amount of tax you'll pay and the money you'll be able to set aside for retirement. It's a question that's best answered by you and your lawyer or accountant, but in the meantime, here are some of the pros and cons of each form.

SOLE PROPRIETORSHIP
Advantages
Easy to get started
Less expensive
Total control
Easy to terminate

Disadvantages
Unlimited liability
Business and personal assets are combined
Hard to get financing
Illness endangers business

PARTNERSHIP
Advantages
Simple to set up
More decision makers
Additional capital available
Minimum legal paperwork

Disadvantages
Unlimited liability
Vague lines of authority
Hard to get financing to launch business
Difficult to dispose of partnership

CORPORATION
Advantages
Limited liability
Easier for successful firm to raise capital
Better continuity

Disadvantages
More expensive to start
More paperwork
Taxes may be higher than the owner's personal rate
Must comply with more government regulations
Increased legal and accounting expenses
Less control

THE S CORPORATION. The S corporation is ideally suited for a small or start-up business. If you elect to become an S corporation (previously known as a subchapter S corporation), the company's profits and losses will be distributed to the individual shareholders of the corporation and will be taxed at their personal rates; you may be the only shareholder. You still, however, retain the limited-liability advantage of the corporation. Check with your attorney to see if your company qualifies for this choice

TAKE THEIR ADVICE

Outplacement consultants and financial advisers offer these warnings and suggestions to retirees who are thinking about going into business.

- Don't refinance your home and invest the capital in a business.
- Don't risk pension income and investments in a business in which you have no expertise.
- Don't bankroll younger family members in a business in which neither of you haS any expertise.
- Don't involve yourself in a new business that requires upward of 60 hours of work a week.

INSTEAD:

- Become a consultant in your field of expertise.
- Acquire a business under a game plan to earn the difference between your former take-home pay and your current income.
- Keep your business simple. Let it challenge but not overwhelm you.
- Develop a practical business plan commensurate with your age. Sixty-two-year-olds should avoid overly ambitious corporate objectives.

than 30 years designing electronic products and now does so for himself—but he was hardly entering uncharted waters. Simply put, a retiree should think twice before launching a start-up business. There are other ways to become an entrepreneur.

If you get the itch, be aware that you most likely would fetch a better return on your money in any number of safer investment vehicles. This may be beside the point if you are intent on owning a business, but it's a critical consideration as you approach retirement age. The three to five years it will likely take to establish the business may seem like an eternity to you. Also consider that you no longer have the luxury of 20 to 30 years to recoup any money that you may ultimately lose. Business turnaround expert William Buxton, president of Alpha Partners, Inc., of Chapel Hill, North Carolina, does not court retirement-age people as prospects to purchase businesses up for sale. "Other than those people with extra money to spend or who know a specific business 'cold,' I advise people in their late fifties to sixties to avoid risking it all in buying or starting a business."

Aside from the financial risk, there are serious questions to consider:

- If you've spent 25 to 30 years working in corporate America, how prepared are you for the rigors of self-employment?
- How well do you know the business that you hope to start or buy?
- If you are a newcomer to the field, who is going to teach you the ABCs?
- Are you mentally and physically prepared to be your own boss?
- Are you ready to work longer hours than you most likely did in a previous corporate job?

In spite of the possible financial and personal risk, Sterling Dimmitt, a Lee Hecht Harrison senior vice-president and director of entrepreneurial services, finds that about 18% of downsized executives of all ages surveyed by his firm opted to acquire or start their own business, compared with a 12% rate in 1990. These potential entrepreneurs tend to be in their mid forties or older and were earning more than $100,000 when they left their last job. "Survival in your own business generally requires significant capital and business know-how, which many of these older, experienced people have," said Dimmitt. But unless the individual has sufficient capital to risk, Dimmitt would seriously question the wisdom of starting a business from scratch in one's late fifties. Exceptions are service and consulting fields, where the capital requirements can be rather modest and the entrepreneur is already an expert in the field.

POINTS TO REMEMBER

- The business-as-usual concept no longer applies to the job market.
- Are you mentally, physically and financially ready to start a business?
- Franchising has its advantages, as well as its pitfalls.
- Thorough homework is important for entrepreneurial hopefuls.
- Running a successful consultancy requires a different set of work skills, especially the ability to get out and hustle the work.
- Operating from an at-home office calls for different work habits.
- Opportunities exist by changing careers.

Buying a Business

A more practical alternative is to buy an existing profitable business, with enough sales (perhaps as little as $1 million to $3 million) to provide you with an adequate income. "Although it takes a lot of up-front money, this is the self-employment path most likely to succeed," says Dimmitt. "In purchasing a business and its positive cash flow, people are, in effect, buying a job and a return on their investment." Buying an ongoing business makes sense just as long as the purchaser is in good health and has a desire to work harder and longer than the previous owner has worked in years. This rule has even greater application to retail businesses, where six-day work weeks are standard. If you are considering retail or restaurant ownership, get experience working in the industry beforehand or find a partner who is experienced. According to Dimmitt, running these businesses is an art, and experience is essential. "To succeed, the person should know the field very well, know how to run a business and have had experience operating a similar type of business." In short, we're still not talking about novices flying blind. He also cautions retirees against investing a large part of their retirement savings in a new business venture. The personal risks are obvious.

Is a Franchise a Better Choice?

W hat about franchising for "wannabe" entrepreneurs? Many new-business experts feel that franchising represents a strong start-up opportunity for the 50-plus set with risk capital resulting from severance or golden-parachute payouts to invest. The risks are sharply lower than in starting a business from scratch.

Franchise-industry growth figures are impressive There are approximately 600,000 U.S. franchise-owned businesses with industry sales expected to top $1 trillion in sales by the turn of the century. A new franchise unit opens somewhere in the U.S. every eight minutes. Name a retail or service chain of business and most likely it's a franchise. The roster includes food retailers such as McDonald's and KFC, service companies such as Budget Rent-A-Car and H&R Block, and executive-search firms such as

KNOW THE ANSWERS BEFORE BUYING A FRANCHISE

- What type of experience is required in the franchised business?
- Do you have a complete description of the business?
- How many hours and what level of personal commitment are needed to run the business?
- Who is the franchisor? What is its track record? What is the business experience of the officers and directors of the company?
- How are other franchisees doing?

- What are the start-up and licensing costs? How do they compare with similar franchises from other franchisors?
- Are you required to buy supplies and business services from the franchisor?
- What is the turnover rate among other franchisees?
- Do you know the terms and conditions under which you can terminate or renew the franchise relationship?
- Is the franchisor in good financial health?

Source: International Franchise Association

Management Recruiters International and Snelling & Snelling.

Despite the numbers, however, franchising is not for everyone. Watch out for possible culture shock, especially if you're shifting from a corporate lifestyle to a "mom and pop" business environment. Gone are the 9-to-5 workdays. Hands-on work begins with the boss and is the order of the day in most franchises, as well as in any other start-up business. It can be especially shocking to a former white-collar administrator turned fast-food franchisee. Interestingly, the transition may be easier for older and more seasoned professionals who are less interested in frills and titles, have their feet firmly planted on the ground, and are more willing to do what's necessary to get the job done.

A franchise at best represents an entrepreneurial compromise. The buyer obtains what hopefully is a proven business formula and a strong marketing image, along with training and an array of ongoing support services. In return, the franchisor sets the ground rules on fees, use of the company's logo, quality control, product marketing, advertising and purchasing.

Buying a franchise is not forever, says John Hayes, a consultant to would-be franchisees. "It is not like a family-run business passed along from generation to generation, but rather a business that might be sold after eight years, hopefully at a profit. This might become your retirement nest egg, or you could use the money to buy another franchise." Other franchise owners leverage their investments. They parlay a single franchise unit into a regional chain or create mini-franchise conglomerates. Nearly 20% of franchise operators own more than one unit—sometimes with the same franchisor, other times in different businesses to increase diversification and lower risk if one franchise concept goes sour.

Some franchise operators actively seek former corporate managers as franchisees. ProForma, a distributor of printed items (including promotional printing and advertising specialties), indicates that the owners of 240 of its 310 franchises had prior sales and management experience. What's more, 60 of them are age 50 plus.

It's little wonder that franchise operators run recruitment advertisements in the *Wall Street Journal*. In one ad, AlphaGraphics, a digital publishing specialist, proclaimed that its 330 franchisees "come to us from a variety of industries, professional services and consulting firms."

Some franchise operators look for franchisees with related industry know-how. The Golden Corral chain prefers to recruit experienced restaurant-industry personnel. "When they aren't food people and they still want to invest in our franchise, we get them to partner with a food guy," says Golden Corral's Stephen Fortlouis. Since a single Golden Corral might gross up to $3 million a year and serve about 3,000 meals a day, the franchise company believes it is imperative that franchisees know the restaurant business. Compared with Mail Boxes Etc., which has trained more than 3,000 U.S. franchise owners in two-week sessions at "MBE University" in San Diego, Golden Corral provides food-service training only to the staffs of each franchised restaurant.

Learning how to run most franchise businesses is not that difficult. The good franchisors have developed easy-to-learn operating formulas, and they are experienced in training recruits. If you're interested in someday buying a franchise, why delay learning about it? The education and training in the practical day-to-day operations can start long before you retire or contact any franchisors. Work part-time in the evenings or on weekends for a franchisee in a field that interests you. You will soon learn whether that type of franchising is for you.

Start-up costs vary. It is safer but more expensive to be part of a proven, successful franchise company than to join a newly established franchise operation. Some franchises, due to their success, are naturally costlier. The minimum McDonald's start-up expense typically ranges from $445,000 to $580,000, including franchise fee and the cost of the restaurant and excluding any working capital. Yet a Subway sandwich shop franchise costs from $58,900 to $100,700, including a franchise fee of $10,000 and working capital to start. ServiceMaster, the cleaning operation, charges a franchise fee that may range from $8,700 to $19,700 and requires working capital from $16,600 to $29,900. Storefront fast-food and retail operations are generally more expensive to acquire than most behind-the-scenes business-to-business and customer-service franchises.

More often than not, the franchise fee represents just a part of the start-up costs. If it is a retail operation, there may be the cost of building or renting the store. Bona fide franchisors provide checklists that show the average cost for training; store design; inventory and equipment; leasehold improvements;

TAPPING FRANCHISES FOR INFORMATION

- What was the quality of training that you received?
- What kind of ongoing support and counsel have you received from the franchisor?
- Have there been regular innovations and upgrades to the program to make it more timely?
- How effective is the advertising to which you contribute?
- How much money is realistically necessary to have as working capital?
- How many months did it take to break into a positive cash flow?
- How long was it before you could take a salary from the business?
- If you could do it all over again, knowing what you know now, would you acquire this franchise?

Source: Donald Foltz, Franchise Centre, Inglewood, Colo.

---

working capital; opening-day advertising; legal, accounting and licensing fees; and insurance. In talking with franchisees, ask them to compare their experience on opening-day charges with the franchisor's checklist.

You can also get into business by buying an existing franchise outlet. About 15% to 20% of franchises are resold annually. "Some owners prefer buying an accepted winner, and they don't mind paying a premium for it. Distressed or marginal operations are less costly to buy, but turnaround situations are best left to the experts," says franchise consultant Donald Foltz. One suggested buyout formula: The buyer should expect to pay three to four times net earnings plus depreciated value of assets, the current franchise fee and the liabilities as of the closing.

Protecting Yourself

Due diligence should be the order of the day before making any commitment.

Now's the time to study the marketplace. Attend regional shows where franchisors exhibit. This is a chance to increase awareness of the range of different franchise businesses. Start to read how-to business books on franchising available in most bookstores and public libraries.

Prior to purchase, the franchisor is obligated by law to send all prospective buyers either the Uniform Franchise Offering Circular or an extensive disclosure document, which discuss such basic issues as the history of the franchising company, any bankruptcy records, fees and royalties. For fear of potential liability, most franchisors will avoid being specific about an anticipated return on investment from a franchise.

The UFOC guidelines were revised in 1995. Potential franchisees should have a much easier time understanding the disclosure documents they receive because the information can no

---

FOR MORE INFORMATION

If you seek some additional background on the franchise industry, contact the **International Franchise Association** at 1350 New York Ave., N.W., Washington DC 20005 (202-628-8000; www. franchise. org).

---

longer be hidden behind "legalese" but must be provided in plain English. The new guidelines also require franchisors to reveal the names, addresses and telephone numbers of franchise owners, including all franchisees who have sold out or gone bankrupt. Franchisors must also reveal any litigation in which they have been involved. No longer can they list only the names of successful franchise operators.

Personally check out the franchisor. If the franchisor still operates a company-owned outlet, spend some time there assessing his or her day-to-day operation of the business. Or spend a day or two at the company's headquarters, getting a feel for how management interacts with its franchisees and perhaps even reviewing the UFOC with the principals.

Determine whether you will receive some form of market exclusivity or whether the franchisor has the right to open additional outlets in your area.

Most important, visit other franchises licensed by the same company you're interested in and talk to the owners.

In short, as in any new venture, do your homework and do it thoroughly.

> ### HAVE YOU CONSIDERED?
>
> - How much money you need to earn
> - How much money you want to earn
> - Growth potential
> - Risk
> - Liquidity of the business. How quickly could you sell the business if you needed to?
> - Location
> - Competition
> - Physical working conditions
> - Status and image
> - People intensity, or the degree to which you'll be required to interact with other people. Are you a loner, or do you get your energy from other people? Make sure the business suits your personality.
>
> Source: Lee Hecht Harrison

Consultants Abound

QUESTION: Who is a consultant?
ANSWER: Any unemployed person 50 miles from home wearing a three-piece suit and carrying a briefcase.

There is no shortage of consultants. It doesn't take any particular skill to call yourself a consultant: Just print some business cards and letterhead. Except in a few specialty areas, consultants do not need a state license or professional accreditation.

The reasons for starting a consultancy vary. Sometimes the incentive is purely defensive. Downsized managers and early retirees become consultants as a shelter against further job loss. The start-up and carrying costs are minimal. You establish your own work schedule and business plan consistent with your lifestyle objectives. Above all, a consultancy permits you to sell your expertise to others.

Consultants are independent contractors who work for various employers, with whom the consultant shares certain advantages based on the consultant-client relationship. The client pays no fringe benefits or payroll taxes, and the consultant receives tax advantages and business exemptions. For example, consultants (and any business owner or self-employed person), may shelter 15% to 25% of self-employment earnings, up to a maximum of $30,000, in the most popular types of Keogh retirement plans. This money is fully deductible regardless of how high your income is or whether you or your spouse is covered by another retirement plan. Another fully tax-deductible alternative is the simplified employee pension (SEP or SEP-IRA), which is even easier to set up and maintain than a Keogh. This allows you to contribute as much as 15% of your net self-employment earnings (in practice, about 13% of earnings after subtracting your contribution and any social security taxes) up to a maximum of just under $20,000.

A new form of IRA became available in 1998. The Roth IRA should be of particular interest to the post-boomer set. Although contributions to a Roth IRA are not deductible, this new plan has several advantages. While investors in a regular IRA or Keogh plan usually can't withdraw any contributions until they reach age 59½ without paying a penalty, Roth investors can take their own contributions out before that age tax- and penalty-free, thus offering a potential source of funds for business start-up. And all earnings from the Roth ultimately can be withdrawn tax-free, while those earned in regular IRAs and Keoghs are fully taxed. In addition, investors don't have to start withdrawing money from a Roth at age 70½, as regular IRA and Keogh investors do, and there are further tax-saving benefits that come with the death of the investor.

The Internal Revenue Service cautions employers to avoid using consultants on a nearly full-time basis while specifically excluding them from their tax roll and benefits program. Similarly, consultants should avoid any relationships with clients that appear to be a subterfuge designed to avoid tax consequences of full- or part-time employment. That could affect your status as an independent consultant and your ability to take business-related tax deductions.

Some 50-plus-set ex-managers flower as consultants, with incomes eclipsing their highest corporate achievements. They're able to both market their services and do the work. Other consultants are only marginally successful. In fairness to them, strong financial performance may never have been their primary business goal. To many retirees, a consultancy represents a way to stay active, maintain business or professional skills, and, most important, bridge the earnings gap between their former salaries and their retirement benefits and investment income.

> ## MUSTS FOR NEW BUSINESSES
>
> - Do your homework before going into business.
> - A preliminary, one-year, realistically written business plan is mandatory.
> - Avoid blue-sky proposals; they accomplish nothing. Remember, the planning is not an exercise in fiction writing. You want to set realistic and achievable goals.
> - Prepare a tentative operating budget.
> - Decide whether you need additional financing.
> - Decide whether you have the income to support the business and your personal needs during the start-up period.
> - Decide whether the business needs any other full- or part-time employees.

Birds of a feather sometimes stick together and build a consultancy based on their past experiences. For example, Hickok Associates—made up of retired senior-level financial managers and auditing partners from large accounting firms—offers a range of financially related services to small-to-midsize businesses and nonprofit organizations. And Multinational Market Services Group was launched as a consultancy by ten senior-level retired and downsized IBMers. It seeks to help companies anticipate and manage market changes.

SOME COMPANIES AVOID "DOUBLE DIPPERS"

Retirees interested in being consultants or part-timers often have to surmount an extra hurdle. They may discover that their former employer shuns hiring its own retirees as consultants, referring to them as "double dippers" because they have received a severance package to leave or are receiving a pension, as well as a consultant's fee. This is probably more true in the case of a severance or other buy-out agreement. Your company may feel that if you had really been needed, it shouldn't have paid you to go in the first place. So if it did, there's no reason to hire you back as a consultant.

If you're interested in consulting after retirement, check with your employer's human resources department beforehand to find out what your company's policy is.

Some Consultancy Guidelines

Many of the ABCs of consulting apply to other businesses as well.

THE CONSULTANT'S LIFEBLOOD IS NEW BUSINESS. The consultant's first rule of survival is to obtain business. Signing the first client is usually not the problem. Many times, it is a former employer. For example, if you're a recently downsized corporate public-relations director, your former employer has an immediate problem. Who is going to write its annual report—the one you wrote for the past five years? Your former boss contracts with you to write it. Client One surfaces. But a consultancy needs other clients and their business, perhaps writing annual reports for other companies or offering a range of public relations services. Where will they come from? You'll have to learn to market yourself.

AVOID DOING BATTLE WITH THE "BIG GUYS." Consultants come in all shapes and sizes. The large national and international firms can afford to be generalists, offering clients what seem like an unlimited range of services. Smaller consultancies need to pursue a different strategy because they can rarely compete across the board with the larger firms. The successful one-person consultancy wisely becomes a niche specialist and, more often than not, a sub-niche specialist, obtaining new business by convincing clients of its unique expertise.

THE CONSULTANT MUST BE SELF-SUFFICIENT. Many consultants go into business directly from a sheltered corporate environment. Staff assistants previously handled simple tasks like ordering stationery, maintaining office equipment and billing customers. A consultancy and, in fact, nearly all start-up businesses operate differently. Unless you do your own word processing, printing, photocopying, faxing and telephoning, nothing gets done.

THE CONSULTANT NEEDS TO KNOW MORE THAN HIS BUSINESS. Take nothing for granted. Know the basics of running a consultancy. You may be an authority in your area of business or technical expertise, but chances are you are not an authority on running a consulting business. Develop new checklists for yourself, and don't overlook things you most likely never did as a corporate employee, such as billing and collecting fees. Learn the consultancy fundamentals, well in advance of opening day. Take a trip to the library or bookstore and get an array of books and magazines on running a small business or consultancy (see the list on page 196). Talk with other consultants. And consider taking courses at a local college or community college.

How are your writing and presentation skills? Consultants need to express their views on paper and on their feet. Do you like to lead and command? Do your people skills need polishing? Only in Hollywood movies do consultants pound the table to make a point. Effective consultants use tactful terms such as "suggest" and "recommend," and they take charge by "counseling" and "advising." If you're too heavy-handed, you might be a consultant without any clients.

IT PAYS TO BE FRUGAL. Control your expenses. Remember, it might take up to 90 pays to get paid by some clients, and cash flow can be a problem. Don't overspend on equipment and supplies. One alternative is to lease office equipment and furniture for a few months with an option to buy. By then, you'll know whether you really need the equipment. Though you might have been taught in corporate America to "think big," this caveat works in reverse for start-ups. If you mail five letters a day, why rent an automated postal meter? Postage stamps will do.

Life in a Home Office

Whether you are an engineer or technician starting a high-tech company in the garage, or a marketer who launches a consultancy in the den, you've probably considered the immediate advantages of an at-home office. Folklore aside, not everyone wants or is suited temperamentally to work at home. Thomas Roeser, a retired Quaker Oats executive and now a Chicago-based columnist and public affairs consultant (profiled in Chapter 8), enjoys commuting from suburbia to a downtown Michigan Avenue office; and James Duffy, (profiled in Chapter 5), a corporate lawyer turned mystery writer, prefers walking a few blocks from his East Side New York apartment to a separate office to write.

But the at-home office has become an acceptable venue for many 50-plus-set consultants, as well as for start-up entrepreneurs of all ages. There are some obvious advantages, such as eliminating office rent, avoiding a commute and enjoying the ambiance that comes with a more informal business lifestyle.

There is also a slight home-office tax advantage, but it is hardly enough motivation for working at home. You can

---

HOW MANY AT HOME?

It is anybody's guess how many people work at home. Depending on the report, the number of at-home workers vary. IDC/LINK, a market researcher that conducts an annual survey, reports that the number of home-office households reached 34.7 million in 1997, a nearly 15% spurt from 1995. And it predicts 40 million at-home offices by the end of 1999. The home-office contingent consists of two segments: self-employed full- and part-timers, and corporate telecommuters and after-hours workers.

The 1997 survey shows that 25% of all small companies began as home-based businesses. They grow, and like college students, many leave home.

deduct only that portion of your home—determined by square footage or number of rooms—that is totally dedicated to an office. For example, if you live in a seven-room house and devote one room to your work, and your work only, then you may deduct 14% of the operating costs for the home, as well as 14% of your monthly mortgage payment minus the interest, which you deduct separately.

The availability of low-cost computers and communications equipment means that even the most remote home office is only microseconds away from customers and important business hubs.

Some Home-Office Do's and Don'ts

Before you start to redesign an attic or spare bedroom into an at-home office, alert yourself to some of the realities and myths of this workplace.

- **Find out whether your community, condominium or landlord permits your business to operate in the home.** Zoning regulations, for example, may prohibit posting a business sign or causing increased traffic or parking in front of your home. Environmental rules usually ban chemical processes in residential areas.
- **Working at home is more than trading in wing tips for Docksiders.** Business is still the order of the day, despite the informality of attire.
- **Can you resist the temptation of the 24-hour workday?** With an office across the hall from your bedroom or in the basement, you may find it hard to separate your business from your personal life. Modern technology can help you on that front, too. After-hour telephone calls can be intercepted by an answering machine, and the fax machine can operate unattended.
- **There's no reason to be a recluse.** Unless you are a peripatetic consultant who only returns to the office to read mail, make telephone calls and prepare reports, you may find it lonely working at home. Make a point of meeting regularly with business friends and associates. Also, keep up with trade and business groups, and attend their meetings. This serves another

THE AT-HOME OFFICE TOOL BOX

There's no need to overspend when you equip an at-home office. Buy the basics; avoid the frills. A good basic start-up package costs under $5,000, including the following items. Add to this stationery and other consumable supplies, such as paper clips and note pads. Also, budget for office furniture, though this is one area where you can make do with what you've got or purchase used. Once again, don't be excessive.

- **A few years ago, a modem was an accessory.** Now it is a basic communications tool. New software packages require enormous amounts of memory, so don't try to save a few dollars by buying too little RAM or your computer will be obsolete before you know it. Is a laptop more appropriate for your business?

- **Word processing and application software packages.**
- **Dot-matrix, inkjet or laser printer.** Consider the advantages of each machine. Dot-matrix printers have a letter-quality mode and are cheaper to operate, but the final product doesn't look quite as professional as inkjet or laser output.
- **Self-standing fax** or one that is integrated into desktop telephone equipment or your computer.
- **Photocopier,** though for occasional copying it may be just as well to take a break and run out to the nearest copier.
- **Telephone answering device or voice-mail service** from the phone company. Depending on the business, a cell phone is no longer an optional communications device.

purpose, too; networking usually leads to new business prospects.

- **Don't be defensive about your at-home office.** If you are a consultant, you are supposedly an expert in your field. The location of your office was rarely a factor when you were considered for the assignment before. It's no more important now that you work for yourself at home.
- **Avoid routine household chores during working hours.** This is another angle on separating business from home life. It is as fundamental as refusing to answer the family telephone during business hours. It went unanswered when you worked outside the home, so why change the pattern? The same guidelines apply to trees that need pruning and closets that plead for cleaning.

Changing Careers

areer-changing is not rampant among the 50-plus set. Compared with the baby boomers, who are making 180-degree career changes—from teaching to medicine, or from investment banking to the ministry—the 50-plus retiree or downsized manager tends to use existing skills as the basis of a new career. The reporter becomes a publicity writer, or the teacher resurfaces as a corporate trainer—hardly dramatic, but career-changing nonetheless at this or any other age.

The media thrive on publicizing the dramatic career changes: the physician who leaves medicine to enter law school (see Erle Peacock's profile in Chapter 4) or the medical technician who realizes her high school ambition and enters medical school at 57. But professional schools and education statistics confirm that the number of students over 50 is rather small. Few are prepared to face the academic demands, the dual rigors of learning a new trade and obtaining professional accreditation, or the cost in time and money.

When someone does switch to an entirely different field, it usually involves shifting gears from a demanding job to a less pressured one. That's the route taken by Roald Young, a one-time bank officer in Arizona who described himself as burned-out and seeking a fresh start after a 32-year banking career. He took a nine-month program in restaurant management and has been employed as a cook and baker ever since. After so many stressful years in banking, he says, "I feel as if I've been let out of the cage."

Teaching as a Career Change

How many times have you said or heard a friend say, "I'd like to teach when I retire"? If you pursue it, you'll soon discover that colleges and universities are inundated with employment applications from would-be teachers in the 50-plus set. They, like the corporate world, have few openings as they reduce the size of their faculties. What about elementary and high schools? Perhaps they might be interested in a chemist as a science teacher or an editor to teach English composition? Practical as it sounds, the concept never flourished, and the U.S. Department of Education acknowledged a teacher shortage. The shortfall was projected because of an increase in the school-age population and a corresponding rise in teacher retirement.

A few years ago, educational leaders reasoned that the entry of mid- to later-life career changers into education could offset that shortage of classroom teachers. A number of colleges developed teacher-training programs to attract to the classroom early military and corporate retirees, particularly those with engineering and scientific skills. And 41 states plus the District of Columbia have implemented alternative teacher-certification programs to quicken the transition. To date, approximately 75,000 teachers have been licensed this way, says Emily Feistritzer, president of the National Center for Education Information. California, New Jersey and Texas lead the way with aggressive alternate certification programs.

SUGGESTED READING

OWNING YOUR OWN BUSINESS

- Friedman, Robert. *The Complete Small Business Legal Guide* (Dearborn Financial Publishing, 1993)
- Cohen, William. *The Entrepreneur & Small Business Problem Solver* (John Wiley & Sons Inc., 1990)
- Zoghlin, Gilbert. *From Executive to Entrepreneur* (AMACOM, 1991)
- Burstiner, Irving. *The Small Business Handbook* (Simon & Schuster, 1994)
- Anthony, Joseph. *Working for Yourself* (Kiplinger Books, 1995)

WORKING AT HOME

- Edwards, Paul and Sarah. *The Best Home Businesses for the '90s* (Tarcher/Putnam, 1994)
- Gordon, Kim. *Growing Your Home-based Business* (Prentice-Hall, 1992)

FRANCHISING

- Green, Carol. *The Franchise Survival Guide* (Probus Publishing, 1993)
- Mutsky, Gregory, and the Philip Lief Group. *The Best Home-Based Franchises* (Doubleday, 1992)
- *Franchising: The Complete Guide to Evaluating, Buying and Growing Your Franchise Business* (Dearborn, 1998)

CONSULTING

- Shenson, Howard. *The Complete Guide to Consulting Success* (Enterprise/Dearborn, 1993)
- Kelley, Robert. *Consulting: The Complete Guide to a Profitable Career* (Macmillan, 1986)
- Tuller, Lawrence. *Cutting Edge Consulting* (Prentice Hall, 1992)

FOR MORE INFORMATION

For additional information on how to obtain public-school teaching accreditation, contact your state's department of education. If you're interested in receiving information on teaching careers in independent schools, contact the National Association of Independent Schools, 1620 L St., N.W., Washington, DC 20036 (202-973-9700; www.nais-schools.org). The NAIS holds an annual conference that includes several days of workshops on such topics as leadership, teaching and learning, and career paths. The conference provides an opportunity to network with administrators and teachers from independent schools across the U.S., as well as the Employment Exchange, a job bank that can put you in touch with potential employers.

Dr. Feistritzer, who has surveyed what has taken place in alternative teacher certification since 1983, has found that the teacher shortage anticipated by the Department of Education has not developed because the supply of teachers has risen to meet demand. There has been an outpouring of interest in the teaching occupation from numerous sources—people in other careers who wish to get into teaching; military personnel facing retirement or being relieved of their duties due to the projected downsizing of the military in the next few years; former teachers trying to get back into teaching; people who trained to teach some years ago but never taught; and current students.

AN ALTERNATIVE. Don't be too disheartened. Teaching opportunities are more readily available for the 50-plus set in independent schools, where state licensing and accreditation are not required, and prior work and professional credentials are accepted in lieu of teaching experience. What's more, the independents, unlike most public schools, can set salaries for entry-level teachers based on past work experience. Want to know more about alternative certification? Contact the National Center for Education Information at 4401 Connecticut Avenue, N.W., Washington, DC 20008 (202-362-3444; www.ncei.org).

Some Who've Taken the Leap

Some of the victims of downsizing or forced early-retirement plans have been soured by their recent corporate experiences. Others in the 50-plus set are seeking a challenge commensurate with their age. As an alternative to uncertain corporate employment, they reenter the workplace on their own terms—as their own bosses. The profiles you are about to read illustrate a variety of ways to start all over again in your own business.

GETTING A GOOD HEAD START

Mitch Badler

CORPORATE PUBLIC RELATIONS EXECUTIVE TURNED NEWSLETTER PUBLISHER

Long before the reality of downsizing dawned on most managers, Mitchell Badler was playing "what if" games. What would happen if he lost his job as a corporate public relations executive with Eastern Airlines or, later, with Amax, a mining and energy conglomerate? Mitch's newsletter-publishing sideline was his cushion. For nearly 20 years, he worked evenings and weekends on first one, then two newsletters dealing with imaging technology. How Mitch handled his dual careers could serve as model for the early wave of baby boomers who are pushing 50, anticipating the possibility of downsizing and plotting their next move.

For more than 20 years, Mitch combined days of corporate life with nights and weekends of self-employed publishing. All the effort paid off.

"It began for several reasons," said Mitch. "To see if I could make money, to keep my hand in editorial work since my PR responsibilities were becoming increasingly more managerial, to have a possible fallback because I instinctively distrusted the corporate world, and for something to do, if and when I ultimately 'retired' from the corporate world. Looking back, it worked on all four counts."

Mitch started to hedge as far back as 1969, when he launched the *Microfilm Newsletter* as a part-time activity. He learned about the microfilming industry earlier in his career as the editor of several photography trade magazines. At the time, Mitch was working as a public relations writer for Eastern Airlines.

Even though his career had proceeded steadily uphill, Mitch had good reason to distrust corporate employment. Prior to Eastern Airlines, he had worked four years for Citibank editing the bank's publications. "When I was at Citibank in the mid to late 1960s, I got caught in a power struggle between two executives competing to be CEO." His boss straddled the fence during this succession fight. Realizing that the new head of public relations would reorganize the department, Mitch left before it all happened. He joined Eastern Airlines and stayed with the company until it relocated to Miami.

Mitch was hired by Amax and a few years later was named its director of public relations. In the 1980s, Amax suffered a reversal in fortunes and lost $2 billion in three years. Heads rolled, but Mitch kept his. In 1991, he left Amax after it was acquired by another mining company. He retained a lawyer and negotiated a favorable severance package in the form of a one-time payout along with lifetime health care benefits.

Other executives might have looked for another corporate job, but not Mitch. "I decided that enough was enough. No more corporate jobs; I don't need that anymore." Neither did Mitch need to retire. He held some valuable trump cards.

Throughout his corporate career, *Microfilm Newsletter* "went its merry way" as a sideline endeavor. In the early days, it was strictly part-time for Mitch and an assistant, another moonlighter, who handled circulation. After a few years, Mitch hired a full-time office administrator while he continued to write and edit the newsletter.

As a part-time editor and publisher for more than 20 years, Mitch's life was hectic. "My routine until I left Amax was to work on the newsletter at least one full day each weekend and most evenings." His one-newsletter company grew. He introduced a biannual industry directory. He started, then dropped, two other newsletters, and in the late 1980s, he spun off *Imaging Technology Report*, previously a supplement in *Microfilm Newsletter*, as a separate monthly. The newsletters were Mitch's long-term security blanket, a way to control his destiny. It was employment that he totally controlled.

Newsletter publishing rarely conflicted with his corporate life. He spent vacations at microfilm industry trade shows. There were few problems with either Eastern Airlines or Amax because the subject of the newsletters did not conflict with his line of work at either company.

When he left Eastern Airlines, Mitch briefly considered becoming a full-time editor and publisher, but the income from newsletter publishing wasn't sufficient to support his family. It did, however, produce enough supplementary money to send his children through college and graduate school.

FINALLY FULL-TIME

The corporate workplace behind him, Mitch now works as an editor and publisher five days a week. His staff consists of a full-time office manager, a part-time circulation manager and freelance editorial correspondents. Compared with his former schedule, Mitch notes, "it's like being on a part-time holiday. I actually have time to watch TV at night. I get to work about 10 in the morning and I'm home about 6." He supplements his newsletter income by tapping his investment portfolio, so that his lifestyle hasn't changed since he left Amax.

Looking back at his dual corporate and publishing careers, Mitch knows that the relationship, though complex, gave him career options. "My employer never owned me on a full-time basis. Above all, publishing was something that did not depend on the whims of other people."

As he got older, it furnished still another benefit. "I never considered retirement. I'm not a golfer. I want to keep my hands in something useful."

MID SEVENTIES AND HE STILL INVENTS

Harry Wayne

CORPORATE RESEARCH DIRECTOR TURNED OWNER OF
A PRODUCT-DEVELOPMENT COMPANY

Harry Wayne has been an inventor his entire adult life. He officially retired from the corporate world when he was in his mid fifties, and because retirement wasn't really his goal, he launched right into entrepreneurship. Harry and his wife, Elaine, started Wayne Engineering as a product-development company.

An electrical engineering degree from the Illinois Institute of Technology and a master's in physics from Northwestern University provided Harry with a technical education, though he was motivated to be something more than a theoretical scientist, as his many patents show. He was granted 28 patents while working as a researcher with J.B. Seeburg, the jukebox manufacturer, and with Chicago Aerial Industries, maker of sensors and controls. As research director of Beltone, a producer of hearing aids, he received patents for the first all-in-the-ear hearing aid.

Harry was also a pioneer in fiber optics, and his invention, a device for photographing the moon, was used on NASA's first Surveyor mission. Harry's list of accomplishments includes inventing an instrument for measuring the moisture in houseplant soil.

Harry's focus on optically related products began with his daughter. He hired his kids' friends. The family lived with punch presses in the living room.

He also holds the first patent for a color copier. "I even created a toy lie detector. It was a good product, but it proved too dangerous to have in the home." More than 100,000 units were sold.

New-product development has been Wayne Engineering's forte, with a keen eye to developing and manufacturing sports-vision and general-vision equipment, as well as other products. Harry's interest in inventing and producing optical products arose when one of his four children developed an eye problem that doctors were unable to solve. Some Chicago optometrists said Harry's daughter had an ocular motor disorder and prescribed vision exercises. Though somewhat skeptical about following the regimen, he built a facility in the basement of his home to help his daughter exercise her eyes. Her condition improved, and today she is a nurse.

A series of vision-related products followed, such as the Talking Pen, an instrument with special-education applications that sounds a tone when the user strays from a predetermined path, and a peripheral-awareness trainer, a multipurpose training instrument. Having found its niche, Wayne

Engineering has introduced more than 25 new products, unveiling at least one new item a year.

THE FAMILY THAT WORKS TOGETHER

Wayne Engineering began in the Wayne home. For the first two years, Harry and Elaine financed the business out of savings. They employed friends of their children, then in college, to do some assembly work. "Our home was somewhat of a social embarrassment," Elaine said. "One of our daughters was engaged, and we invited the boy's family to the house on Sunday. We had punch presses in the living room and equipment all over the place. It must have created some impression. Fortunately, we also had good relations with our neighbors. Nobody ever complained about delivery trucks coming to our house or shipping crates in the driveway." After two years, the Waynes started to pay themselves a regular salary, and after seven years, in the early 1980s, they moved the company into its own engineering and production facility.

Wayne Engineering's management formula is simple: "I invent and Elaine manages," says Harry. Now employing eight people, the company is unusual in its approach to designing and manufacturing products. "We make everything ourselves. We do our own silk screening, make computer circuit boards and do software programming. Very little of our work is subcontracted." His approach is based on experience as a tool-and-die maker, physicist and electrical engi-neer, and a desire to totally control the quality of his products. Harry and Elaine jointly handle sales and distribution, and in a typical year they travel to professional meetings and trade shows throughout the U.S. and overseas to introduce new products.

A WONDERFUL RETIREMENT

When Harry left his last employer after 15 years of service, he was without a pension because the company went out of business. Elaine, a social worker by training, invests in stocks and mutual funds as they continue to build their retirement portfolio.

The Waynes have four married children—a son and three daughters. None has sought the education or training to head a technical product-development company. Harry and Elaine, however, are planning for the future when they can no longer work. Selling the business is always a possibility, but Wayne Engineering, like most businesses closely identified with the owner, will have little resale value. Why buy Wayne Engineering when Harry Wayne is no longer working there?

Harry continues to table any thoughts of retirement. "After you've worked all your life, when you can make a career change into something you really enjoy doing, that is my definition of retirement." For his inventions, the Sports Vision Section of the American Optometric Association awarded Harry with its first-ever industrial appreciation award. He responded to the award by thanking the optometrists for a wonderful "retirement."

THE EDUCATOR EDUCATES HIMSELF

Thomas Lutton
COAST GUARD CAPTAIN TURNED TEACHER

The day after Thomas Lutton retired from the Coast Guard, he started a new career in education. Tom's move was actually a pretty natural segue from his career. After 30 years as an officer, a role that required him to train personnel, he finds teaching to be an equally rewarding career. "You're on stage for 50 minutes at a time. You're the entertainer, and it takes a lot of preparation to be good. Since I'm a late starter, I'm also more enthusiastic than most teachers my age."

Growing up, Tom wanted to be an engineer. By chance, during his senior year in high school, he saw a Coast Guard Academy brochure, "Career for Tomorrow." It represented an opportunity to combine many interests in a single career.

While he spent many years working in line, staff and technical assignments, Tom was continually looking ahead, planning for the future and engaging in personal "what if" exercises. As a result, he earned a bachelor's degree in electronic engineering from the Naval Postgraduate School in Monterey, California, and a master's degree in engineering administration from George Washington University, both of which were suitable for

> **Despite his training and technical skills, Tom encountered the usual impediments to this postretirement career change. Persistence paid off.**

conversion to the corporate marketplace.

After 20 years of service, Tom was eligible to retire, but a number of assignments were too challenging to refuse. One was as the Coast Guard's chief of avionics, a job that requires a technical knowledge of both electronics and aviation. When he finally retired at age 50 as a captain, Tom was chief of staff for the Atlantic Area, based on Governor's Island in New York, a command responsible for all Coast Guard operations east of the Rocky Mountains.

A few years before his 30th anniversary, a normal time for many senior officers to retire from military service, Tom began to play "what if" again and considered future job opportunities. "Working within the military-industrial complex would have been the logical step, but I soon discovered that the jobs they offered were only a civilian counterpart of my Coast Guard jobs. There were few new challenges.

"Above all in looking for work, I did not want to face the day and say, 'What's next?' I wanted to have a plan." Income wasn't an issue in Tom's decision-making because he had a full Coast Guard pension and investments, and his two sons were grown. He could afford to take an entry-level job.

FINDING A WAY IN

Tom was interested in teaching. Besides having had some specific teaching assignments in the Coast Guard, he says, "It's part of an officer's life to teach because you're held responsible for training personnel in your command." In his last year in the Coast Guard, Tom attended a job fair conducted by the National Association of Independent Schools (see page 197). By then he had discovered that even with his technical background, it would be difficult to become certified to teach math or science in a public school. He encountered the kind of bottleneck in obtaining state teaching certification that too often foils otherwise capable applicants.

"My credentials were more readily accepted by independent schools where state licensing and accreditation are not required. What's more, independent schools are more flexible because they are not tied into the unions or large administrative systems. The pay is also based on academic skills and life experiences."

When he started in his new career in education, it wasn't in the way he had hoped. "I received several offers. I wanted to get going and do something." He took a job as business manager of Woodmere Academy, an independent school on Long Island. "While I wanted to teach science and math, Woodmere thought my past executive experiences were better suited to administration." A year later he got the chance to teach math, along with handling some administrative assignments, when he transferred to the Collegiate School in New York. Two years later he left Collegiate to become a full-time math teacher at the Buckley School, another New York City independent school.

THE TEACHER STUDIES, TOO

To further increase his professional skills while teaching at Buckley, Tom enrolled in the doctoral program at Columbia University's Teachers College. He was part of the Operation Plowshare program, now ended, that was designed to help military retirees like Tom train for second careers in education.

For his doctoral thesis, Tom drew on his experiences as a Coast Guard officer. He surveyed more than 1,600 retired or eligible-to-retire senior-level Coast Guard officers regarding their interest in teaching math or science in the public schools. About half of the 1,000 officers who completed the survey said they would like to teach, preferably math or science. Tom's findings supported the popular view that qualified math and science teachers could be recruited from nontraditional sources such as the military and other industries.

The results of the survey paralleled Tom's own experiences. "Teaching is an excellent second career, whether you're in the military or industry. But training should start before you retire. In fact, you can't get started early enough. In anticipation of retirement, start taking education courses and complete your [state's] teaching requirements." While math and science teachers are usually in demand, he warns other early retirees that there is less interest in English and history teachers.

Tom's training did not stop with his doctorate. He subsequently received a second master's degree, in curriculum development, and pursued another in math education, both useful professional tools for someone who hopes to teach indefinitely.

Tom left Buckley nine months after his wife died. He moved to northern Florida, nearer to his two sons and their families. Now remarried, Tom does some substitute teaching, which leaves time for traveling with his wife.

FROM BANKING TO ACADEMIA

Leo Rogers, Jr.

BANK PRESIDENT TURNED COLLEGE ADMINISTRATOR

When Leo Rogers, Jr. found himself unemployed for the first time in 27 years, his career search was guided not by an out-placement firm but a passage from the New Testament: "For unto whomsoever much is given, of him shall be much required: and to whom men have committed much, of him they will ask more." This verse from the book of Luke inspired the search that led to Leo's job as a college administrator with Fairleigh Dickinson University.

Leo's résumé is impressive, summarizing a record of high achievement in business and community life. But at age 55, Leo's bubble was deflated. The bank where he was president fell victim to the collapsed metropolitan New York real estate market.

Leo's marketing know-how had helped to build the bank to a network of 74 branch offices. "I went into banking in 1965 as a marketer, and my job as president resulted largely from my work in marketing, advertising and public relations. I was part of the changeover when banks decided to alter their image and the ways they did business."

When the bank went into receivership, Leo's credentials attracted the interest of other banks, but he wanted to change

> **Leo didn't just get a lucky break. He focused on his needs and desires, updated his computer skills, and got out there and hustled.**

fields and careers. Throughout his banking career, Leo also served on a number of boards of trustees, including a hospital, Rider University, and Blue Cross and Blue Shield of New Jersey. Those experiences later propelled him to look for a job in the nonprofit field. "I realized that nonprofit work is just as challenging as business, but there is more of an opportunity to serve others."

Fortunately, Leo qualified for early retirement from the bank, which gave him options in seeking a new job. "I didn't want a job just to say I got one. I wanted to be selective at this stage in my life," Leo says. "As a starter, I determined those things I like to do, do well and would like to continue doing in the future."

As an executive, Leo had been somewhat pampered by the corporate lifestyle. Without employment, these perks were no longer available. He had to learn some basic office skills just to hunt for a job. "I was computer-illiterate. Others did that type of work for me." Carole, his wife, is a freelance writer who does her own word processing, and she encouraged him to develop computer skills and coached him. "I learned WordPerfect and Lotus 1-2-3. I did my own letters. This was important because I would most likely be joining an organization where these skills would be necessary. I had to learn how to make ordinary things happen because nobody else will do them for you."

Nearly eight months of networking and interviewing started to produce results. Leo was offered a job with one of the nation's larger outplacement firms to counsel other downsized senior-level executives. Though the business wasn't nonprofit, he liked outplacement because even there he would be involved in helping others. But after living and working in New Jersey most of his life, he was reluctant to commute to New York. "I took several practice commuting runs to the firm's offices. If they had offered me the same job in their New Jersey office, I would have taken it, but I had little interest in commuting three hours each day."

A GREAT BREAK

During the same time that he was negotiating with the outplacement firm, Leo received an offer from Fairleigh Dickinson University to direct the George Rothman Institute of Entrepreneurial Studies.

"I had had my eye on this job ever since I left banking. I had heard about a possible opening from the university's president. When I learned officially that the institute's director was leaving, I called the university, received a job description and sent in a résumé along with a cover letter summarizing why I felt I was suited for the job. I was told that a search committee had been established, then I got a letter saying that I

was among 75 very qualified candidates for the job. I said good-bye to this one. Then another letter told me that they had screened the résumés and that I was one of six selected to meet with the committee."

Leo met with the committee and soon afterward learned he was one of two finalists. "They invited me back to make a presentation. I worked on it for four days. The day after the outplacement firm's offer, I heard that the Fairleigh Dickinson job was mine."

Similar to his banking days, Leo serves as the institute's key representative in the New Jersey business community. Now, however, he's an advocate of entrepreneurship rather than banking services. Leo is also the institute's representative in the academic community. He finds that getting things done here differs greatly from business. "At the bank, we would meet, discuss an issue and reach a decision. In a university, one needs to be patient because decision-making is more collegial and takes much longer."

Since Leo has been at Fairleigh Dickinson, he's succeeded in making innovations in the curriculum. All undergraduate and graduate business school students are now required to take a course in entrepreneurship, a recognition of the growing interest on the campus in small-company management. Another innovation is a certificate-of-entrepreneurship program for small businesses and entrepreneurs.

All in all, it's been a satisfying transition. Leo had longed to return to academia since he left it in his twenties. Now he feels like he's home again.

FROM KODAK TO COFFEE

John Salviski
CORPORATE MANAGER TURNED FRANCHISEE

John Salviski took early retirement from Eastman Kodak at a time when many corporate managers and professionals were revising résumés, looking over their shoulders at younger up-and-comers in their company or still struggling to climb the corporate ladder.

He could have found another corporate job or bought an existing business. John took a gamble. He switched from corporate manager to entrepreneur, bought the rights to two Coffee Beanery franchise locations, relocated from New England to South Carolina and, though not as much as he might have wished, has changed his lifestyle.

Just eight months after he left Kodak, John opened his first Coffee Beanery in an upscale downtown Charleston mall. "After working for 26 years, I wanted to get going again." Shortly thereafter, he opened a second Coffee Beanery store in a Columbia shopping center, about 120 miles west of Charleston. He subsequently expanded in Columbia by introducing a free-standing Coffee Beanery cart in the shopping center's food court. It's a distance from the main store and sells only a limited number of products. The first two outlets cost him

Signs said John would be "good for a long time" at Kodak. Wrong. But he took the early-out offer and ran with it. He's still running.

$25,000 each, not including the cost of the stores, set-up and inventory.

John found that his sales management experience at Kodak had carry-over value. "Even though I worked for a large company, I knew how to manage, prepare and control a budget, and work with people." Operating two stores has increased his work load, but he applies his corporate managerial style to that dilemma, too. "My job is to pick good store managers and train them. When I was a Kodak district manager, I was responsible for sales in several cities and for training the local managers. I didn't think there was any reason why this approach wouldn't work in franchising." And it has.

John spends a considerable amount of time with vendors. It's one way to improve the bottom line. Though contractually required to buy coffee from the franchisor, he is free to purchase other products—mugs, aprons, tea, electric coffee makers and teapots—from his own sources. If John purchased these items directly from the Coffee Beanery, it would charge him an additional 10% for the same merchandise.

John captures the names and addresses of his credit card customers, especially those who are among the 4.5 million tourists who visit Charleston each year, and markets directly to them. From its inception, this marketing tactic has boosted his monthly profits.

NO GUARANTEES

John is a product of corporate America. Except for one-year job teaching school after graduating from the University of Buffalo, he spent 26 years with Kodak specializing in selling bar-code, electronic-imaging and optical scanning devices. In 1991, he was sent to a management development program at Duke University. "No question about it, I thought I was good for a long time at Kodak." The next year he was gone.

No sooner had he returned from Duke than Kodak offered an early-retirement package to 8,900 managers and professionals. "The plan was too tempting to reject. I was only 48, but it brought me up to 100% of my retirement benefits, guaranteed life insurance, a social security override to age 62 [Kodak pays John an annual amount equivalent to what he will get from Social Security beginning at age 62.], and free medical and dental care for life. When I added things up, I couldn't afford to stay. So I took a lump-sum distribution, rolled one-half into an IRA and decided to put the rest into my own business."

In looking at career options, John was not anchored to the metropolitan New York area. He owned a home in Weston, Connecticut. His wife, Maureen, a medical assistant, has a highly portable skill, and two of their three children had already graduated from college. "My first reaction was to look

for another job, and I actually got two offers, one in Chicago and the other in Allentown, Pennsylvania. The jobs were interesting, but they were in the wrong direction."

RECOGNIZING THE BUSINESS OWNER WITHIN

As part of his buyout package, he was assigned to an outplacement firm. Some of the outplacement tests confirmed John's aptitude for self-employment. He had confidence resulting from over 25 years of sales and sales management.

John started to consider career alternatives such as buying an existing business or a franchise. When an offer to buy one business fell through, John, at the suggestion of the outplacement firm, turned to franchising. He read how-to publications that evaluate franchises. "Up to then I was never conscious of franchises. It's like buying a new car. You never notice the model on the road until you buy the same car."

In reviewing different types of franchises, John hadn't narrowed his search to any particular field, but he avoided businesses that would demand 100% of his time—a tune he would eventually change once he was actually in business. His lifestyle plans included playing golf on a year-round basis. If the Salviskis were to move from Weston, they wanted to go south, to a warmer climate.

Several newspaper articles on the growth of the gourmet coffee market piqued his interest. One article listed the four major retail franchisors. John read their literature, analyzed the comparative data on the four franchisors on his home computer and reviewed the findings with his financial adviser. He visited coffee franchise sites, talked with their owners and, a few months later, acquired his first Coffee Beanery franchise. He selected Coffee Beanery on the basis of a favorable cost analysis, income potential for himself, the quality of the product, what it would cost to build a store, talks with other franchisees, management's attitude and the locations available. Both John and Maureen had visited Charleston a number of times and liked the community, and Coffee Beanery wanted a franchise unit there. Within the year, they had moved and John had his first Coffee Beanery in operation.

A GROWING ENDEAVOR

John hopes to operate a few more franchises, Coffee Beaneries or others, within easy driving distance of Charleston. Having multiple units has its advantages. The lessons he has learned in opening the Charleston store—how to train employees, develop customer lists, select vendors and establish a bank credit line—were applied in Columbia and will be again elsewhere.

The Salviskis' income is based on income from the Coffee Beanery stores, savings, and the one-time windfall of profit they enjoyed from the sale of their Connecticut home. Rather than rolling over the profit into the purchase of their new home in South Carolina and deferring the capital-gains tax that was in effect when he sold the house, they chose to take the profit and pay the tax. (Because John was not yet 55, he wasn't eligible to take the then-current one-time exclusion of $125,000 of profit from the capital-gains tax, even if he had wanted to.) John can't touch his pension funds until he turns 59½.

John's earlier fantasy about working part-time has vanished indefinitely. He works at least five full days a week. He plays golf on the weekends and occasionally at 7 A.M.—before going to work.

DOING BUSINESS IN THE DESERT

Al Croft

PUBLIC RELATIONS EXECUTIVE TURNED INDUSTRY CONSULTANT

For decades, Al Croft read *Arizona Highways* and dreamed of someday living in the Southwest. The dream began to become reality when Al and his wife, Irene, bought a second home in Sedona, Arizona, about 110 miles north of Phoenix. Though they rented it out to start with, someday, Al mused, it would be their full-time residence and the site of an at-home office for Al. He put the next phase of his plan into effect, somewhat unexpectedly, the next year. At 61, he left his job as a senior manager in the Chicago offices of one of the nation's larger public relations firms following what Al describes as a "difference of opinion" with some of the firm's managers. A 25-year veteran of the public relations agency business, Al had already decided to use his agency management skills to start his own consultancy, one that focused on ways to better operate and manage public relations firms.

Al invested his severance package in office equipment and direct-mailing costs to launch his consultancy the day after he left his job. His objectives, then and now, were to offer a range of management services to public relations firms of all sizes, work at his

> **A public relations veteran, Al took up counseling the counselors on better ways to operate and manage their PR firms.**

own pace, and, above all, live and work in Sedona. Being familiar with PR agency management and marketing practices, he felt confident that there was a ready market for his niche specialty.

The Crofts waited four years, long enough for their daughter to graduate from college, before they moved to Sedona. By then Al's consultancy was well established. Sedona became their permanent residence and the headquarters of A. C. Croft & Associates.

Sedona, a community of approximately 10,000 people, is a tourist haven, drawing more than three million visitors annually. The mountain landscape is the prime attraction. A number of other small consulting firms in other fields call Sedona home for reasons similar to the Crofts'. Most of these consultants find that they can carry on their work as easily in Arizona as in a metropolitan center.

The area is hardly isolated in the computer age. Computers and telecommunications have eliminated geographic isolation, and overnight delivery services are omnipresent. "On a trip to Falstaff, 32 miles away, I counted nine United Parcel Service trucks making early-morning business deliveries along the route," says Al. His clients are scattered throughout the U.S. and can be readily serviced through personal visits, e-mail, fax and telephone.

No formidable snags occurred in moving from Chicago to rural Arizona, and Al has found many pluses. "Clients like to take a few days off from their offices and meet with me in a leisurely fashion in Sedona. Some come from as far as Washington, D.C."

The nature of Al's work has changed dramatically from his days as a PR agency executive. "I don't do public relations for companies. I counsel the principals of public relations firms, write an occasional speech for an agency executive, represent a buyer or seller in an acquisition, conduct in-house account-management seminars and produce a monthly newsletter. Everything I do is geared to help agencies market their services and manage their operations more effectively."

Marketing is critical to building his client base. Toward that end, Al actively promotes his business with a newsletter on management strategies for PR firms, and a guest column that he writes on agency management for the *Public Relations Quarterly*. Al also sponsors the Sedona Roundtable, an annual two-day management workshop for the principals of public relations agencies. He has written a book, *Managing a Public Relations Firm for Growth and Profit.*

Being a niche specialist has certain advantages. He can bill clients up to $200 an hour. And, of course, because he is working at home his overhead is minimal. Irene, who has a sales and marketing background, handles the administration of the Sedona Roundtable.

Even with his good cash flow, Al had to make some adjustments when he became self-employed. "After 35 years of regular paychecks and several years as an independent consultant, I'm still not used to not knowing exactly what my income is going to be for the next month, or from year to year."

By corporate standards, Al might appear to be semiretired. "I work as hard as I want to, traveling outside the area two to three times a month. I make almost as much money as I did in the agency business but I also play tennis a few times a week. The most important thing is that it keeps my brain active. I couldn't imagine being retired, and I'm not the volunteer type. Why retire, when I like what I'm doing and I'm making money at it?"

While Sedona has a reputation as a retirees' haven, Al points out that he's not alone in his active lifestyle. "One of my tennis partners is a 76-year-old plumber. After two hours of doubles, he goes back to work for another six hours."

RETIREMENT "A BLESSING IN DISGUISE"

Paul Sharar
YMCA EXECUTIVE TURNED CONSULTANT TO NONPROFITS

Imagine the difference: Rising at 6 A.M. and commuting into New York City by train or bus every workday for 30 years. Or traveling from the bedroom to an at-home office and cutting out at midday for a three-hour bike ride.

Even if you're not a bicyclist, it's not too hard to appreciate why Paul Sharar, a former program manager for the New York YMCA, is enjoying this part and more of his "retirement." Though his retirement came five years earlier than expected, Paul's career specialty has become the key part of a consultancy practice that allows him to continue working for his former employer from home.

Operating from an office in a converted bedroom, Paul by design works 40% of a normal workweek. He could handle additional assignments, but his current workweek meets his professional and financial objectives. He continues to work in the areas he knows best, spending about half his time in the field working with clients and researching projects, and the balance at home analyzing the data on his computer, summarizing the results and writing reports.

Paul's career as a YMCA executive opened innumerable paid and volunteer consulting opportunities. He also knew

> **Paul returned to his "root" skills and consults with the YMCA and other clients gleaned from his community contacts.**

other players and the marketplace through such community groups as the United Neighborhood Houses of New York City and the New York City Human Services Taskforce. The YMCA continues to be his most active and consistent client, and he has conducted a number of market research and membership studies for YMCAs throughout the tri-state area (New York, New Jersey and Connecticut). He limits assignments to those that he can handle on day trips.

It might have seemed inevitable 40 years ago that Paul would end up working with youth and youth-related programs. In his hometown of Clinton, Iowa, both parents worked for this community of 35,000 people: his father as the founder of the community college and his mother as a teacher. His parents' involvement with people and community helped steer Paul toward a related career.

After he graduated from Ohio Wesleyan University with a degree in psychology and religion, he went on to Boston University to receive a master's degree from its School of Theology. Paul then became a youth director at the Ridgewood, New Jersey, YMCA. The New York City YMCA recruited Paul to direct counseling and testing services as well as corporate executive development and management programs. He earned a PhD in organizational psychology from Columbia University in 1974. His doctoral dissertation was based on a youth training and employment program involving a Fortune 500 company. And for a number of years he taught counseling at New York University.

By the late 1980s, the YMCA, like many other nonprofit organizations, faced deep operational and financial problems. Recession reduced its income and the New York City YMCA had to cut staff. "My goal was to retire at 65, but when the staff reductions took place five years earlier than I anticipated, it proved to be a blessing in disguise. I could retire on nearly full salary. I was given a choice: I could leave, get six months' additional pay and go through outplacement, or work another six months and have several thousand more dollars added to my pension plan. I stayed on for six more months.

"While I was preparing to leave the YMCA, I thought about a number of job options—teaching and counseling for outplacement firms—but I decided to stay with my root skills in counseling and my work with community groups. I'm a career psychologist by training and experience, so I simply followed the advice that I would give to others my age: Make a list of things you like to do and things you feel qualified to do. And try to find paid or volunteer assignments that use your past skills."

Paul could have retired altogether. His retirement plan was excellent. He owned his home in Glen Rock, New Jersey, and his four daughters were self-supporting. His wife, Helen, did not work. Instead, Paul decided to use his knowledge of YMCA operations and other nonprofits to launch a consultancy based on his ground rules.

"Why retire when consulting keeps me active in my profession, and it provides us with a source of additional savings and a chance to travel more frequently?"

TEAM RETIREE: LEAVING THE CORPORATE LIFE BEHIND

Erford Porter II

PURCHASING EXECUTIVE TURNED PETROLEUM INDUSTRY CONSULTANT

When Erford Porter II turned 50, he was tiring of corporate life. After 28 years with Union Carbide, Erf's career was anything but lackluster. But even with his corporate success, he felt that he had become a corporate nomad and in the process had made himself expendable. Erf took the bull by the horns. He opted for early retirement and set up Supply Planning Associates Inc., a nationwide consulting firm with a contemporary pitch. Erf demonstrates how a one-person consultancy can provide sophisticated services to major companies.

Besides personally handling consulting assignments, Erf is the firm's primary salesperson, traveling about 40% of the time, marketing SPAs' services to companies who purchase, market or transport raw materials, fuels and electricity. About 90% of the work is repeat business.

If SPA had an organizational chart, it would show that Erf is the only full-time employee. The balance of his staff consists of three part-timers—his wife, Jane, who is the bookkeeper; a secretary; and a computer analyst. Nearly all of SPAs' work is done at client sites. The "paperwork" and communications between the firm's offices and the consultants is handled by e-mail.

About 50 professionals a year work under SPAs' umbrella as independent contractors. Most are retired chemical engineers in their sixties (a few are in their seventies) who have escaped from retirement. Though they want to continue working to maintain their technical skills, many feel that social security income caps limit the amount of work they can do (see the discussion of earned-income limits on page 272).

Erf stresses informality as a way to increase creativity. In a memo to associates, he said: "Supply Planning Associates Inc. was started on a handshake understanding, based on trust, a pattern that has not changed over the years." Erf's philosophy may reflect a reaction to his many years of experience with big company administrative practices.

When Erf graduated from Alfred University with a degree in chemistry, he spent an obligatory two years in the Army to fulfill an ROTC commitment. He joined Union Carbide as a technical sales repre-

> **Erf is founder and the only full-time staffer among the some 50 consultants who work for Supply Planning Associates. He runs his business informally from home.**

sentative, and during the next 15 years he worked in field sales, sales management and corporate training.

In the mid 1970s, the company assigned him to the hydrocarbons purchasing group, where he was initially responsible for crude oil, offshore trading and shipping, and hydrocarbon planning and forecasting. Erf received successive promotions. In the early '80s, he coordinated Union Carbide's worldwide hydrocarbon needs and played an active part in assessing the feasibility of and developing the supply portfolio for numerous cogeneration power projects across the U.S. Little did Erf know then that a number of the suppliers and other companies he studied would someday become clients or associates of his consulting firm. Until he left Union Carbide, Erf had never even considered going into his own business. "Why should I when I was doing challenging work?"

That changed when Union Carbide began downsizing and slated a 25% reduction in force in Erf's planning group. Erf and his cohorts acted first and planned their own departure; they all retired or left for jobs elsewhere. Erf's retirement offer did tack three years onto his age and service, but this didn't quite bring him up to full retirement benefits.

Once he made the decision to leave, Erf wasn't sure of the next step. "I knew I was good at keeping a number of balls in the air, and from what I knew about consulting that was an important criterion for success." Erf's marketing, corporate-planning and business-development positions gave him an edge, as

did his corporate-training experience. Erf says the clincher in his decision-making was the support and encouragement of two of his former bosses. So, in 1987 Erf established SPA as a consulting firm. He recruited about eight other independent consultants to work with him on a project-by-project basis, and he went into business. He looked for work and found little interest. Nobody called.

REDEFINITION PAYS OFF

Erf and his associates recognized the need to differentiate themselves from other players in the consulting field. They studied market needs and changed their direction from general consulting to a specialty—the strategy and planning behind buying and selling of hydrocarbon raw materials, feedstocks and fuels. This is what Erf and his associates knew best, and the phone began ringing. "We were very fortunate to develop a unique group of clients with distinct interests. They don't compete, but their broad strategic interests are quite compatible with what we have to offer."

Using personal savings to capitalize the business, Erf started SPA in his home, then moved the following year to an outside office when he found the business was interfering with household routines. He moved to a new house where loft space was converted to an office over the garage. Erf and his wife moved in about the time that Greenwich, Connecticut, in recognition of the growing trend to home-based offices, changed its ordinances to permit consultancies and other small service businesses to operate from home.

NETWORKING IN TUSCALOOSA

John Blackburn

UNIVERSITY ADMINISTRATOR TURNED CONSULTANT

John Blackburn describes his "retirement" in glowing terms, but don't let him fool you. He's as busy today as he was 20 to 30 years ago. "Retirement is the greatest experience in one's life. It's the first time in my adult life that I'm working purely for the fun of it.

"I retired voluntarily, even though I was not asked to. I saw too many of my friends who stayed on the job too long.

"When my friends ask me for advice on retirement, I tell them to go out and do something they always wanted to do. Forget about how much money you will or won't make. Remember, it's as important to keep yourself mentally fit as physically fit."

When John stepped down as vice-president for educational development at the University of Alabama, he jumped right into his own consulting business. "When I retired, I would have lost my sense of direction if I hadn't set up my consulting firm, which is a full-time job and then some.

"All my adult life, on Monday morning I woke up and said, 'I wish I didn't have to go to work today.' Then I reached the point where I didn't have to. I woke up on Monday and said, 'What am I going to do

now?' I could play tennis, which takes an hour, or I'd take a two-week trip. I found I would rather be working."

John was raised in Missouri during the 1930s. The family farm did not produce enough income to pay for him to go to college, but World War II and the GI Bill made it possible. John graduated from Missouri Valley College in 1950, received a master's from the University of Colorado in 1952, and 16 years later he earned a doctorate from Florida State University.

John's entire career was spent in college administration—as a student counselor at Florida State, dean of men at the University of Alabama, vice-chancellor of the University of Denver, and back again to the University of Alabama as vice-president for development. As the university's chief fundraiser, he raised more money in ten years than the university had brought in during the previous 148 years.

When John decided to retire, he began to make postretirement plans. His initial interest was to start a computer software business, relating PCs to home education. "I still like the concept, but I've put it on the back burner. It would have taken too much

> *After he retired as a college administrator, John formed his own company to do what he knows how to do best: fundraising for nonprofits.*

of my money and time."

Instead, John drew on what he knew best. "I use my college know-how and apply it to consulting and fund raising. Most nonprofit organizations need money, but few know how to get it. Others need managers but can't afford a permanent staff. We raise the money and do the staff work. Plus, getting into consulting calls for a minimum cash investment." Blackburn Educational Technologies, which operates from a Tuscaloosa corporate office park, has a staff of four including John, and his wife, Gloria, who works full-time and gets an honorarium as the firm's treasurer, and two part-timers. "To date, I've not made too much money. I've invested in some staff people and new computer equipment. But, more important, I'm having fun doing what I like to do."

John is a natural networker. He uses his Tuscaloosa and University of Alabama credentials to attract a client base of community and educational organizations that includes an antebellum museum, a local historical landmark and a medical research center. His long-time membership in national groups has paid off. When the American Association of University Administrators was looking for a firm to provide back-office services, it named Blackburn Educational Technologies. John was familiar with the association's operations, having been one of its officers and directors for 15 years.

AND, NOW, "RENT-A-DEAN"

John looks to new services that his company can offer. He is developing an interim administrative service designed for colleges and universities that want to fill a staff academic or administrative vacancy on an interim basis. John notes that universities are becoming more cautious about rushing job searches lest they result in bad appointments. Rather than leave the job vacant or move someone in temporarily from another job, they can "rent a dean" through John. "It is the perfect assignment for a retired administrator or professor who wants to work for only six to 15 months until a full-timer is on the job."

John finds that universities, unlike corporations, are not averse to hiring retirees on an interim basis. "It's a practical way to avoid giving the wrong person lifetime tenure and not being able to get rid of him." This way the search for a competent pro can be made at a more leisurely pace.

A NATURAL MOVE FOR A SPECIALIST

Thomas Cassidy
PUBLISHING SALES MANAGER TURNED INTERNATIONAL BOOK MARKETER

"I'm in my mid sixties and I'm making more money today than I ever dreamed," says Thomas Cassidy, president of Cassidy and Associates, the nation's leading book-publishing sales representative in China.

Tom averages about two trips a year to China, spending about one month in residence on each visit in Beijing and Shanghai. From his New York office, he visits with distributors and special-book project officials and readies the upcoming season's sales and marketing program. Starting with Random House as the first customer, Cassidy and Associates now represents nearly 50 small to large American and European travel, reference and mass-market fiction publishers. He even sells for John Wiley & Sons, his former employer.

Cassidy and Associates has two offices: one in New York and the other in Beijing. Computers and fax machines connect them. When Tom went into business, he knew nothing about computers and had little time to learn. "I bought books on word processing and spreadsheet analysis, and taught myself." In the New York office, Tom and his small, Chinese-speaking staff prepare catalogs, advertising and other promotional materials in English as well as classical and simplified Chinese. He has a working knowledge of the Mandarin dialect.

> **With a few shoves from interested parties, Tom set himself up to do business—in China and Hong Kong.**

In 1988, Tom's career in publishing seemed to be at an end. Due to corporate restructuring, he had just lost his job as international sales manager with Wiley. He found job-searching through headhunters who specialized in the publishing field unproductive. With his headful of gray hair and hefty salary requirements, he says, "publishers didn't want to meet my requests. It was my outplacement consultant who goaded me to consider going into business on my own representing publishers in China. After all, in the past 11 years I had been to China 24 times representing Wiley. It seemed like a natural fit."

When Tom graduated from Fordham University, he expected to become a lawyer. He completed two years of law school but dropped out to return home to Stamford, Connecticut, to help run a family insurance agency. Tom then started his own insurance brokerage firm. Though he liked the independence of being his own boss, he never fully enjoyed the business. In his early thirties, Tom made a career change into book publishing and joined Macmillan's sales staff. By the time he left the company

16 years later, Tom had spent his last four years there in international book sales.

Tom joined Wiley in 1976 in its international division, traveling the world. Little did he realize that he would be meeting many of the players who would become useful in starting his own business.

"I sort of expected something to happen to my job because Wiley was being reorganized and the work of the international division was being distributed throughout the company. Up to now, I had never considered going into business again. Even though I was yearning to do something more creative than I had been doing at Wiley, I knew what it was like to run a business."

When his suspicion became reality, Tom took his severance in a lump sum along with a rather small pension that didn't become effective until he was 65. He doesn't receive medical benefits through Wiley but is covered through his wife, Jeanne, an executive at MTV Networks.

A GREAT LEAP THAT MADE PERFECT SENSE

"My wife encouraged me to go into business. 'You do what will work for you,'" she said. With his employer-provided outplacement consultant, Lee Hecht Harrison, and Jeanne cheering him on, Tom bought a plane ticket for China and set himself up as a freelance sales representative. He met with his contacts at the Chinese Ministry of Education and with the book distributors, sources of potential purchasers of books, and began to represent foreign pub-

lishers to markets in China and Hong Kong. Because Tom already knew the marketplace, it took him only two weeks to get his first customer.

"I used my severance money to help bankroll the business, set up offices in New York and China, and to pay my expenses in China. I borrowed from my IRAs and my two grown sons, and I refinanced my home. It was costing me about $8,000 a month to get by." Tom retired his loans after seven years and is now saving for the time when he might consider retiring.

Starting a business from scratch, as discussed earlier in this chapter, can be disastrous for many people in their late fifties and older if they sacrifice their retirement savings and have little time to recoup them. Tom, however, is an exception. He had something to offer: accumulated know-how and skills in an identifiable niche. Tom has been selected for special projects by the World Bank to sell books in China, and, in a sort of role reversal from book seller to book buyer, by the Chinese Ministry of Education to purchase books for 150 universities. In both instances, the payment is in U.S. currency.

"I never believed that when I was in my sixties I would be doing so many important things. But I was lucky. I had a niche specialty and I took advantage of it. I followed my outplacement consultant's advice that I would have a better chance to do it on my own. But when you've lost your job and you're older, there's not too much you can do. The specialists have a decided advantage."

Escaping From Retirement

FOR SOME OF US, RETIREMENT CAN'T COME TOO soon—but when it does, it isn't what we expected. Consider my friend the manager, who retired at age 61 and moved to a rented apartment in Florida. Soon after, he went to the swimming pool and was greeted this way by one of his new neighbors: "Welcome to God's waiting room." That capped his impression of his new life. Disillusioned, he returned to New York the following day, and asked for and got his old job back. My friend escaped from retirement.

Then there's Henry Nigrine, who spent 32 years as a violist and retired with a full pension from the New York Philharmonic. Though he didn't want to go back to work full-time, he missed the routine and excitement of orchestra life. Each season, Henry now looks forward to filling in as a substitute violist. He receives advance programs, looks for music and conductors he enjoys, and indicates his availability. Then he waits to hear if there's an opening among the Philharmonic's 12 violists.

Early retirees and others who thought their working days were over are changing their tune. They are finding ways to go back to work, either as their sole pursuit or as one part of their retirement portfolio.

This is hardly a surprise to Dr. Letitia Chamberlain, who directs

New York University's Center for Career, Education and Life Planning. She finds it normally takes people at least two to three years to settle down into a retirement lifestyle. They want to stay productive and above all be active. Some in the 50-plus set want to return to the workplace to fill an income shortfall between their cost of living and their retirement income. But many others miss the challenge of the workplace and its camaraderie, or they want to maintain technical and professional skills. As Dr. Chamberlain observes, there are many people who are not satisfied working as volunteers or hobbyists. Employment is what they knew and what they like. Paid work is their antidote to a "retirement lifestyle."

The Sidelines Weren't for Him

Take Dr. Lawrence Walker, a downright miserable spectator. When Larry retired in 1991 as superintendent of schools in a rural North Carolina county, he learned some real-life lessons about early retirement. Following his retirement, he managed a statewide political campaign for a friend. His friend lost the election, and Larry was out of work.

Fortunately, Larry's expenses were pretty well controlled. He and his wife, Mary, a nurse, owned their home in Yanceyville, a town of 2,000 and the county seat of Caswell County. Too young to collect social security benefits, Larry had a pension, health care benefits and savings. He worked a few hours each day in a convenience store that he had acquired in 1987 as an investment and had had others manage, previously working there only once in a while.

But Larry's retirement would soon turn into a litany of disappointments.

"I got tired of tending my garden. Working in the store full-time was not for me. My golf is miserable, so it made me feel even more miserable.

"My hobbies, collecting antique fountain pens and old American coins, are not the type of activities that keep you too busy.

"Neighbors and friends hearing that I retired thought I left due to illness. Their concerns made me concerned. I'm an optimist but I got down.

"I missed the camaraderie of school work. I found that I was starting to lose education and government contacts. It doesn't take too long to be out of the loop, and once you are out of it it's hard to get back in.

"I also did some consulting, but it's not the same as a full-time job. I needed a more solid base of operation."

Larry attended a meeting of retired school superintendents and returned home depressed. Mary said: "You don't belong in that group yet."

Less than two years after retiring and as a result of networking among his fellow educators and government officials, Larry was reactivated as executive director of the Central Carolina Consortium, one of seven regional groups established in the state to link schools at all levels with industry and business. To take the job, he had to temporarily forgo a pension based on 33 years' service as a North Carolina educator. When he leaves or retires from his present position, he can resume receiving pension payments. As a first step toward increasing their mobility, Larry and Mary sold the convenience store because neither of them wanted to work in the store any longer, even on a part-time basis.

> **POINTS TO REMEMBER**
>
> - Boredom is an important factor that draws the 50-plus set back to work.
> - Many retirees miss the challenge, competition and collegiality of the work place.
> - There's stiff competition to get part-time or interim management jobs.
> - Avoid obsolescence. Upgrade your skills before looking for a job.
> - If you're willing to accept a lower salary, you can use that as an advantage in the marketplace.
> - To get a job, you need to learn new ways to "sell" yourself to a potential employer.

It's Great to Be in Demand

Reactivation—and for some retirees that's exactly what it is—can be a big motivator for midlevel managers and corporate chieftains alike, especially for those who would otherwise find serving on corporate boards and doing volunteer work a poor substitute for the excitement of the actual workplace. And for some institutions and companies, reactivating retirees is a boon.

The Hastings School of Law in San Francisco, for example,

has long recognized the value of employing retired law professors. More than 50 years ago, Hastings mobilized the talents of retirement-age law professors when a faculty shortage occurred during World War II. The school recruited retirees from other law-school faculties. Nearly all had been stars in their fields before their first retirement. What started out as an interim solution at Hastings during the mid 1940s became a long-standing tradition, called the Sixty Five Club. While the club is not expected to survive since its last three faculty members are in their eighties, Hastings is not abandoning the idea. The school has created a new program to attract senior professionals. The criteria for appointment as a Distinguished Professor are similar to those of the Sixty Five Club. The difference is that no minimum age requirement is imposed. Senior faculty, regardless of age, will be considered for the openings if they offer "substantial experience in legal education" and are nationally recognized leaders in their fields. And other law schools have created similar programs, at least in part due to the fact that tenured faculty can no longer be forced to retire due to age.

Everyone Can't Be a CEO

Paul Rizzo retired from IBM in 1987 at age 59. In 1985, he had been considered a prime candidate to become CEO. Passed over, he left two years later and was named dean of the business school at the University of North Carolina, where he had graduated and had been a football star 40 years earlier. In mid 1992, Paul retired from UNC. Within four months he was summoned back to a troubled IBM on a full-time basis to help run the company as a "counselor and adviser" to then-chairman John Akers. When Akers was ousted, Rizzo was promoted by the new CEO, Louis Gerstener, to vice-chairman. Rizzo retired from IBM a second time at the end of 1994.

Stanley Gault's career has a similar ring. After he lost out to Jack Welch for General Electric's top job in 1980, Gault left the company at age 54 and joined Rubbermaid in Wooster, Ohio, as its CEO. Eleven years later, he retired from Rubbermaid after building it into one of the nation's most admired and profitable companies. Like Rizzo, who could have spent his retirement years joining boards of directors, Gault wanted to stay active in business, but he had achieved all he had hoped for in corporate America. He intended instead to put his talents to use in a small venture-capital start-up. But after Goodyear approached him several times to take charge, Gault finally conceded because he wanted to see this troubled American tire maker survive.

Unfortunately, the mobility that permits older, high-profile CEOs to slide into another corporate job does not readily apply to many 50-plus-set managers. Odds are stacked against their getting another high-paid job in corporate America.

There are some notable exceptions: As midlevel management jobs are abolished, it is ironic that hands-on technical, financial and sales people are in far greater demand than their immediate supervisors. To confuse matters even more, it is easier to place a 54-year-old downsized executive who has worked for four different companies over 27 years than someone who has worked for a single employer during the same period. Compared with a decade ago, says executive recruiter Randall Bye of Elinvar, a Raleigh, North Carolina–based executive search firm, employers now seek managers who have worked for several companies and have proved that they have the flexibility to adapt to different types of corporate cultures.

> ### BACK IN THE SADDLE—WHEN?
>
> There's a split of opinion on returning to the workplace after downsizing or retirement. Though your family's finances may influence the decision, take your choice: Start the job search immediately. Get to work just as quickly. You don't want to lose momentum and skills. Out of sight, out of mind rules the day for these folks.
>
> Or take a break. You might tell yourself: "I haven't had more than an annual ten-day vacation since I graduated from college 35 years ago. I'm going to take a few months off, enroll in a course in music theory and just relax. Then I'll start looking for a new job."

A New Way of Doing Things

Bleak as the situation may appear, it does not mean there is a total absence of job opportunities. Rather, the rules have changed and early retirees need to acquire new habits. The job-search winners are those applicants who recognize the need for new tactics and have updated their game plan.

Outplacement consultant Temple Porter of the Raleigh Consulting Group advises clients to disregard old road maps in favor of nontraditional and alternative routes to the job market. "Clients need to show their 'unique leverage' in terms of reputation, special knowledge and professional skills. If a company is looking for a turnaround expert, Lee Iacocca assuredly doesn't need to revise his résumé [to apply for the job]."

Avoid shooting yourself in the foot when trying to get a new job, says James Challenger of the outplacement firm Challenger, Gray & Christmas. He finds that job prospects for the 50-plus set rise when they follow a few simple rules:

• Sell them on your expertise.

• Look and act young.

• Avoid looking dowdy at interviews.

• Address yourself to the employer's needs, not your own.

• Above all, do not announce personal timetables such as a desire to work for only four more years before retiring.

STAYING SMART IS THE KEY. Executive recruiters and business professionals all agree that keeping yourself informed through educational courses and corporate training programs is a key factor in your business success after the age of 50. In its study, *The Untapped Resource,* the Commonwealth Fund urges corporations to offer training to older workers so they can continue to make as great a contribution to the organization in later years as they had in earlier ones. If your company doesn't offer training programs or have a tuition-reimbursement program, check with local universities to see if they offer courses at a reduced cost to seniors. For less expensive courses, check with your local public school system for information about its adult extension program and with community colleges in your area.

WORKING FOR LESS. Susan Lawley, who downshifted from a $250,000 human-resources position on Wall Street to open the Camelot Group, a human-resources consulting firm in Fairfield, New Jersey, maintains that escapees from early retirement often find jobs if they are willing to take a significant pay cut, are flexible in geographic location and can offer a variety of skills. Money is always a bargaining tool, especially in negotiating with small- to midsize companies. While a controller for a billion-dollar company might easily have earned a six-figure salary, such a salary rarely exists in a $20 million to $40 million company. Compared with a younger person seeking the

> ### THE ABCs OF GOING BACK
>
> - Don't think like a "Pampered Corporate Baby " (see Chapter 1).
> - You will need to convince a company that it should hire a 62-year-old.
> - Don't expect to get a prestigious title.
> - Be prepared to do hands-on work, even in a manager's job.
> - Be prepared to accept less money than you are used to.
> - Above all, be flexible.

same job, the 50-plus-set applicant should expect to work for less money, should not require a full menu of fringe benefits and should not feel a loss of identity if the job does not carry a title. The bottom line for a midsize company? Getting a senior executive at a bargain price.

If you're still concerned about the loss of prestige in taking a new job, then the best suggestion is to start your own consultancy or other business (see Chapter 7). You become your own boss and can act accordingly.

Alternatives to Business as Usual
The National Executive Service Corps—
Nice Work If You Can Get It

The Senior Careers Division of the National Executive Service Corps Executive Search Division deals with retirees every day who have had their retirement fling and want no more of it. They seek employment for different reasons. Money, though a factor, is usually not the driving force, although many retirees find they need additional income to maintain a desired lifestyle. One retiree noted that "after my retirement, I thought all of my knowledge would be locked up like concrete in the brain, never to be used again."

A RÉSUMÉ TELLS THE STORY

The résumé for the 50-plus set is practically an art form.
- The résumé is a selling document. Tell the reader what makes you unique. Simply put, what assets do you bring to the party?
- Above all, give readers a fast career overview. Stress what happened over the past 20 years. The rest is ancient history, and chances are the earlier ones were stepping-stone jobs anyway.
- A similar rule applies to education. List the college degrees, but you can omit the graduation year.

Like so many organizations dealing with retired executives and professionals who want to return to work, the NESC has a backlog of 3,000 résumés of applicants and a comparatively small number of interested companies. NESC applicants who get an assignment in the nonprofit sector typically receive between $40,000 and $80,000 per year, which is frequently 25% or less of their former salaries. Applicants placed in the for-profit sector can see salaries ranging from $60,000 to $150,000 for corporate jobs that are usually with family- or closely-held companies with sales under $250 million. What most companies receive is a seasoned manager at a bargain price. What the retirees get is a return to the workplace, where they find the excitement, challenge and sense of achievement that they miss in retirement.

David Willcox, who directs the NESC program, says that retired managers often feel uneasy during job interviews, particularly when they're twice the age of the person conducting the interview. In reviewing job opportunities, he tells retirees that they must be willing to do hands-on work, often using sub-skills from their past career. As a former human-resources manager, Willcox cites his own employment history. "Like a number of people I place, I'm using a subset of my human-resource skills. In this case, it is executive search."

Perry Vascallera was an NESC placement who wanted to escape from retirement. After 40 years with the Yellow Pages division of Reuben H. Donnelley, Perry retired when the company downsized. "I was out of work for more than 13 months. I enjoyed golf and tennis but missed the involvement of business. There was no concern about paying the bills. But I still wanted to achieve. The job I got at Bunn Coffee Service was perfect."

The company needed him to put together a new sales compensation plan and to upgrade its sales training program. Perry took the job when he was 65, and 19 months later he completed the assignment and "retired" from Bunn. "I worked five days a week, often ten hours a day. I got the job because I had the sales background, came cheap, did not need benefits and already had my pension." If nothing more, the Bunn job and the feeling of being useful helped to ease Perry into retirement somewhat more gracefully than when he had been ushered out of work five years earlier. What's next? "Perhaps I'll stay retired, but if some interesting work comes along, I might take it."

FOR MORE INFORMATION. Contact David Willcox, Managing Director of the NESC's Senior Search Division, 120 Wall St., New York, NY 10005 (212-269-1234; www.escus.org).

The Part-Time Alternative

Make sure you know the differences between part-time and temporary work. The part-timer is a company employee, while the temporary worker may be an employee of a temporary agency. Part-timers, depending on the number of hours worked, may receive fringe benefits and may be eligible for paid vacations.

Some employees, particularly those who are nearing retirement age and whose skills are in demand, are switching from full- to part-time employment as part of a phased retirement plan. Some part-timers are also working at home, participating in the trend toward telecommuting for workers of all ages. The best bet for part-time employment at your skill level is your present employer, but make sure that you make arrangements while you're still on the payroll. Chances of making as good a deal are lessened once you've retired.

Also make sure that you won't reduce your eventual pension pay-out by continuing to work part-time with your present

TEMPING FOR YOUR EMPLOYER

Several years ago hospitals began building their own in-house lists of temporary workers to call on when they found themselves short-staffed. Some other businesses have followed suit. For example, Travelers Corp., the insurance company, set up a job bank to keep track of retired employees who are interested in temping for the company. Travelers now places several hundred temporary workers in assignments each business day, from unskilled production to professional. Check with your current or previous employer to see whether it offers a similar program or has a similar need that you could meet.

employer. This might occur, for example, if your pay-out was based on your highest salary for three consecutive years within the last five years of your employment. If the years when you're working part-time count in the five-year period, you run the risk that your highest-paying years—presumably those when you were working full-time—will drop out of the equation.

If part-time employment is for you, decide what form will best suit your needs. Permanent part-time positions are a traditional option in which the employee spends something less than a full workweek at the job, however the employer defines that.

Job sharing allows you and another employee to split a full-time job. Perhaps you will work two days and your co-worker will put in three days, allowing for some overlap time so that you can communicate about details and divide projects.

With telecommuting, thanks to advances in communications, many people find it possible to perform the same tasks they used to do in an office setting at home. You cut back not only on your hours but also on commuting time and daily expenses.

With each of these options there are disadvantages, so find out more about them and consider your choices carefully.

Once you know what sort of arrangement you think you want, you have to convince your boss that it's a good idea. Things you should consider include:

• **Can your job realistically be redesigned to fit a part-time schedule?** How often do you need to meet face-to-face with your employer, clients, and others? What will you be giving up? What difficulties, if any, might you be imposing on your employer?

- **What are your unique talents or skills?** Why is the employer better off keeping you on part-time instead of hiring someone new full-time?

- **What is your employer's attitude toward part-time work?** Are there other employees on the payroll who have worked out similar arrangements? What sort of precedent for other employees would you be asking your employer to set? Is there a set policy regarding flexible work schedules? What will happen to your salary and benefits?

- **If others have gone the part-time route before you, what happened to them?** What hurdles did they encounter? How are their arrangements working out? What do you need to know to be successful?

- **Who makes the decisions?** Draw up a political game plan: Who can you safely use as a sounding board for your idea? Who should you discuss it with first in earnest? Who can you appropriately and effectively enlist as an ally if you anticipate a touchy situation?

ONE WOMAN'S STORY. At age 63, Jane T. was more fortunate than many of her retired contemporaries. A year after she retired, Jane went back to work three days a week, earning proportionately what she had been paid as a full-time employee. She also continued to receive her pension payments. What made Jane so attractive to her employer, a communications conglomerate, was her specialty as a legal expert on rates and tariff law.

When she retired, Jane's job was eliminated, but her responsibilities were divided among

THE NEW NETWORKS

You might not have expected to find a job through a local church or synagogue, but about 5,000 congregations nationwide are holding networking meetings each week. These informal networks are great sources of leads, support and job-searching tips. Their success in helping people find new jobs has been remarkable, so check for such a group in your local area and join up.

other staff members. Then, due to changes in government regulations, there was an increase in the tariff-law work load. The company needed professional assistance. It viewed retaining a law firm to handle the work as too costly an alternative, and when it tried to hire a replacement for Jane, it found the candidates lacked expertise. When it approached Jane, the company found a perfect candidate who was "thrilled" to return to work as a part-timer on an assignment that lasted another 30 months.

You Don't Have to Be a Kelly Girl

When you think of a "temp," you probably remember those folks who came to your office to answer the phones, do copying or perform some other necessary but low-level chore when a regular staff member was ill or on vacation. The temp field has expanded, however. Now there are executive temporaries who are politely referred to as interim managers. Kelly Services, employer of the temps you used to know as Kelly Girls, has a professional and technical division.

Even with the growth in temporary employment services, temps account for only about 2% of the total workforce. The National Association of Temporary and Staffing Services found in its 1997 survey that 10% of temporary workers are 55 and over. The difference these days is the increase in the number of professional and management positions being filled by temps, many of whom are in the 50-plus set.

THE PROS AND CONS OF INTERIM MANAGEMENT JOBS

THE PROS
- Provides income during a job search
- Allows for networking while on the job
- May be a good fit with your lifestyle
- May lead to a permanent position
- Could fill in while doing own consulting or self-employment work

THE CONS
- Can make it difficult to actively search for a permanent position elsewhere while on the job
- Odds are low for placement
- Income can be uncertain
- No benefits

Source: Executive Recruitment News

The temporary service field has benefited from downsizing, early retirement and the trend toward getting retirement-age employees off the corporate books. As staffs are thinned, though, the corporate appetite for skilled managers and professionals hardly diminishes. Thus the birth of interim-management firms that place managers, staffers and professionals in temporary jobs. These agencies supply the manpower and handle all the employment-related paperwork. The typical assignment lasts from three months to one year and pays from $30 to $75 or more an hour. The U.S. Department of Labor reported that the 1997 median weekly salary for temps was approximately $329.

Kennedy Publications, which tracks corporate human-resources trends, notes that "candidates over age 55, who may have difficulty finding permanent posts, are, with their wealth of experience and expertise, ideal for executive temporary placement. As the demand for specialization increases along with the need for mentoring, their skills increase in value. Interim executives who are placed are often over-qualified for the jobs they perform."

Still, finding an interim-management job is a long shot. The best candidate for a temporary job is the highly skilled professional in a niche that's in demand, but the chances of getting a job as an interim executive are slim at any age and even slimmer if you're graying. The ratio of applicants to job openings on file for people of all ages at the 110 or so firms that specialize in placing management and professional personnel is staggering, sometimes as high as 1,000 to 1. Dahl-Morrow International, a suburban Washington, D.C., specialist in the information systems and communications fields, has little difficulty attracting candidates to add to its database of more than 12,000 names. At Dahl-

---

MORE ON INTERIM PLACEMENT

If you'd like to meet with an interim-management firm in your area, consult the Yellow Pages of your telephone directory, or request a listing of member firms from the National Association of Temporary Services, 119 S. Saint Asaph St., Alexandria, VA 22314 (703-549-6287; www. natss.com/staffing).

Another helpful resource is The Association of Part-Time Professionals, 7700 Leesburg Pike, Falls Church, VA 22043 (703-734-7975; www.mbinet .mindbank.com/aptp).

Morrow and most other interim-management firms, temporary assignments range from three months to one year.

Even with the low odds of success, retirees should not overlook the interim-management market. If nothing else, you might find it more efficient having an employment firm market your talents than trying to reach out to corporate America yourself. If you get an assignment, you may find it gives you a leg up on a permanent job—if that's what you really want. At Dahl-Morrow, 50% to 60% of the interim-management assignments turn into full-time jobs. Because it's such a good opportunity for the employer to get to know the worker's skills, there's a growing trend toward converting temporary positions to full-time.

Forty Plus Organizations

When your company doesn't offer outplacement services or you have already used your allotment, where do you turn? Since 1939, when Forty Plus of New York was founded, offices in 21 other U.S. cities and metro centers have been established to help managers who are age 40 and over to find a job. Don't

VISIT A LIBRARY

Job seekers will find public and university libraries to be gold mines of employment-related information. You can expect to find plenty of how-to and self-help career books, as well as countless directories and even on-line information that may be of help. Don't hesitate to ask the reference librarians for help in locating the information you want. That's what they're there for. The New York Public Library, for example, has taken an additional step to help patrons. It established Job Information Centers in a few branches with a collection of books, directories, pamphlets and periodicals covering such topics as career choice, the job search process, résumé writing and interviewing techniques. Job counseling is also offered at its branch in the Bronx. Call 212-340-0836 or access the Library's Web site at www.nypl.org.

THE FORTY PLUS CLUBS

CALIFORNIA

Forty Plus of Northern
California
7440 Lockheed St.
Oakland International Airport
Oakland, CA 94621
510-430-2400

Forty Plus of Northern
California
1150 N. First,
San Jose, CA 95112
408-288-3555

Forty Plus of Southern
California
3450 Wilshire Blvd.
Los Angeles, CA 90010
213-383-2301

Forty Plus of Southern
California
23172 Plaza Pt. Dr.,
Laguna Hills, CA 92653
714-581-7990

Forty Plus of Southern
California
8845 University Center Lane,
San Diego, CA 92122
619-450-4440

COLORADO

Forty Plus of Colorado
3842 S. Mason St.
Ft. Collins, CO 80525
303-223-2470

Forty Plus of Colorado
5800 West Alameda
Lakewood, CO 80226
303-937-4956

Forty Plus of Colorado
2555 Airport Rd.
Colorado Springs, CO 80910
719-473-6220, ext. 271

DISTRICT OF COLUMBIA

Forty Plus of Greater
Washington
1718 P St., N.W.
Washington, DC 20036
202-387-1582

HAWAII

Forty Plus of Hawaii
126 Queen St., Suite 227
Honolulu, HI 96813
808-531-0896

MINNESOTA

Forty Plus of Minnesota
14870 Granada Ave.,
Suite 315
St. Paul, MN 55124
612-683-9898
(voice mail and fax)

NEW YORK

Forty Plus of Buffalo
701 Seneca St.
Buffalo, NY 14210
716-856-0491

Forty Plus of New York
15 Maiden Lane
New York, NY 10038
212-233-6086

OHIO

Forty Plus of Central Ohio
1100 King Ave.
Columbus, OH 43212
614-297-0040

PENNSYLVANIA

Forty Plus of Philadelphia
1218 Chestnut St.
Philadelphia, PA 19107
215-923-2074

TEXAS

Forty Plus of Dallas
13140 Coit Rd., Suite 300
Dallas, TX 75240
214-783-2300

Forty Plus of Houston
2909 Hillcroft, Suite 400
Houston, TX 77057
713-952-7587

UTAH

Forty Plus of Utah
P.O. Box 9820,
480 27th St.
Ogden, UT 84409
801-399-2181

Forty Plus of Utah
1550 N. 200 West
Provo, UT 84603
801-373-7500

Forty Plus of Utah
5735 S. Redwood Rd.
Murray, UT 84145
801-269-4797

WASHINGTON

Forty Plus of Puget Sound
300 120th Ave. N.E., Bldg 7
Bellevue, WA 98005
206-450-0040

CLUES TO WINNING INTERVIEWS

You're scheduled for a job interview. Now don't blow it.

- Act your age but don't overdo it. Start by leaving the grand children's pictures and similar bric-a-brac at home.
- Watch the narrative. Avoid talking about 1970 or even earlier business trends. The date might predate the interviewer's own date of birth.
- This is a job interview, hardly the time to tell "war stories" about the old days.
- Talk in the present and future tense. Emphasize what you've done recently and what your goals are.
- Above all, be yourself. The interviewer is well aware that you didn't graduate from college in 1980.

be misled by the organization's title. A large proportion of members are in their fifties and some are in their early sixties. Membership is limited to men and women who earned more than $40,000 a year in either a managerial or professional job. The organization will not get you a job, but it will provide the road maps leading to it. Run by its members as a nonprofit organization, Forty Plus offers low-cost executive-search services, computer training in word processing and spreadsheet analysis, résumé preparation, guidance on performing in a job interview, and psychological counseling. Depending on locale, members pay an initial entry fee that ranges from $200 to $450, plus a monthly fee of $30 to $75. In New York City, a member pays a one-time $100 application fee and a $299 membership fee plus $75 monthly dues. The fee entitles the member to all the organization's job-preparation services at no additional cost. There are also lots of "look-alike" organizations that offer similar self-help programs.

How They Resurfaced

Some people retire eagerly, looking forward to a leisurely lifestyle. In a little while—a few weeks, maybe a few months later—boredom sets in. A lifestyle based on golf, volunteerism and hobbies is not for them. They miss the competitiveness of the workplace or, frankly, the chance to make some more money. Whatever the reason, their solution is to return to work. They find a new job or opportunity by networking and by virtue of their proven skills. Opportunities exist for those willing to explore and take a chance, like the group of unretirees you'll meet on the following pages. These include three former mid-level bank executives who took different routes to the job market after losing their jobs to downsizing.

Leonard Barishansky, George Manitzas and Louis Lagalante worked for New York City banks until the companies were downsized when the men were in their mid to late fifties. Only Leonard was a banker by trade. George was a computer expert and Louis a back-office financial controller. They resurfaced in three different careers with, at best, indirect ties to banking.

SUGGESTED READING

- Laqueur, Maria and Donna Dickinson. *Breaking Out of 9 to 5* (Peterson's, 1994). If you are interested in re-designing your job, this book is full of useful information concerning job trends, proposal writing, negotiation tactics and locating a flexible job.

- Trialkill, Diane. *Temp by Choice* (Career Press, 1994). Good background on working as a temp.

- U.S. Department of Labor, *Occupational Handbook 1998-99* (VGM Career Opportunities). Published in alternate years. Provides vital information on dozens of professional and management careers that you might never have thought of.

- Bolles, Richard. *What Color is Your Parachute* (Ten Speed Press, 1998). A perennial for job seekers of all ages.

- Petras, Kathryn and Ross. *The Over-40 Job Market* (Poseidon Press, 1993). Lots of good practical hints on the workplace.

- Bird, Caroline. *Second Careers: New Ways to Work After 50* (Little, Brown, 1992). This book was based on responses to an AARP survey.

- Moreau, Daniel. *Take Charge of Your Career* (Kiplinger Books, 1996). A comprehensive guide to renewing and revising your job-hunting strategy.

- Wendleton, Kate. *Through the Brick Wall* (Villard Books, 1993). The book's subtitle sums it up: "How to job-hunt in a tight market."

A SMALLER POND IS JUST FINE

Leonard Barishansky
BANK EXECUTIVE TURNED CFO AT AN IMPORT-EXPORT BUSINESS

When Leonard Barishansky was a panelist at a Manufacturers Hanover forum for former bank employees, he told many of his former co-workers, "Don't be one-dimensional in your job search and think that banking is the only thing that you can do. Above all, you have other business talents." It's a strategy that worked well for Leonard when he found himself out on the street after working 28 years for one of the nation's largest commercial banks. Then in his mid fifties, he had not planned to retire for at least another eight to ten years. Unlike many of his associates who called it quits, Leonard looked for another job and found one that has been more than mutually beneficial for him and his new employer, a small import-export firm.

Working for one company for so many years has its advantages, but Leonard learned that it can also lull you into a sense of false—and maybe unnecessary—security. "I've actually become a stronger person. Once you've lost your job and found another one you get the confidence that you can do it again if you have to."

An assistant vice-president at Manufacturer's Hanover, he managed about 60 commercial accounts, a job that required a

After 28 years with Manny Hanny, Leonard played role reversal, from banker of small businesses to CFO of one.

range of banking, marketing and customer relations skills. Downsizing meant more than losing a job. Leonard knew that he most likely would not find another comparable job in banking.

With the encouragement of his outplacement counselor, Leonard explored opportunities to apply his financial and managerial skills in other business surroundings. "She helped me evaluate myself. She built upon my strengths and helped me to broaden my horizons. I never thought I was stepping backward, only moving ahead."

Manufacturers Hanover was not Leonard's first employer. He went to work in the credit department of an apparel company but found that the job offered little opportunity for growth. Leonard left and was hired by Manufacturers Hanover, where "I learned that I was not just a money man but a good people person. Over the years, I lived much of my business life through my customers."

In his case, customers were mostly mid-size, family-owned and -operated companies that looked to the bank as their prime financial resource and to Leonard as their banker. He got close to customers, thrived on the relationships and, in turn, was promoted. Even with a forthcoming merger, he felt that his job was secure. Then his luck ran out.

Going to outplacement was a new experience. "I didn't even have a résumé. It took me two months to put 28 years of work on two sheets of paper. It was the hardest thing I ever had to do." In the process, he eliminated banking from his career plans and restricted his job search to smaller and mid-size companies that he thought could use his finance and credit know-how.

Seven months later, far fewer than those spent by many of his downsized associates at the bank, Leonard found a job as the chief financial officer of a 20-year-old family-owned company, an importer and exporter of general department-store merchandise.

Leonard found the job by networking with former bank customers, and with accountants and lawyers with whom he associated. One of these customers was the company that would become his new employer.

While the salary was comparatively modest, Leonard's finances were in good shape. His wife, Marcia, was employed as a special-education teacher. He had minimal debt, he left the bank with a severance package and was still covered by its major-medical program, and he could draw on his pension. The combination of his pension and his salary produced an income comparable to what he had made at the bank.

ONE TITLE, MANY ROLES

Leonard works in a business world far different from the structured environment that he knew in banking. Then, he had a clearly defined job description; now Leonard does everything and anything. He is the liaison officer with the company's bank and accounting firms. "When I ghostwrite letters to exporters, I become the export manager; when I work out a financial deal with a bank, I'm the chief financial officer."

What he particularly enjoys is the work atmosphere. "There is no such thing as red tape. My job is to free the two owners, brothers in their forties, from the day-to-day administration and let them concentrate on the business. Management meetings consist of three people—the two brothers and myself—and we make decisions on the spot. As the only outsider in management, I voice my opinion without hesitation."

And after years of working as an intermediary within a very large organization, Leonard is getting to see how a small business actually operates. "That's a real eye-opener—to learn that there is more to learn, that there is more to business than what is needed in a bank relationship."

Leonard still works nine to ten hours a day. He misses the camaraderie of the bank and the contacts he once had with a variety of companies. But, somewhat fortunately for a manager in his late fifties, he is developing new skills and has become an integral part of the operation of a smaller company.

"I have no desire to retire. I'm continually learning new things about smaller business as an insider.

Age is actually to my advantage. I'm the oldest person in the company. I'm presently working as the unofficial mentor to the son of one of the owners, teaching him some of the business graces and skills I learned in banking."

NOTHING LIKE HAVING PORTABLE SKILLS

George Manitzas
BANK PROJECTS MANAGER TURNED COMPUTER PROGRAMMER

"It's not too hard to guess my age, even though I removed some dates from my résumé," says George Manitzas, a downsized bank project manager. "I had one search guy who interviewed me for a couple of different jobs who wasn't even born when I started doing computer work."

George was 55 when he left one of New York's major banks, where he was project manager in the global securities/information technology department. George simply became a victim of the bank's urge to merge. But he was in a more favorable position than many downsized managers his age, who knew only a narrow specialty area. George offered potential employers, especially financial services companies, more than 30 years of industry-related communications, hardware and software experience and skills.

George was not surprised when the bank announced its intention to merge with another major New York bank. "We started to hear rumors of some type of deal a few years before. They started playing the 'yes, we're going to do it'; 'no, we're not going to do it' game." During this period, it was business as usual. Few people in the bank were affected, and George was involved in developing some new software applications. But he looked at these projects in light of possible job elimination. How would the projects prepare him to find future work?

> **"I started to look for a job where I could work another ten years. Then I woke up and smelled the smoke. It's not going to work that way any longer."**

When it comes to computers and information services, George is an early entrant, with experience dating back to his graduation from Texas A&M University. For 30 years, he worked for a string of stockbrokers and banks, creating computer software and communications systems. These were boom years as financial services companies automated nearly every phase of their operations and skilled professionals like George had little trouble finding employment.

George was developing a new system in the foreign-exchange department, one of the bank's more profitable business units, when the ax fell. "It didn't seem reasonable to lose my job. Why should this happen when my department was a money-maker? Sure, I was getting up in years but I was still working like a 21-year-old. Nor was I making that much money."

George didn't actually leave the bank for two years after being downsized. Because his skills were in demand, he continued on the payroll as an independent contractor doing the same type of work as before. As a consultant, George had an agreement that he could conduct his job search so long as his performance didn't suffer. He was dropped from the bank's medical plan, but his wife, Meredith, a computer programmer in the insurance industry, picked him up on her company's benefit plan.

THE ADVANTAGES HE HAD

George eventually needed to find something more permanent because the consulting relationship appeared to be ending. "I started to look for a job where I could work another ten years. Then I woke up and smelled the smoke. It's not going to work that way any longer. The job market has changed."

George was well aware of the consequences of not being able to make the shift. "I saw people at the bank with 20 years' experience who were never being interviewed."

Fortunately for George, his varied work history prepared him for the hunt. "During my career, I had worked for seven different companies, and now I was unemployed. I knew how to move from one company and one job to another company and a new job.

"I knew how to network. My data base included more than 1,000 names, everyone I could think of—friends, relatives, vendors, former bosses—going back to my first job. I listened to everyone, got a lot of advice and discovered that the scenario for jobs had changed. I found that too many jobs were short-term. No longer can you have the attitude that you can put your feet on the table

and relax for the next five or ten years."

He also had the advantage of what he calls "straightforward" outplacement assistance. "My consultant kept me motivated. When I relaxed, she told me to get off my butt. And she taught me some of the tricks of salary negotiations."

His job-searching techniques paid off when he was hired as an independent contractor by a 50-person communications systems consultancy in New York. "I knew the president when we worked together in the mid 1970s. What started out as an informal talk turned into a job interview. We danced around. We talked about money and the work to be done. I made some offers; he countered. We reached a compromise. My pay as an independent consultant would equal what I was making at the bank."

George was not concerned that he wouldn't be a salaried, full-time employee. "It might be the only way that older guys like me can find work."

IT'S NOT OVER 'TIL IT'S OVER

When George began his new assignment, he thought it would last several years. But uncertainty became apparent when some contracts never materialized or were reduced, and the need for George was eliminated. His computer career, however, did not come to an end. He went back again to networking, talked to people at the bank, and was selected for other consulting assignments.

"I speak to the folks I know at banks and financial institutions. They know my skills are still up-to-date. We have three PCs at home. Meredith and I talk about computers, I read the computer publications, attend computer workshops and am constantly learning new things."

With more free time than before, George spends about a day a week with the Nassau County Library System. While the job is unpaid, George, as the volunteer treasurer of this countywide 55-branch library network, became involved in the introduction of some new computerized management systems.

George no longer is assured of five days of work a week but he seems to feel that his skill as a hands-on computer specialist will continue to keep him in demand as an independent contractor. "Considering what's taking place in the job market, this is how I and others will be working in the future."

THE THEATER BECKONS

Louis Lagalante
BANK OFFICER TURNED ACTOR

Louis Lagalante has two heroes, Danny DeVito and Joe Pesci. Unlike either of them, Lou, a one-time bank officer, is still waiting to be discovered by either Broadway or Hollywood. Lou credits his long-time interest in music with helping him at age 55 to make a career switch from business to acting.

Lou grew up in New York's Queens County, where he attended high school, college and graduate school, and he still lives there. His career, nearly all of it in financial management, was spent with an oil company, a motion picture distributor and, for 14 years, the Manufacturers Hanover Trust Co., as an assistant controller. When the bank downsized, Lou took advantage of its early-retirement plan.

He accepted the bank's offer because it included lifetime health care coverage for his wife, Sarita, and himself. Up to then he had anticipated completing his career with Manufacturers Hanover so as to be eligible for a pension based on at least 20 years of service. As things turned out, his pension benefits were reduced because he had worked for the bank for only 14 years.

What's more, he had given little thought

> **Like any postretirement endeavor, acting takes patience, a well-formulated plan for success and an ability to bounce back after being turned down.**

to what he might do in retirement. Lou looked for work. "I went out on 40 interviews, but few companies were interested in anybody my age. I was considered too old for the job. I had two alternatives—get a New York City substitute teaching license or become a tax consultant." He combined the two by teaching accounting and bookkeeping part-time in a branch of a community college, but he disliked the long commute to work and the job prevented him from going to auditions.

Lou, the banker, also played the trumpet, an interest that dated back to high school. He felt comfortable being on stage. Over the years, to make extra money to support a family of seven children, he had worked evenings and weekends as a musician. He had had a six-piece band, had gotten a few songs published and was a member of the musician's union, Local 802.

A son, Paul, an actor who appeared regularly on a popular TV soap opera, realized his father's stage presence and encouraged him to attend an audition at a community playhouse. Paul told him they needed a person to play the part of a radio announcer. But when the director heard Lou's guttural New York accent, he hired him instead to play Max Levine, a fight manager, in *Heaven Can Wait*. This small part in a community theater production was the start of Lou's acting career.

WORKING HARD, WAITING FOR DISCOVERY

It is a tough regimen to be accepted as a professional actor. It takes lots of patience, a well-formulated plan for success (just as in any business), and an ability to bounce back after being turned down for a part. These facts are at the heart of Lou's approach to acting, one that he would suggest to others who are considering either an acting career or any other postretirement endeavor.

More often than not, Lou is typecast for parts as a detective or gangster. To break the mold, he takes speech courses to "correct" his accent. He reads trade papers for leads and sends bulk mailings of his portfolio to casting directors. He might receive two or three replies from a mailing of 130 pieces. While Lou still does not have a full-time agent, he expects that will come when an agent feels he's producing sufficient income to justify a commission.

Even with what appears to outsiders as slow progress, Lou feels he is gaining some recognition as an actor as he is selected for somewhat larger roles in dinner, regional, community, off-off- Broadway theater, television, TV commercials and even independent, low-budget motion pictures.

To make ends meet, Sarita works as a para-professional in a local high school, and Lou has prepared income tax returns. The Lagalantes live modestly and at times draw on savings. "If I didn't want to take the risk of being an actor, I'd still be teaching accounting or doing some temporary office work," Lou says. While his acting income is still marginal, Lou wouldn't exchange it for a full-time corporate job.

On one audition, Lou, the bank financial manager with an MBA in management, was turned down to play an accountant in a Merv Griffin commercial. "I was told I didn't look the part." Even as he struggles to gain recognition, Lou remains optimistic. "Whenever the phone rings, I tell myself maybe it's Bob DeNiro asking me to be in one of his movies. Remember, Danny DeVito was discovered by Michael Douglas in an off-off-Broadway play."

WORKING FOR HIS DAUGHTER-IN-LAW

R.J. Freeman
SALES MANAGER TURNED EMPLOYMENT AGENCY COUNSELOR

With the best of intentions, R.J. Freeman visited three temporary employment agencies following his corporate retirement from a career in sales. "They didn't have the time of day for a 62-year-old, even one who was willing to do anything—customer service or even a manual job. After the third brush-off, I politely suggested they keep their attitude and decided I would do something about it." R. J. Freeman took the initiative. The following year, he went into business with his daughter-in-law, Valerie, and helped her start Prime Timers as a division of her office temporary service, Imprimis Inc.

Prime Timers concentrates on placing workers age 40 and over in office-support jobs, especially those requiring computer-related skills. In the Dallas–Ft. Worth market, there are nearly 250 temporary-service firms, and about seven of them are staffed to handle work similar to Prime Timers'. Perhaps it is R.J.'s age and work experience, not just those of Prime Timers' employees, that make the difference in such a competitive marketplace.

As an employee of Prime Timers, R.J. is still out doing what he knows best: selling. When he meets with potential employers, he focuses on the usefulness and capability of older workers. "It's an easy sale to convince employers of the caliber of our work force. I tell them prime timers are retired. They aren't looking for competitive positions. They are content with lower wages and fewer fringe benefits. They have a positive attitude toward work and, above all, they want to be part of the workforce.

"Our success also dispels the myth that older people can't learn computer skills. If they don't have them, we train them." Prime Timers uses its ACE (Accelerated Computer Education) training program to train applicants in different software packages. "We have an inventory of at least 900 applicants, and we place about 200 people a week in jobs where they earn from minimum wage to $30 an hour."

R.J. also speaks to retirees. "I go to job fairs and community programs to talk to retirees, pushing the idea of their returning to work and revitalizing their self-esteem." Some of the people he speaks with are interested in returning to work but rule it out because the job might be at a lower level, offering less money and no title. "They

> **When R.J. couldn't join the temp agencies, he beat 'em at their own game, helping to found Prime Timers, a temp agency placing 40-plus workers.**

are being totally unrealistic. Chances are they'll never replace the type of job they just left. I tell them they need to be flexible. Until they recognize this, it's hard to place them in a job."

FLUNKING RETIREMENT

Even then it may be no picnic, as R.J. himself found out in his first and unexpected brush with retirement.

Following military service in World War II, R.J. spent his entire career in Texas in the advertising and apparel business. He joined Warner Brothers, a clothing manufacturer, when he was 41 and became a regional manager responsible for apparel sales in five of the southwestern states.

Warner reorganized when R.J. was 62 and working for its Hathaway Division, the shirtmaker. The company presented R.J. with two options: relocate to New York or take an early-retirement package. "Until then I had planned to work until I was at least 65, but the decision was an easy one to make." At his age, he had no intention of working in New York. He'd done that earlier in his career, when he had worked there for one year and commuted on weekends to Texas.

"I retired for three weeks. During the third week, as I was shaving, I asked myself 'Is this all I've got to look forward to, playing golf and going fishing?' It's okay for the weekends but not every day for the rest of my life. I had just flunked retirement." His wife, Patricia, recognized that there was something missing from his life and encouraged him to return to work.

R.J.'s goal was to work part-time. He had sufficient income from his pension and investments. "I'd do anything in a service business. I needed very little money, just a token amount, but I wanted to get back working with people. I went to three part-time employment agencies and didn't even get the time of day. Two didn't offer me an application. If I hadn't been a salesman used to hearing people say no, my self-esteem would have been even lower."

Most 62-year-olds who get rejected sadly accept the fact. R.J. was more resilient and fortunate. He finally talked to his daughter-in-law, Valerie Freeman, who already owned and operated Imprimis Inc., a staffing agency in the Dallas area that specialized in placing temporary workers in jobs requiring word-processing skills.

R.J.'s interest in finding part-time work and his experience with other temp firms coincided with Valerie's plan to expand into office services provided by workers age 40 and over. She had been reviewing demographic studies that pointed to a shortage of trained workers, yet she knew that companies in Texas were then laying off and retiring large pools of experienced older employees.

At first, R.J. and Valerie were reticent about mixing family and business but they decided to give it a try and started Prime Timers. They have succeeded to the point where Prime Timers has had multimillion dollar billing years.

Others became interested in the company as a business opportunity. Prime Timers caught the attention of Cable News Network after a reporter heard about how it helped older people return to work. A TV feature resulted in telephone calls from around the world. Viewers wanted to know if they could franchise Prime Timers' formula or join forces. "We considered the idea and decided against it. We'd lose quality control over a franchise operation. Instead, we show others how to do it and never charge a fee for this service just as long as they operate under a different name and in a different marketplace.

I'm thrilled that I can get others to want to help older people get jobs."

In deference to his age, R.J. reduced his workweek from seven days when he started Prime Timers (so much for working part-time) to four days, commuting 60 miles each way from home on Lake Kiowa to his downtown Dallas office. R.J. admits that he's beginning to slow down, but he vetoes the idea of retirement. A man with a mission, he still enjoys what he's doing.

"WORK IS STILL MY ONLY HOBBY"

Harry Olson

INVESTMENT COMPANY EXECUTIVE TURNED COMPUTER GURU

"As I see it, there are three groups of people when it comes to retirement. One group can hardly wait to retire so they can do their own 'thing'; others don't want to do anything; and then there are people like me who just can't stop working." So says Harry Olson.

Harry's first job following retirement from American Express was with the National Executive Service Corps, where he was paid an honorarium to build up the network of field offices in the U.S. Doing something useful in the workplace was his objective. Although he needed to work to support himself, a high salary was not his prime concern.

At the same time, he became a volunteer with New York City Partnerships, a nonprofit group concerned with jobs and education. This exposure to urban problems led Harry to do something more directly to help youthful offenders. He sold his home and bought a larger one in Brooklyn. "I renovated it, and over the years, I had as many as seven young men living in my home at the same time, all referred by a youth center. They stayed from three months to three years. Most times they had their own room. They were responsible for cooking and cleaning,

> **Harry has enjoyed a variety of paid and unpaid jobs, combined with helping others, in the years since his retirement. His work ethic just won't quit.**

and they either went to school or worked." Harry financed this project out of his own pocket and never asked for government assistance since it meant interference. It was Harry's way of saying thanks in a practical way, or as he puts it, "I wanted to be more than a once-a-year Christian."

Even with so large a responsibility, Harry still had little interest in withdrawing from the work force. He spent three years as co-owner of a start-up software company but sold his 50 percent ownership and returned to the National Executive Service Corps. Through NESC's placement service, Harry joined the Diocese of the Armenian Church of America as its chief administrator to head all nonreligious functions for the diocese. Harry, a Unitarian, was the only lay person on the staff. In exchange for a moderate income, the diocese received a seasoned financial executive for far below market value, and Harry remained in the active work force. Unlike in his corporate days, Harry's staff was very small. His office was a cubicle where he maintained financial records on his own computer.

Even by Harry's work standards, the job

at the church was too confining, and after two years he withdrew from it. Harry rekindled the formal business ties with his one-time software partner, whose company was developing and marketing a software package that provides the communications link between insurance companies, self-insurers and their law firms. His ex-partner offered him some consulting work, and Harry now works from home on a computer that is linked with the software company's offices in Seattle. This way he also saves 80 minutes a day that he once spent commuting by subway to and from his office at the Armenian Church. His software assignments are varied and utilize his background as a financial executive and lawyer. One task is to develop ways that insurance companies can use computers to effectively measure the performance of the lawyers who work for them. His income now surpasses what he made working for the Armenian Church.

Unlike so many retirees, Harry is computer literate. "From the early '60s, I was always a big user of computer services, but I never was at a keyboard until I retired. I taught myself to operate a PC because I knew I was going to be on my own from here on in. If you didn't know how to use a computer, who would bother to hire you?"

By the time Harry left his job with the church, he had already sold his Brooklyn home to increase his cash equity, and he replaced it with a three-bedroom apartment. He still continues his work with the youth center, but space allows him to accommodate only one house guest at a time.

Harry's lifetime creed of work and doing for others grew up with him in his hometown of Nashwauk, a small Minnesota iron-mining town. "Nashwauk taught me an important lesson that I've never forgotten. We were pretty badly hit by the Depression. You grew up with few, if any, pretensions. If you had any, they weren't tolerated."

Harry squeezed in two years of junior college before he entered the Navy in World War II. Following service, he returned to school and received his law degree.

His first job was with Minnesota Mutual Life Insurance as an investment clerk. Three years later he joined another insurance company as a utility industry analyst. "This proved to be the best education in my career. I worked for an 'SOB,' but he was a good teacher. Any person who survived him had no trouble getting another job. I stayed there three years." A law-school classmate asked him to join his law firm, but after ten months Harry decided that a legal practice wasn't for him.

He returned to investments and a job in Minneapolis at Investors Diversified Services, which was subsequently acquired by American Express. When he left IDS in 1961, he was 38, director of the investment division, earning $30,000 a year and managing a $3 billion portfolio. "I decided to take a risk as an entrepreneur, and I bought into a small financial services company where I lost my money. The relationship ended when I negotiated the sale of the company."

Harry then joined the Fireman's Fund Insurance Co., which was owned by American Express. Until his retirement 17 years later, he was associated as a senior executive with American Express or its various corporate holdings. Even though he had a reputation as a hard worker, he found at age 60 that he could no longer work at the demanding pace expected of American Express managers.

When he left American Express, his personal responsibilities were few. He was divorced and his children were all grown. He spent the first few months traveling in the U.S. as a way of unwinding. "I then realized that it was time to find a new niche for myself and that work is still my only hobby.

"People always ask me when I'm going to retire. Never."

THE MAKING OF A COMMUNITY ACTIVIST

Gerard Stoddard
PUBLIC-RELATIONS EXECUTIVE TURNED HOMEOWNERS ASSOCIATION LEADER

When Gerard Stoddard walks down Fifth Avenue in New York, he could be easily tagged as a successful corporate executive. And, for many years, he was. But a corporate merger and an abiding interest in his home-away-from-home put him on his present career path. Jerry made the transition from corporate executive to volunteer president of the Fire Island (New York) Association and most recently to paid president. Defying retirement, Jerry converted the position into a demanding career using much of his professional experience and skills.

For 20 years, Jerry's career was closely associated with SCM Corp., once the nation's premier typewriter manufacturer. When SCM was acquired by Hanson Trust, a British conglomerate, Jerry's job as vice-president for corporate communications became redundant.

Jerry was protected financially by a contract, a fully vested pension and savings and investments resulting from an excellent salary. In addition, he executed his stock options at a very favorable price. What's more, his expenses were contained. The townhouse that he owned and lived in

> **Job-hunting didn't turn up much. Consulting for law firms didn't cut it. With the Fire Island Association, Jerry found his calling in retirement.**

in New York's Chelsea section also included some rented apartments. His wife, Patricia, was employed as a contributing editor to various publications of the Girl Scouts. Their oldest daughter had completed graduate school and their youngest daughter was helping to finance her pursuit of a PhD through fellowships.

In the public relations field, an occupation noted for high job turnover, Jerry had had only two employers over a 25-year span. When he graduated from Cornell University, he was interested in public affairs and public policy, and took a job with the American Petroleum Institute, the oil industry's prime lobbyist. While an API employee, he obtained a law degree at night from New York University and passed the state bar exam, but never practiced law. In future years, he was, however, able to leverage his legal education.

He joined SCM as director of shareholder relations and six years later was named a corporate vice-president. While responsible for the company's full range of public relations activities, Jerry personally handled its lobbying activities in Washington and New York, a job that required a knowledge of public relations and the law.

When he left SCM, Jerry was much too young to consider retiring. Until the acquisition, he felt he had a secure and satisfying job, so in many ways he was unprepared for his departure from SCM. Unemployed, he looked for jobs through traditional search methods and even received a few offers, including one that, in effect, represented a career demotion. "At the time, I realized that this might very well be my last job offer. I would most likely never find a job equal to the one I had at SCM."

Jerry was not idle professionally as he looked for a full-time job. He started a public relations consultancy firm in his home. Law firms were then just beginning to market their services, and as a lawyer and public relations practitioner, Jerry received assignments from several large New York law firms. But lawyers, he soon concluded, are fine if they work for you—and not so fine if you work for them.

THE SUMMER PLACE CALLS

In the meantime, Jerry and his family, like so many New Yorkers, had had two residences. During the school year, they lived in New York City. In the summer, the family moved to their cottage on Fire Island, 55 miles from midtown New York. Jerry spent weekends on Fire Island with his family.

As is typical of many resorts, Fire Island's population soars in the summer to 25,000 residents and declines in the off-season to about 500 year-round occupants. The swing in seasonal population places pressure on the island's environment and its relaxed lifestyle. This has led to a division among residents—those who want to see more commercial development and those who are opposed to it. Automotive vehicles are banned from the island. Walking or biking are the only modes of transportation. "I began to get interested in community life when someone wanted to build a hotel, something I didn't feel was in keeping with community living," Jerry says. "This activated me, and I got the local property owners to buy the land and make it into a park."

NEW CAREER
FROM COMMUNITY CONCERN

About the time he was leaving SCM, Jerry was elected president of the Fire Island Association, which represents the island's 3,000 homeowners. "As a professional lobbyist, I knew that our association was too small to have any impact in either Washington or Albany." To build a bigger political power base, he helped to form the Long Island Coastal Alliance, consisting of similar beach communities on Long Island's South Shore. The alliance gave him the incentive to start *Coastal Reports,* a paid bimonthly subscription newsletter devoted to coastal property owners, as well as an annual conference on coastal matters. Jerry had taken another step away from retirement.

As the association's president, Jerry has a varied job description. He has been involved in a number of environmental issues, including finding ways to control the influx of deer and the Lyme disease they can bring. The association also faces other challenges as many of the island's residents near retirement age and opt for year-round residence. The growing year-round population needs better transportation facilities and ways to realistically extend the season beyond the normal five months from May to early October.

At first, Jerry served on a volunteer basis as the association's president, but growing responsibilities and the expanding time commitment led the association's board of directors to begin paying him a $25,000 honorarium. Since receiving the honorarium, Jerry has sidelined his public relations consultancy and instead concentrates on his paid work with the Fire Island Association and on his volunteer leadership of the Long Island Coastal Alliance. He still edits his newsletter and runs the annual conference. The work uses his varied professional skills, including writing, knowledge of government operations and lobbying in Washington and Albany with the state legislature and executive offices.

"There are many psychic pleasures with my job. I testified a couple of times before the U.S. Senate on the need for greater shore protection on Long Island, helped win a major victory to enable coastal property owners to obtain flood insurance, and I constantly meet and work with important people."

Jerry finds his present work is a much better alternative than retirement, but there are still drawbacks. "Volunteer groups can be as demanding as any client— or corporate president, for that matter. But the issues are fascinating, so I guess I'll stay on as president until the board gets tired of me and kicks me out."

COMPUTERS, AN ALLY IN REAL ESTATE SALES

Dorothy Arnsten
SCHOOL PSYCHOLOGIST TURNED REAL ESTATE BROKER

"Larry (her husband) and I do not like to hang out. I don't like going to lunch with the girls and I'd don't like shopping. We have lots of interests but other than work no other single activity can fill up a day," says Dorothy Arnsten.

When Dorothy retired several years ago as a psychologist with the New York City public school system, she took a retirement route normally not associated with someone with a doctorate degree and over 25 years of classroom and counseling experience. Like many retired psychologists, she could have concentrated on her private practice, and enjoyed the income from an ample New York pension. Dorothy, however, was looking for a different stimulant consistent with her attitude toward retirement.

Dorothy started to plan a career switch several years before she left the school system. Her husband, an accountant, also owns and manages some property. "Larry would give me papers to look at. He asked me to read and then sign them. I discovered that I was the general manager. When I asked about the title, Larry said, 'I work for you, sweetheart.'" This whetted her appetite to learn more about real estate.

She subsequently met Ileen Schoenfeld at

> **Interestingly, Dorothy finds that real estate sales combine a number of different skills, including psychology and teaching.**

a party and learned that Ileen, also a one-time teacher, was selling New York City co-op and condo apartments. "The work interested me. Selling real estate would add something different in my life. I took a real estate course and was licensed by New York State." Real estate added a third dimension to an already busy lifestyle as a full-time school psychologist with a part-time private psychology practice.

Her big break came when Ileen had to go to Florida to visit an ailing mother. She asked Dorothy to be her proxy, and in her absence Dorothy sold two apartments. Eileen and Dorothy became partners. "It's a great relationship since I can work my own schedule and we can spell each other on weekends and vacations." She admits, however, that she'd like to reduce her current 40-hour work week.

While many retirees would be satisfied with a single post-retirement job, Dorothy works as both a full-time real estate broker and as a part-time psychologist. She purposely limits her psychology practice to no more than eight patients, all in short-term relationships, six hours for six weeks. "I don't take on patients with deep emotional problems. They're mostly people who are going through bereavement, an affair or have problems at work." Interestingly, Dorothy finds that real-estate sales combine a number of different skills including psychology and teaching.

As a real estate broker, Dorothy brings strong research and computer skills to the workplace. She was introduced to computers in the early 1980s when she took several courses in conjunction with her doctorate studies. Computers provide a key research and marketing tool for real estate brokers. It didn't take much to convince her that in-depth research on behalf of clients helps to clinch a sale. Either from a home or office computer, Dorothy feeds information on clients' needs into the computer, which generates lists on apartments or townhouses that fit the client's specifications. Her computerized listings are read by potential buyers in places as diverse as New York, Hong Kong and London.

JUST GOT BORED IN RETIREMENT

Danny Winston
FABRIC SALESMAN TURNED EXTERMINATING-SERVICES SALESMAN

Danny Winston has always been a people person. He relishes meeting new people, making new friends and keeping them. That was true when he attended summer camp in the 1920s, when he was an officer in the Eighth Air Force in World War II, throughout his various sales jobs over the past 50 years and in his current one with a New York exterminating company.

Danny enjoys sales, creating goodwill with customers and giving them good service. He works a five-day week except in the winter months when the exterminating business is generally slower.

In many ways, Bliss Exterminating, one of the oldest and largest independents in the field, offers Danny ideal working conditions. Danny and his wife, Suzanne, who retired in the early 1990s, live on New York's East Side, only two miles from his office. His workday routine fits his New York personality. He rides the bus to work but walks home. Considered a fashionable dresser, Danny finds his daily walk lets him window-shop and stop in the boutiques and men's clothing stores along the route. And he still has time for the other New York activities he enjoys. "Suzanne and I like how we live. We're members of several muse-

> Danny tried retirement decades ago. "I was bored, I missed the people and the excitement of going to work." He's been selling ever since.

ums, we go to the theater, we eat out several nights a week, and we travel."

Other than World War II duty as an intelligence officer in England, Danny has lived in New York his entire life. He inherited his local mannerisms from his parents who, he says, could have been characters in a Damon Runyon story: "My mother was a bookmaker and my father was a professional gambler."

Danny's first "romance" and oldest friendships began when he was 7 years old. He was sent to Camp Moween, near New London, Connecticut, where he was a camper and counselor from 1923 to 1937. Others might forget summer camp, but not Danny. "Camp was one of the most important parts of my life. At camp, I was motivated to do well and to take care of myself. It taught me to be a regular guy. I still speak to many of the 'boys' at least once a month."

Even though Camp Moween closed in 1963, Danny is one of the camp's more active alumni, as a *New York Times* article pointed out. "The former boys gather to retell the familiar stories over catered chicken dinners, to sing the old songs after a couple of scotches and, well, to remind themselves of one another and the shared days gone by."

The second major event in Danny's life was the Eighth Air Force. While the atmosphere was dramatically changed in most ways from Camp Moween, Danny nonetheless feels that "it was another extension of the camp spirit and the atmosphere of fellowship." And in that spirit, Danny has attended Eighth Air Force reunions for more than 50 years.

Following his discharge from service, Danny worked in appliance sales for 11 years until he joined his father-in-law's textile company in 1957. Danny liquidated the business, a supplier of linings to the fur industry, in the mid 1970s due to declining fur-industry sales. "I was in my fifties. I tried retirement for a few months and was bored. I missed the people and the excitement of going to work. I saw a classified advertisement from an exterminator looking for a salesman. I knew nothing about the business, but the owner of the company invited me to visit his office. We talked for three hours and I got the job."

Danny remained with the company for nine years until the owner moved the business to Florida. He wanted Danny, then in his mid sixties, to join him there, but Danny

had no desire to leave New York. Though his two children were grown, Suzanne, about 12 years younger than Danny, was still busy teaching school. What's more, their life was too closely tied to New York City to consider leaving.

After a brief stint as a mortgage broker, Danny found the names of some other exterminators while scanning the Yellow Pages and was soon selling for Bliss. "When I went to work at Bliss, it was a throwback to the spirit I enjoyed at summer camp. I felt like I was once again the new boy on the block, meeting people and making new friends."

As long as he is healthy, Danny has no plans to retire. He still enjoys going to work and helping people with their real-life problems. His boss is in his seventies, so Danny's age is hardly an issue from that end. And while other workers Danny's age might have difficulty dealing with younger customers, this is hardly a problem because customers have never personally met him. He sells exterminating services by telephone.

Danny generally sums up the idea of retirement this way: "I find Florida boring, shopping malls depressing and the entire retirement atmosphere not to my liking."

OUT OF THE FRYING PAN AND INTO THE FIRE

Thomas Roeser
CORPORATE VEEP TURNED PUBLIC AFFAIRS ADVOCATE

Thomas Roeser, at 62, was the oldest executive in a senior management position at Quaker Oats' headquarters in Chicago. As its vice-president for government relations, Tom felt no pressure to retire. "For a while, I thought I would stay until I was 70 and really be the company's grand old man."

But the idea of retirement was accelerated when Tom was injured so seriously that he received the last rites of the Roman Catholic Church. He had fallen while getting out of a shower and a blood clot formed on his brain. He recovered rapidly and was back at work in ten weeks. "But it got me to think about the future and what I might do if I retired."

This was not the first time that Tom had thought of leaving Quaker Oats and perhaps going into business for himself. He knew instinctively that if he ever left he would use his skills in public affairs as the basis of any new career. "Quaker Oats' chairman gave me a long leash and let me say publicly what I wanted to on issues as long as I kept the company out of it. But I still had to be careful. There's always a need as a company executive to be

> **After years of speaking for Quaker Oats, Tom found his own voice. He debates and writes about the issues, and represents public affairs clients who appreciate his point of view.**

discreet. By comparison, I knew that the owner of the smallest business has the freedom to speak his mind."

Tom has been speaking his mind in a variety of ways since he left Quaker Oats. His public affairs work became the basis of his consultancy practice and a patchwork career. He flourishes in the limelight as a lobbyist, public affairs consultant, newspaper columnist and radio talk-show host.

Tom is a paid columnist for the *Chicago Sun-Times* and the host of three radio shows each week on WLS, morning and evening. "If you're up to date on the issues there's little preparation that is needed, but it is still demanding. One of the shows involves a McLaughlin Group–like, no-holds-barred discussion of local and state politics. And there are drawbacks. Even though it pays well, it keeps me from traveling on some lobbying assignments. Nobody knows how long the Ty and Tom Show will last. If nothing more, it's gotten me some public affairs clients who share my views and want me to represent their companies."

Tom's radio shows and writing now

occupy more and more of his time, but this builds name recognition with future clients. Tom sees his specialty as public-affairs consulting to midsized companies. When he went into business, he had already arranged to represent Quaker Oats as a public affairs consultant. It helped get him started and provided him with an immediate source of income and a major company to include on his client list. The arrangement lasted about two years. "By then my successor no longer needed my assistance. I don't blame her. I wouldn't like my former boss looking over my shoulder, either."

Tom's clients tend to be companies with specific equal-employment or environmental problems that need to be brought to the attention of a government agency or elected official. These firms normally are too small to have a public affairs manager on staff, and their lawyers are usually trained in corporate law, not public affairs. They're the ideal candidates to retain a consultant. "I try to solve their problems by making things happen in either Washington or Springfield (the capital of Illinois)."

Tom still commutes to work from the suburbs to a downtown Chicago office that he shares with several other corporate retirees. He subleases space with a one-time business colleague, who is also retired and a consultant. The arrangement gives him an office, use of photocopy equipment and a conference room, and the part-time use of a secretary. "I need the discipline of an office where there are no distractions, no grandchildren to play with or snow blower to use. Going downtown to the office every day charges me up, and I want to continue doing this as long as I remain in good health."

PUBLIC AFFAIRS IS IN HIS BLOOD

Tom admits to working as hard as he did in his peak years but enjoys the freedom of being his own boss. He attributes his drive to his being a Depression-generation child. "It's an attitude that's hard to shake loose and one of the reasons I'm a political conservative. I'm uncertain about the future. I always knew that I didn't want to follow in my father's footsteps. He died at 68, tired and under self-generated pressures."

Tom began his career after graduating from St. John's University in Collegeville, Minnesota. He started out as a political reporter in Minnesota but left soon afterward to become research director and publicist for the state's Republican party. "I enjoyed being a reporter, but it was like being a stenographer; I wanted to be a newsmaker and political insider." He became a speechwriter for two members of Congress, then was assistant to the governor of Minnesota before joining Quaker Oats as a public affairs specialist.

Tom took a sabbatical from Quaker Oats in 1969 to serve as an assistant to Maurice Stans, President Nixon's first secretary of commerce, and spent about two years in the government. "When I left Quaker Oats, my boss said that I would not like working in Washington and he told me that I could have my job back whenever I wanted." Tom spent the next 20 years, until he retired, as the company's senior lobbyist and public affairs officer.

While still a Quaker Oats employee, Tom was involved in a number of outside activities that eventually provided an ideal bridge into retirement and his patchwork career. As a conservative public affairs analyst, he wrote newspaper and magazine op-ed pieces and appeared on radio and television. He also became the first business lobbyist to be named a John F. Kennedy Fellow at Harvard.

"I went into business the day after I left Quaker Oats. I advise others to do the same thing. Don't even take a vacation. That way you have no time to feel sorry for yourself or become depressed. I find my friends who need to unwind before taking the next step never get back to peak efficiency again."

MAKING ENDS MEET

Tom left Quaker Oats with a pension, stock options and a good investment portfolio. To bring his monthly income up to a preretirement level, he supplements his pension payment with a fixed monthly withdrawal from his investment account. "But even with my good pension, I continue to worry about money. The Depression syndrome kicks in. When I'm overly concerned about needing more work, my wife, Lillian, counters by saying that it's time to forget about money and enjoy what I'm doing."

The income that Tom receives from writing, radio and consulting goes into a separate account to cover the costs of maintaining a downtown office and other business expenses. He reserves the remainder against downturns in business.

Even with Tom's busy daytime schedule, he has been a student during evenings at the University of Chicago, where he has taken a course in Western literature and philosophy. "It's fun reading Plato at my age. It leads to lively discussions with the younger students." During the past year, Lillian, who was an aide to a congressman when Tom held a similar post in Washington, graduated from Loyola University with a degree in English literature.

"I don't feel I'm ready in the slightest to retire," says Tom. "If I ever do, it will be for one purpose: to have more time to reflect and write some books.

"There are so many things I wanted to do and I've done them—visit Israel, get a dog because I never in my life had one, and write. Above all, I like actively debating the issues. It beats my retired friends who have nothing to do all day."

How Will You Foot the Bills?

THE PRIMARY THRUST OF THIS BOOK IS TO HELP you answer the question, "What will I do if I retire?" Questions that may be looming equally large in your mind are, "How much money will I need to live in retirement?" "Do I have enough?" and "Where is it going to come from?" While whole books have been written on these subjects, this isn't one of them. This book would be the perfect companion to a book on financial planning for retirement and to one on managing your investments to meet your goals. We recommend some appropriate resources in the box on page 36. And, of course, you've gotten at least a glimpse of how each person profiled in this book is financing his or her "retirement."

That said, this section will help you begin to assess the current and future status of your nest egg and the income it will provide you in retirement. You may realize that the funds you've accumulated for retirement are, in fact, enough and you can devote your energies to developing your new life in "retirement." Maybe you can afford to retire early and devote yourself to an unpaid labor of love or to work for the sheer joy of it, without regard to income. Perhaps accepting a buyout offer will provide the funds necessary to supercharge your retirement nest egg, allowing you ultimately to retire early, if not immediately. You may realize that if you just hang on for another few years and increase your rate of saving and investing, you can afford the travel you had always hoped for. You may learn that you're going to need to work after you retire, but maybe not the 50-hour weeks you've been putting in for the past 15 or 20 years.

The Income You Will Need at Retirement

No two individual or family budgets are the same. What one family calls "just getting by" is luxurious living for someone else. However, one common rule of thumb is that you will need 80% of your preretirement income to maintain your "standard of living" after your regular paychecks stop. Some people may be able to do what they want on 70% or 75%, but unless you're looking forward to a more Spartan life than before, aim for the higher figure to help ensure that you'll achieve your retirement lifestyle dream.

Accounting for Future Dollars

The 80% of your income that you will need annually in the future isn't 80% of your income today. It's 80% of your income at the point when you are ready to retire, whether that's a year away, or five, ten, or 15 years from now. The further out you're looking, the more your income is likely to grow due to raises and cost-of-living increases, and the less your purchasing power will be, due to inflation. All of this adds up to the need for a bigger nest egg than you might think. But you don't have to panic. The same forces that make your needs grow will help your nest egg grow, too.

Predicting the Unpredictable: How Long Will You Live?

Knowing how much money you will need in retirement also depends on how long you're going to need it—ten years, 20,

30, or even 40? Life expectancy is on the rise; the average woman retiring today at age 65 is expected to live another 19 years, and the average man can look forward to another 15 years. Those who have just entered the 50-plus crowd can expect to live even longer.

Assessing Your Resources

The cornerstone of your retirement nest egg is likely to be your pension (or other employer-provided defined-*benefit* plan) or a 401(k) or 403(b) (or other defined-*contribution* plan), together with social security. The rest of the gap between preretirement and postretirement income will be filled in by your own savings and investments, and from other resources such as profit from the sale of your home. If you're close to normal retirement age, you've probably accumulated a substantial chunk of your retirement savings. You may know precisely what you can expect from your pension and social security, but you may not be fully aware of all the resources available to you, or even how to figure out how long you can expect your nest egg to last. If you're just 50-plus, you've probably got a retirement savings plan under way and you just need time as your ally to fill it up and out. This section will show you what a difference you can make.

AVERAGE REMAINING LIFETIME

| | Average Number of Years of Life Remaining | |
Age	Male	Female
40	35.1	40.6
45	30.7	35.9
50	26.4	31.3
55	22.3	27.0
60	18.5	22.8
65	15.1	18.9
70	12.0	15.3
75	9.4	12.0
80	7.1	9.0
85	5.2	6.4

Source: Vital Statistics of the United States, 1990, from the Centers for Disease Control and Prevention/National Center for Health Statistics, Vol. II, Section 6. Based on April 1, 1990, U.S. census data.

Your Pension

Chances are that if you're close to retirement or you've been contemplating leaving early, you've already received an estimate of your monthly pension benefit from your company's pension administrator. If not, you might be interested in knowing how a defined-benefit pension is typically calculated. The formula looks like this:

final average monthly earnings x 1.5% x years of service (the benefit accrual rate) = monthly benefit due

Final average monthly earnings might be the average of the five consecutive years you earned the most—that will probably be your last five (add income for each of the five years and divide by 60 months).

So, for example, if you have worked for 30 years, your benefit accrual rate is 45%. If your final average monthly earnings is $5,000, then you would get $2,250 per month.

What percentage of your preretirement income will your pension likely replace? The answer varies greatly by employer, but a typical benefit is 50% of income at retirement minus 50% of social security, which works out to 37% of income for a 30-year worker retiring at a salary level of $50,000. Usually the longer you stay on at work, the greater the percentage of replacement, though there is usually a maximum period of service allowed for the computation.

To receive the maximum pension, most plans require that you work at the company for 30 years and wait until "full retirement age," which is usually 62 or 65. Some companies use a point system that lets you retire at full benefits once your age plus years of service total a certain number of points. An early retiree would probably see benefits reduced, depending on his or her age.

Social Security

You can still begin collecting your full social security benefits at age 65, although this will change in the future (see the table on the next page). For an estimate of your social security benefit based on your earnings history, request a personalized benefits estimate from the Social Security Administration. Call 800–772–1213 and ask for Form 7004-SM, "Request for Earnings

WHEN YOU CAN RECEIVE FULL BENEFITS

Year of Birth	Age Years	Plus Months
pre–1938	65	0
1938	65	2
1939	65	4
1940	65	6
1941	65	8
1942	65	10
1943–54	66	0
1955	66	2
1956	66	4
1957	66	6
1958	66	8
1959	66	10
1960 and later	67	0

and Benefit Estimate Statement." You should receive your estimate in about six weeks. The estimate you receive will be based on your retiring at age 62, retiring at full retirement age, and waiting to retire at age 70. (The SSA has begun automatically sending the benefits estimate annually to everyone age 25 and over.)

The soonest you can begin collecting monthly social security checks is age 62, but if you do, your benefits will be reduced by as much as 30% for life. Using the table on page 266, you can calculate your reduced benefit. Multiply your estimated benefit at full retirement age by the reduction percentage for the number of months early that you plan to retire.

On the other hand, if you expect to delay retirement, see the discussion on page 272.

Once you begin receiving social security benefits, your spouse can also receive benefits based on your record, even if he or she never worked in a job covered by social security. A nonworking spouse is eligible to begin receiving benefits at age 62. At your full retirement age, you will together receive 150% of what you would receive on your own.

If your spouse works, he or she will receive a benefit based on his or her actual earnings or 50% of your benefit, whichever is more, assuming that you're the first one to retire.

Other Current Savings

Add up what you've got socked away in any of the following, whether yours or your spouse's:
- profit-sharing or any other company-sponsored defined-benefit plans,
- 401(k) or 403(b) plans,
- Individual retirement accounts (IRAs),
- Keogh plans
- other retirement savings.

Your Home

And don't forget the house. If you own a house and plan to use the equity in it to help finance your retirement, you're further along to your goal. Of course, for a realistic picture, you'll need to subtract from your home's market value any mortgage you expect to still owe at retirement, sales commissions and closing costs and any part of proceeds of the sale of the home you'll use for the down payment on a retirement home. Thanks to a provision in the Tax Act of 1997, chances are you won't have to pay

HOW EARLY RETIREMENT WILL REDUCE YOUR BENEFITS

Months Early	% of Full Benefit	Months Early	% of Full Benefit
2	98.9%	32	82.2%
4	97.8	34	81.1
6	96.7	36	80.0
8	95.6	38*	79.2
10	94.4	40*	78.3
12	93.3	42*	77.5
14	92.2	44*	76.7
16	91.1	46*	75.8
18	90.0	48*	75.0
20	88.9	50*	74.2
22	87.8	52*	73.3
24	86.7	54*	72.5
26	85.6	56*	71.7
28	84.4	58*	70.8
30	83.3	60*	70.0

* As full retirement age rises to age 67, these early retirement percentages will apply.

a dime in taxes on the profit when you sell (see page 274), so any-thing remaining can be added to your nest egg.

Figuring the Gap Between What You Need and What You Have

Let's say that you're age 62 and you plan to retire from your employer of 32 years at age 65. Your wife, a late-blooming professional five years younger than you, expects to continue working for five years after that.

Your current salary is $60,000, and you expect a 4% cost-of-living increase for each of the next three years ($2,400 in year one, $2,496 in year two, and $2,596 in year three), putting your preretirement income at $67,492.

Your wife's current income is $40,000 per year. Between merit raises and cost-of-living increases, she thinks that she can reason-ably expect an average income increase of 7% for each of the eight years until she reaches retirement, setting her preretirement income at $68,800.

For the first five years of your retirement, you will need to replace 80% of your annual preretirement income, or $53,994 per year ($67,492 x .80) and in the following 20 years, 80% of your and your wife's preretirement income, or $109,034 per year ([$67,492 + $68,800] x .80).

Now, where's that money going to come from?

Social Security and Pension Benefits

THE FIRST FIVE YEARS. As a top wage earner by social security standards, you know that your annual social security benefit will be $16,404 ($1,367 a month x 12; for the purposes of this example only, the monthly figure is based on estimated social security ben-efits for the year 2000).

You know that your annual pension benefit will come to $25,544 (50% of preretirement income minus 50% of social secu-rity; [.50 x $67,492] – [.50 x $16,404]).

Between what you will get from your pension and social security, you will have accounted for $41,948 per year, which is short by $12,046 of your estimated need of $53,994.

THE NEXT 20 YEARS. Now your wife retires and claims her social security benefit; she doesn't have a defined-benefit plan, but we'll account for the value of her deferred profit-sharing later.

When your wife retires, she will also be considered a higher-than-average wage earner and she qualifies for an annual benefit of $18,024 ($1,502 x 12).

You and your wife's combined annual income from social security and your pension benefit thereafter will be $59,972 ($16,404 + $25,544 + $18,024). That leaves you with a $49,062 gap between your needs and what your defined benefits will provide ($109,034– $59,972).

Your Retirement Savings and Investments

How will you fill that gap? Let's take a look at the retirement savings and investments that will be available following your retirement:

- **Deferred profit sharing.** You estimate that account at retirement will hold $256,448. You plan to take the money and reinvest it.
- **Your individual retirement account.** By the time you retire, your IRA will be worth $26,000.
- **Investment portfolio.** Over the years you've invested in blue-chip stocks and bonds currently valued at $250,000. At an 8% rate of growth, you estimate that your portfolio will be worth $315,000 in three years ($250,000 x 1.26; see the table on page 270 for an explanation of how to figure money growth).

That gives you a lump sum of $597,448. Off the top you draw about $60,000 to cover the annual income gap of $12,046 you'll have the first five years and put it in a money-market IRA. You leave the rest to cook until your wife's retirement; at 8% per year for five years, you'll end up with $834,149 ($537,448 x 1.47).

THE NEXT 20 YEARS. You estimate that when your wife retires, she will have $125,592 in her 401(k) plan and $36,000 in her IRA, making your total assets $995,740.

Your Home

There's one more resource you haven't yet taken into consideration—your home. When your wife retires, you are planning to sell your house in suburban Philadelphia and move south to your hometown in North Carolina. Your home's current value is $280,000, and you believe you can expect a 3% average rate of appreciation each of the next eight years. By the time you're ready to sell, the house should be worth $355,600 ($280,000 x 1.27 [for money-growth factors, see the table on page 270]). Your mortgage is paid off. Thanks to the 1997 tax act, which exempts from taxation $500,000 in profit from the sale of a home for those filing joint returns ($250,000 is tax-free for those who file single returns), you'll pocket the whole sales price, except for commissions and other sales expenses. That's $326,637 ($355,600 sales price minus $28,963 for commissions and other expenses). You know that you can purchase the home you want in North Carolina for $70,000 in cash. That leaves you $256,637 to pad your investment portfolio.

The Final Tally:
How Long Will It Last?

You now have a grand total of $1,252,377. Will it generate the income that isn't covered by social security and your pension? And how long will it last? You can use the table on page 272 to figure that out.

You know that you need to come up with $49,062 a year ($4,089 per month) for 20 years. You expect that your nest egg will continue to earn 8% annually. The point where 20 years and 8% intersects is $119,550. That's the amount needed to produce $1,000 in income per month for 20 years. (The $1,000 will be exhausted at the end of the period.) Because your monthly requirement is 4.09 times that amount ($4,089 ÷ $1,000), multiply $119,550 by 4.09 and you get a total nest-egg requirement of $488,960. You have more than twice that!

But wait: Before you assume that you're on easy street, keep in mind that you need to account for what inflation will do to your nest egg over those 20 years. A safe rule of thumb is to add

25% to 40% to your total nest egg as an inflation cushion. In this example, that would bring the total required nest egg to between $611,200 and $684,544 [$488,960 + .25($488,960); $488,960 + .40($488,960)]. So, even with inflation, your nest egg is more than sufficient.

Taxes will also take a bite out of your retirement income. The taxes you pay will depend upon many variables including: your tax bracket in retirement; the extent to which your social security benefits will be subject to income tax; the share of your income that comes from savings that have already been taxed; and how long you postpone withdrawing funds from tax-deferred accounts, such as 401(k)s and IRAs. In the early part of your retirement, you and your wife might depend on your investment portfolio, on

HOW A LUMP SUM WILL GROW

This table is useful for anticipating how money you've already accumulated will grow over various lengths of time at various rates of return, compounded annually. Choose the appropriate number of years from the left-hand column and the assumed rate of return from across the top, and multiply the starting amount by the factor that's shown where the two columns intersect. For example, say that you have $20,000 in a mutual fund that you expect will pay 12% per year for the next 8 years. At the end of that time, you'll have $49,600 ($20,000 x 2.48).

Future Growth Factor

Year	3%	4%	5%	6%	7%	8%	9%	10%	11%	12%	13%	14%	15%
1	1.03	1.04	1.05	1.06	1.07	1.08	1.09	1.10	1.11	1.12	1.13	1.14	1.15
2	1.06	1.08	1.10	1.12	1.14	1.17	1.19	1.21	1.23	1.25	1.28	1.30	1.32
3	1.09	1.12	1.16	1.19	1.22	1.26	1.29	1.33	1.37	1.40	1.44	1.48	1.52
4	1.12	1.17	1.22	1.26	1.31	1.36	1.41	1.46	1.52	1.57	1.63	1.69	1.75
5	1.16	1.22	1.28	1.34	1.40	1.47	1.54	1.61	1.69	1.76	1.84	1.93	2.01
6	1.19	1.26	1.34	1.42	1.50	1.59	1.68	1.77	1.87	1.97	2.08	2.19	2.31
7	1.23	1.32	1.41	1.50	1.61	1.71	1.83	1.95	2.08	2.21	2.35	2.50	2.66
8	1.27	1.37	1.48	1.59	1.72	1.85	1.99	2.14	2.30	2.48	2.66	2.85	3.06
9	1.30	1.42	1.55	1.69	1.84	2.00	2.17	2.36	2.56	2.77	3.00	3.25	3.52
10	1.34	1.48	1.63	1.79	1.97	2.16	2.37	2.59	2.84	3.11	3.39	3.71	4.05
15	1.56	1.80	2.08	2.40	2.76	3.17	3.64	4.18	4.78	5.40	6.25	7.14	8.14
20	1.81	2.19	2.65	3.21	3.87	4.66	5.60	6.73	8.06	9.65	11.52	13.74	16.37
25	2.09	2.66	3.39	4.29	5.43	6.85	8.62	10.83	13.59	17.00	21.23	26.46	32.92
30	2.43	3.24	4.32	5.74	7.61	10.06	13.27	17.45	22.89	29.96	39.12	50.95	66.21

which you've paid income tax right along. If you delay tapping your IRAs and deferred profit-sharing for as long as possible—or until age 70½, when you must begin to withdraw the money—those accounts can continue growing tax-deferred, and you put off the inevitable tax bill. (If you start a Roth IRA, or convert a traditional IRA to a Roth, you avoid the tax bill altogether, and there is no requirement to begin withdrawals at age 70½.)

Regardless, you're lucky. You've got some options. Maybe you would like to retire now, rather than later. Maybe your wife would like to retire earlier than planned. Maybe you'll be able to do things in retirement that you hadn't imagined. You could give more to your favorite charities or leave more to the kids. Bottom line, you don't have to worry if you live longer than expected.

Ways to Fill in a Gap

Well, nice for the guy in our example, but what if you end up with a gap that you must fill?

YOU CAN RETIRE ANYWAY AND SEEK OUT A NEW WORK ARRANGEMENT. Look for a situation that offers some of the satisfactions of retirement—say, a more flexible schedule—as well as income. This book is filled with examples of people happily pursuing this strategy, whether they have started a business, become consultants (in some cases selling their services back to their former employer), chosen to work part-time, turned volunteer interests into paid positions or created other options.

You can postpone leaving your current employer beyond your hoped-for retirement age. This option will allow you to contribute more to your savings and investments for as long as necessary, and while you're at it, be thinking about and planning for what you will do next.

YOU CAN RETIRE ANYWAY AND LOWER YOUR POSTRETIRE-MENT STANDARD OF LIVING. Some 50-plusers may take certain steps in this direction anyway, by simplifying their lives. For example, some 50-plusers whose kids are out of the house may trade in their larger, high-maintenance home for a smaller,

HOW BIG A NEST EGG YOU NEED TO COVER AN INCOME GAP

Years in Retirement	Savings Needed to Permit Monthly Withdrawals of $1,000 at Each Rate of Return							
	5%	6%	7%	8%	9%	10%	12%	14%
5	$52,990	$51,730	$50,500	$49,320	$48,170	$47,060	$44,960	$42,980
10	94,280	90,070	86,130	82,420	78,940	75,670	69,700	64,410
15	126,460	118,500	111,250	104,640	98,590	93,060	83,320	75,090
20	151,530	139,580	128,980	119,550	111,140	103,620	90,820	80,420
25	171,060	155,210	141,490	129,560	119,160	110,050	94,950	83,070
30	186,280	166,790	150,310	136,280	124,280	113,950	97,220	84,400

lower-maintenance one. From their point of view, they're not lowering their standard of living, but improving it.

YOU CAN GAMBLE THAT HIGHER-RISK INVESTMENTS WILL PROVIDE YOU WITH HIGHER RETURNS, NOT LOSSES. This isn't a smart idea if you don't have plenty of time to recoup a loss. This advice applies to business start-ups, too (see Chapter 7).

YOU CAN WAIT TO CASH IN ON SOCIAL SECURITY. Social security now offers a bonus, the delayed-retirement credit (shown in the table on the next page), for each year that you continue working or delay applying for social security past your full retirement age. This can mean significantly larger monthly checks when you do decide to call it quits or cash in. Of course, the longer you work, the larger the wage base that your benefit will be calculated on to begin with. Plus, for every year you wait to collect your benefit, the bonus is compounded; that is, each year's bonus percentage is applied to the base benefit plus any previous years' bonuses that you've already earned. And that's on top of cost-of-living increases in social security, if any. A financial planner, accountant or the Social Security Administration can help you figure out how waiting will boost the size of your nest egg.

If You Work and Collect Social Security

Until you turn age 70, if you work and collect social security, the government takes away some of your social security benefits if your earned income exceeds certain limits. In 1999, if you're age 62 through 64, the government reclaims $1 of benefits for every $2 you earn over $9,600; from age 65 through 69, the limit is $15,500, after which the government deducts $1 of every $3 you earn. (The limits go up each year, and there's increasing talk about eliminating the limit altogether.) If you are collecting social security, or soon will be, you won't be alone if you view that as an unfair 33⅓% "tax" on top of your regular income taxes. You'll find that many social security beneficiaries profiled in this book have limited their paid work to avoid being "shorted" on the money they're due. But believe it or not, the final effect of the earnings limit isn't as bad as most people think it is. That's because it's offset by the delayed-retirement credit, described above, and something called automatic benefit recomputation.

Let's say you're 67 and you earned $50,000 in 1998 from a consulting job. That's enough to eliminate all $11,500 of your social security benefits ($50,000 – $14,500 = $35,500; $35,500 ÷ 3 = $11,834). But because you didn't get any benefits, the government treats you as if you had delayed applying for social security by one year, and your future benefits will be hiked by 5% (see the table below). That would add about $575 a year ($11,500 x .05)—plus future cost-of-living increases on that amount—to your benefits for the rest of your life. This will apply each year that your benefits are withheld before you reach age 70. Once you're 70, you can earn as much as you want from a job and still collect your full social security benefits.

Even so, this bonus doesn't entirely make up for the loss of benefits you'll incur. Assuming an average life span, the

THE LATE-RETIREMENT BONUS

Year You Were Born	Annual Bonus for Working Beyond Full Retirement Age
1929–30	4.5%
1931–32	5.0
1933–34	5.5
1935–36	6.0
1937–38	6.5
1939–40	7.0
1941–42	7.5
1943 or later	8.0

higher benefits resulting from the credit will pay back just over half of what you lose to the earnings test. As you can see from the table, the situation will improve over the years for younger 50-

plusers, with the credit rising to 8% for those retiring in 2008.

Automatic Benefit Recomputation

This practice helps if, in a year when you lose benefits, your annual earnings exceed the lowest yearly income (adjusted for inflation) originally used to figure your monthly benefit. Plugging a higher number into the formula pays off in a higher level of benefits. That can be particularly valuable if you have fewer than 35 years of employment. In that case, your earnings after retirement would replace a year without earnings earlier in your life.

While you may want to review your income-producing plans with a financial adviser, your choice on this issue may ultimately come down to principle: You'll have to decide which means more to you—working for pay or collecting the full amount of the social security you're due. It's up to you.

Using the Equity in Your Home

The Tax Act of 1997 included a wonderful break for home owners. It excludes up to $500,000 of profit on the sale of every principal residence you own—provided you've occupied it for at least two of the last five years prior to the sale—if you file a joint return ($250,000 is tax-free if you file a single return). Until that new law was enacted, those over age 55 had a one-time opportunity to take the first $125,000 of profit on the sale tax-free. And there were a few strings attached:

- **You or your spouse had to be at least 55 years old** before the date of the sale.
- **The home had to be your principal residence**—not, say, a vacation home.
- **You had to have owned and lived in the home** three out of the five years leading up to the sale.

If you own your home outright, another way to get at your equity in it is a reverse mortgage. A lending institution sends you a monthly check against the equity in your home. The older you are when you apply for a reverse mortgage, the more money

THINKING OF RELOCATING?

A common consideration in planning for retirement is whether to move to a new location. The motivation may be to live closer to family members, to achieve a new lifestyle, to return to a home from years past, or to live someplace that's always been a dream. Whatever your reason, ask yourself these questions while making the decision.

- Most important, why are you moving? Moving under any circumstances is wrenching and a lot of work. Moving for less than well-considered reasons may be an expensive boondoggle.
- Is the climate comfortable for you on a year-round basis?
- Will this be your only residence, or will you maintain another?
- Are any members of your immediate family nearby? (That could be a plus or a minus, depending on how you feel about your family members.)
- Do you make friends easily?
- How many miles from where you're now living is the new location? Does that matter?
- Is the area served by a major air line, not only for your convenience but for that of family and friends who want to visit?
- How do you rate the area's health care facilities? Do you have any special needs they can't provide for?
- Are cultural and sports facilities available for those activities you enjoy?
- Are there opportunities for part-time and volunteer work of the sort you desire?
- Have you already spent some time in the area—preferably during different times of the year? It's not smart to invest in an unknown quantity.

you're likely to get, because you won't be around as long to collect the monthly checks. When you sell, move or die, the loan comes due. The lender repays itself the balance of your loan plus interest from the proceeds of the sale of your home. The disadvantages of reverse mortgages are the costs associated with getting one and the relatively high interest rate. That's why it's wise to compare the pros and cons of a reverse mortgage with those of a home-equity loan or a second mortgage. However, it can be a good alternative for people with little monthly income who would probably not qualify for a home-equity loan. And, if you do get a reverse mortgage, you'll want to make use of it for long enough (say, not less than a year) to lessen the impact of its costs and maximize its benefits. For more information, contact the National Center for Home Equity Conversion (7343 147th St., Apple Valley, MN 55124) or AARP's Home Equity Information Center (601 E St., N.W., Washington, DC 20049).

Leaving Early

If you want to retire early, as many of the people profiled in this book did, you'll have to figure out not only how much of a nest egg you will have by the time you want to leave but also how much of it will be available to you then. The worksheet on these pages will help you with your planning.

AN EARLY-RETIREMENT WORKSHEET

HOW MUCH INCOME WILL YOU NEED?

First calculate your income goal at retirement. Multiply your current salary by a future-growth factor from the table on page 270. For example, use 4% estimated annual inflation and add that to the amount you expect your salary to rise each year, say 3%, for a total of 7%. If you want to retire early in 10 years, look where 7% intersects 10 years and you find the multiplier 1.97.

Multiplying that by your current salary—say, $50,000—tells you what you'll be earning ($98,500 in this example) at the point you want to retire. Figure on needing 80% of that once you retire, and you arrive at an annual income goal after early retirement of $78,800.

A. $_____ x _____ x 0.80 = $ _____

Your current income   Multiplier from table on page 270   Equals your goal

Example: $50,000 x 1.97 = $98,500 x 0.80 = $78,800

AN EARLY-RETIREMENT WORKSHEET

ANTICIPATED RESOURCES AT CRUCIAL AGES

One of the obstacles to early retirement is that you can't count on all your long-term savings and investments to kick in with income right from the start. You also won't be eligible for medicare until 65 and will have to find some way to cover your health insurance needs until then.

The worksheet below reflects the fact that employer pension benefits are rarely available before age 55, that social security benefits can't start before age 62 and that IRA funds, except contributions made to a Roth IRA, are generally tied up until age 59½. (Regular IRA funds can be tapped earlier if the money is taken via roughly equal installments based on your life expectancy. To use this loophole, you must stick with the lifetime payout schedule for at least five consecutive years and until you're at least 59½. For more information, consult *Cut Your Taxes*, (Kiplinger Books) or IRS publications #590, Individual Retirement Accounts, and #575, Pension and Annuity Income.)

To determine whether you can live on the investment income (before pension and social security payments and certain retirement fund money become available) without depleting capital, multiply your assets by the percent you believe they can earn each year—the example below assumes an 8% earnings rate.

			Target Age			
			50-54	55-59	60-62	62-plus
1. Savings	$_____	X 0.08 = $_____	$_____	$_____	$_____	
2. Home equity	$_____	X 0.08 = $_____	$_____	$_____	$_____	
3. IRAs*	$_____	X 0.08 = $___ NA	$___ NA	$_____	$_____	
4. Keoghs	$_____	X 0.08 = $___ NA	$_____	$_____	$_____	
5. 401(k)s	$_____	X 0.08 = $___ NA	$_____	$_____	$_____	
6. Pension**	$_____	= $___ NA	$_____	$_____	$_____	
7. Soc. security**	$_____	= $___ NA	$___ NA	$___ NA	$_____	
B. Column totals		$_____	$_____	$_____	$_____	
C. Shortfall (A minus B)		$_____	$_____	$_____	$_____	

*You can withdraw your own contributions to the new Roth IRA penalty-free anytime before age 59½.
**When they become available, your pension and social security benefits form the cornerstone of your retirement income. It's assumed you will not be investing them.

Index

A

AARP. *See* American Association of Retired Persons
Adult education programs
alternative learning programs, 6-63
Elderhostel program, 63-64
master's degree programs, 60-61
profiles, 65-83
reading list, 62
reasons for returning to school, 57-59
tuition-free programs, 59
Age discrimination, 12-13
AGLS. *See* Association of Graduate Liberal Arts
Alpha Partners, Inc., 180-181
Alternative teacher certification, 196-197
AMA. *See* American Management Association
American Association of Retired Persons
baby boomer survey, 8-9
community-service programs, 100-101
Home Equity Information Center, 276
membership, 1
Modern Maturity, xvii
American Bar Association, 98
American Management Association
corporate downsizing survey, 10
American Medical Association
retirement planning workshop, 33-34
Art and music

continuing to work after retirement age, 159-161
as retirement hobbies, 137-140, 143-144, 159-161
Association of Graduate Liberal Arts, 60-61
AT&T
volunteer program, 100
Attitudes toward retirement, 1-9

B

Baby boomers
aging of, xvii
attitudes toward retirement, 8-9
Bell Operating Co.
volunteer program, 100
Benefits
reducing level of, 12
Bergen County, N.J., 101-102
Brabec, Barbara, 125
Bush, George, 25
Business Life Transitions, 35-36
Buxton, William, Jr., 151, 180-181
Buyouts, 9-11, 39-40

C

Career changes, 195-200, 206-207, 219-220, 238-260
Career Consultants, 36-38
Carter, Jimmy and Rosalynn, 86-87
Colleges. *See also* Adult education programs; specific college by name
retirement age for faculty members, 16-17

Community college programs, 59
Community service programs, 100-101
Computers. *See also* E-mail
computer illiteracy, 24-26, 43-44
equipping home offices, 194
importance of computer skills, 26-27
SeniorNet, 26, 43-44
Consultants
consulting as a career change, 211-218
consulting in retirement, 19-20, 47-53, 80-81, 113-116
continuing to work after retirement age, 157-158
"double dippers," 190
guidelines for, 190-192
reading list, 196
for retirement planning, 32-33, 35-38
tax issues, 188-189
Contingent workers, 12
Corporate trends
contingent workers, 12
cutbacks in retirement planning programs, 22
desire to continue working, 155-156
downsizing, 10
executives' attitudes toward retirement, 17-20
need for older workers, 11-12
volunteer programs, 98-99
Corporation for National Service, 101
Corporations, 179
Crafting
as a hobby, 125, 141-142